THE DEFEAT OF IMPERIAL GERMANY

1917-1918

MAJOR BATTLES AND CAMPAIGNS
John S. D. Eisenhower, General Editor

I. *The Defeat of Imperial Germany, 1917–1918*
by Rod Paschall

THE DEFEAT OF

IMPERIAL GERMANY

1917-1918

By Rod Paschall

Colonel, United States Army

With an Introduction by
John S. D. Eisenhower

ALGONQUIN BOOKS OF CHAPEL HILL
1989

Published by

ALGONQUIN BOOKS OF CHAPEL HILL

Post Office Box 2225

Chapel Hill, North Carolina 27515-2225

a division of

WORKMAN PUBLISHING COMPANY, INC.

708 Broadway

New York, New York 10003

LIBRARY OF CONGRESS CATALOGING-IN-PUBLICATION DATA

Paschall, Rod, 1935–

   The defeat of imperial Germany, 1917–1918 / by Rod
Paschall ; with an introduction by John S. D. Eisenhower.

       p.   cm.—(Major battles and campaigns ; 1)

   "Published . . . in association with Workman Publishing
Company . . . New York, New York"—T.p. verso.

   Bibliography: p.

   Includes index.

   ISBN 0-945575-05-X

   1. World War, 1914–1918—Campaigns—Western.   2. World
War, 1914–1918—Germany.   I. Title.   II. Series.

D530.P38   1989

940.4'144—dc19   88-29356
                                                      CIP

*This book is dedicated to infantrymen,
particularly those who fought for their nations
in the Great War.*

CONTENTS

LIST OF ILLUSTRATIONS

LIST OF MAPS

INTRODUCTION

by John S. D. Eisenhower

THOSE OF US OLD ENOUGH TO REMEMBER the period just following World War I will recall the great dichotomy of views that the American people held toward that conflict. On one side were the romantics, the survivors who took justifiable pride in having risked their lives for their country and returned safely. To them and to a grateful public, convinced for a time that it had been the "war to end wars," the conflict was the "Great War," great in every respect. Happy stories of Gay Paree, of a mythical "Mademoiselle from Armentières," and of the kindnesses of the French peasants toward American soldiers abounded. Songs such as "Over There," "Goodbye Broadway, Hello France," and "Oh How I Hate to Get Up in the Morning" were still popular. Many brave men had lost their lives in World War I, to be sure, but their sacrifices had made all Americans somehow more heroic.

But by the 1930s—a period I personally remember well—disillusionment had set in. Novels such as Hemingway's *A Farewell to Arms* and Remarque's *All Quiet on the Western Front* made inroads into the public consciousness. Spurred by the Great Depression, which drastically lowered spirits, the veterans of the Great War became pictured as victims, their plights represented by the celebrated Bonus Marchers, who descended upon the nation's capital in 1932. And the fear that the Great War might not, after all, have been the "war to end wars," caused dread. One group, anticipating a fate similar to the veterans of World War I, dubbed themselves the "Veterans of Future Wars," seriously demanding bonuses in advance, before they should be killed in a coming conflict.

Then, at the end of the 1930s, the memory of the Great War was set aside in the agony of a second, even more destructive event, World War II. As a result, the Great War was removed from memory. Events that should have been soberly evaluated were put aside, stamped for future reference (if needed), with labels based upon the prejudices of each individual. World War I became the Forgotten War.

Without a doubt, a contributing factor in the erasure of the Great War from human memory lies in its very horror. An estimated nine million soldiers died in that war, and the carnage turned out to be in vain: victory enabled the Allies to impose the Versailles Treaty on Germany, a dictated peace that was so ambivalent—vengeful in spirit, but not sufficiently harsh to keep Germany in subjugation—as to constitute a direct cause for the rise of Hitler in Germany and another global tragedy. Thus the futility, the feeling that the sacrifices of World War I were in vain, has penetrated the human mind even more than have the numbers killed and maimed.

Even the books of history tend to follow this pattern. Outrage over the mass sacrifice of a futile war encouraged military writers such as B. H. Liddell Hart to treat nearly all the Allied generals with a lofty contempt that they did not really deserve. It is puzzling, when one examines Liddell Hart's history of the war (1930), that so many unimaginative, mediocre minds could be assembled on one side in any war.

Rod Paschall, in this book, has attempted successfully to give a more balanced perspective on the last two years of World War I. Rather than treat the horrors as the product of inferior minds, he assumes the existence of the problem of stalemate along the line from Switzerland to the English Channel, and then examines how various generals, men as capable as those who achieved fame later in World War II, tried unsuccessfully to solve it.

Colonel Paschall's independent, original approach is well taken. He deftly sets out the military situation as it was seen by both sides on New Year's Day 1917, by pointing out that the stalemate on the critical Western Front could be broken only by one of three means: (1) a negotiated peace; (2) the reestablishment of maneuver on the battlefield by the discovery of some way of penetrating the long trench lines; and (3) by attrition. A negotiated peace he quickly rules out, leaving the problem of attaining military victory that of achieving a breakthrough and thus avoiding attrition as the means of resolution. (Attrition, unfortunately, prevailed.)

In so doing, Paschall gives justice to all. "There are no villains in this book," he says. He outlines the efforts of the optimistic French general Robert G. Nivelle in his hopes to break through in the Champagne region of France with one hundred divisions, backed up by a British effort both north and south of the Somme. He describes how the German general, Erich von Ludendorff, anticipated these Allied plans and defeated them with a new tactic, the reverse slope defense. He describes with sympathy the frustration of British general Sir Douglas Haig, in attempting to supplement his attack against Ypres and Passchendaele in the Flanders lowlands with an amphibious landing in the North Sea.

He gives French general Ferdinand Foch credit for helping to save a desperate Italian army after its defeat at Caporetto. He describes the American role, from Ludendorff's spring offensive in 1918 to the battles of St. Mihiel and the Argonne Forest. In the latter he is frank; though he treats the American contribution with charity, he holds no brief for any romantic notion that "one American could lick ten Germans."

Throughout he is professional but readable. He delights in puncturing myths such as the stupidity of all the generals, the alleged rigidity of the German General Staff (which he describes as a "meritocracy"), and the supposed superiority of autocracies over democracies in fighting long wars of attrition. And besides puncturing myths, Paschall points out the continuum between the fighting techniques of the end of World War I and the beginnings of World War II. Without detracting from the abilities of the generals of the latter war, he contends that those of the former were equally imaginative; they were simply faced with an impossible problem.

Rod Paschall has exceptional qualifications to make the judgments he does. He has been a member of the Army Special Forces (Green Berets), a decorated combat veteran of five campaigns in Vietnam, a graduate of the U.S. Naval War College, and an instructor in military history at the U.S. Military Academy (where he graduated in 1959). He holds master's degrees in international affairs (George Washington University, 1970) and in American history (Duke University, 1971). He is currently the director of the U.S. Army Military History Institute, Army War College, Carlisle, Pennsylvania.

The Defeat of Imperial Germany is the first book to be published in the Great Battles series of Algonquin Books of Chapel Hill. For those readers discerning enough to subscribe to the whole series, it will soon become apparent that the styles of these books will vary greatly. That is the intention of this series: to allow each military writer, each one a military student of proven competence, to write in his own distinctive manner. For not only do the techniques of the writers vary, but the wars they write about are sufficiently different as to defy a set format. In progress right now are volumes on the American Revolution, the European campaign of World War II, and the War of 1812 between the United States and Britain. These works in progress should all appear on the market within the next two or three years.

One criterion, besides the length of about 100,000 words, will apply to all the volumes: they will emphasize battles and major campaigns rather than overall national strategies. Sometimes, as with the European campaign of World War II, the vastness makes the differentiation between tactic (battles) and strategies (campaigns) difficult. But to do a whole war justice in all its aspects, including causes, mobilization, logistics, strategies, and battles, would require books of great size. A modest effort to give the general reader some idea of the battles that have helped shape his world is a sufficiently ambitious program in itself. As William R. Hawkins put it,

> We must remember that wars do change things. Nothing equals the difference between winning and losing a war. That the Greeks stopped the Persians at Marathon and Salamis, that Rome destroyed Carthage, that the Christian Theodoric defeated the pagan Attila the Hun at Chalons, that China failed to conquer Japan in the 13th Century, that the English drove the French out of North America, that the North won the Civil War, that the Communists won the civil wars in Russia and China, or that Napoleon and Hitler were defeated are just a few of history's many decisive conflicts. The way millions have lived for centuries has often been determined by a few hours on the battlefield.*

*Hawkins, William R. "Military History: Vital, Neglected." *Chronicles* (November 1987).

ACKNOWLEDGMENTS

ALTHOUGH NOT RESPONSIBLE FOR WHAT these pages say, a number of good people contributed to the effort. Dr. Ted Ropp taught me to discern good sources from bad and Dr. I. B. Holley taught me research techniques. My good friend Jay Luvaas introduced me to the history of World War I when we both taught at West Point. I owe much to the wise counsel of Dr. Edward M. Coffman and Dr. David Trask, both fine scholars of the American involvement in the Great War. I also had the benefit of a few hours of education at the feet of John Toland.

I am deeply indebted to the fine staff at the U.S. Army Military History Institute. John Slonaker, Denny Vetock, and Louise Arnold found many a lost book. Judy Meck also assisted me in tracking down some obscure publications. Mike Winey and Randy Hackenburg helped me with photos, and Dr. Richard Sommers pointed me to some manuscript collections.

John Eisenhower had a hand in reading the first draft and suggested some badly needed changes. I also received considerable assistance from Louis Rubin, Jr., of Algonquin Books. Despite a personal tragedy—the wholly unexpected decline in the fortunes of both the Atlanta Braves and the Baltimore Orioles in the spring of 1988—Dr. Rubin never flagged in his support. I am also indebted to Jim Kistler for cartographic support.

Finally, I owe much to my wife, Pat, and our two daughters, Karen and Chrissy.

The mistakes, however, are all mine.

THE DEFEAT OF IMPERIAL GERMANY

1917-1918

ONE

January 1, 1917

IT WAS A WORLD WAR, BUT NOT THE FIRST. That distinction is held by the Seven Years' War in the eighteenth century. The men who fought in the twentieth-century nightmare would learn to call it the Great War, or the World War. Yet, on a crisp September day during 1931, that too changed when officers of the Japanese Empire in Manchuria created an incident that destroyed the international mechanism to preserve the peace, and the "second" world war began. Thus the veterans of the Great War even lost control of the name of the event they suffered through. There was little protest over the name change, however; for that generation was quite accustomed to its role as a pawn in uncontrollable situations.

The survivors of the 1914–18 war could reflect back on that grim New Year's Day in 1917 when they were all locked into a hopeless, bloody struggle that seemed to have no end. On the first day of January 1917, the people of the West had little reason for optimism. A brutal, worldwide battle had simply stagnated. The adversaries seemed evenly matched. Each military or naval move on either side had been checkmated. It was the same all over the world. The conflict could spread. New fronts could be opened. But each new thrust was parried, and another piece of the earth would be turned into an immovable killing ground.

There was no lack of courage. There was no lack of daring. The missing ingredient was any hope for victory, decision, or conclusion. It is quite likely that some of the world's leaders even secretly hoped for resolution at any cost, including defeat. The rapid collapse of a front, quick negotiations, and an end, however disappointing, would almost be welcomed. Life could then be resumed and some assurance of a future could be secured. As it was, this New Year's Day brought only one certainty—that the already appalling death toll would continue to mount.

The stalemate even extended to the high seas. Some leaders, however, now hoped for decisive results there, in particular the advocates of the German U-boat. In the previous four weeks of December 1916, German submarines had sunk an astounding 300,000 tons of Allied shipping. Erich Ludendorff, knowing that an unlimited submarine campaign was to open in the next month, hoped for a victory at sea beginning in February of 1917. As second chief of the German General Staff, Ludendorff was the controlling mind behind all German operations, and his thinking governed not only German actions, but in many instances those of Austria, Turkey, and Bulgaria as well.

Wiser heads, however, differed with Ludendorff's optimism about the forthcoming U-boat campaign. The British had already transported their colonial armies to war. German submarines in the Channel had not been successful in severing Britain's line of communication to her troops in France. The U-boats might succeed in reducing Britain's vast food imports, but the indigenous British agricultural potential had yet to be fully exploited. Even if the food situation in Britain were to deteriorate, what would that do? The target was obviously the willpower of the British people, and few races had exhibited more dogged determination and perseverance. Moreover, the German submarines were facing the world's most powerful and skillful naval force. If any organization could find an answer to the U-boat campaign, it was the Royal Navy. The German effort might wound, but could not kill Britain's ability to prosecute the war.

Although some German leaders staked their hopes on ending the costly conflict with the submarine, no one anywhere could reasonably argue that an end to the killing would come by some sort of triumph on the surface of the oceans. True, the Royal Navy's blockade of Germany and her allies was effective. But Berlin did not depend on the sea for much of its economy, and its production of the implements of war was reaching all-time highs in January of 1917. There were growing food shortages in Germany, but no Allied leader doubted Ludendorff's continuing ability to mount major offensives. The Allies could not logically hope for another showdown with the German High Seas Fleet, in which they would hold a decided advantage. That had been settled in 1916 at the Battle of Jutland, in a brief foray by the High Seas Fleet from its ports, a naval skirmish with the British, and a return of both fleets to their respective checkmate positions. Admiral Jellicoe, the commander of the British Grand Fleet, was afterward described as the only man who could lose the war in one afternoon. No one, however, thought he could win it in one day's fighting. There could be no rapid termination of the global conflict at sea.

There was also an impasse in the Middle East. On New Year's Day in 1917, all of the British schemes for bringing down the Turkish Empire, opening a southern supply route to Russia, or finding a back door to Austria were defunct. In the previous year the British had lost their entire garrison at Kut-el-Amara, on the Tigris River in modern-day Iraq. The other arm of their offensive against the Turks was based in Egypt and directed into Palestine, but that effort had mired in the sands with little prospect for success. There was a little good news: word had reached Cairo of incidents of Arab unrest and fighting against Turkish rule. However, no British leader believed that the report indicated any sort of decisive movement. The Allied effort was squarely based on its armies, and those organizations in the Middle East not only were stationary, but had been effectively countered by Turkish troops with their German leaders.

Ludendorff could be well satisfied with the performance of his officers serving with Turkish forces. In early 1917, however, his greatest joy probably came from the happy situation created by his Bulgarian allies. The Bulgarian army formed the bulk of the Central Powers' troops arrayed against the large Allied contingent reaching out from Salonika, Greece. During 1916 the Allies had managed to lose 50,000 French, Serbian, and British troops in a failed offensive. Despite this failure, despite open bickering among the Allies and Greek ambivalence about the effort against the Central Powers, the Allies continued to pour in manpower for the questionable enterprise. Allied strength there was approaching 600,000 troops, many of whom would become victims of malaria. Ludendorff could jest with a wry smile that Salonika was his biggest prison camp.

There was, however, little humor to be found among either the Allies or the Central Powers in Italy. There the Italians had taken 273,000 casualties during the year ending in 1916. These grim, morale-sapping totals were the only significant results from five unimaginative, grinding offensives. By December the Italian leaders were asking Paris and London for reinforcements. Their opponents, the leaders of the Austro-Hungarian Empire, had fared no better. They had lost 184,000 men and were asking Berlin for more assistance. No one expected that more resources would actually prove to be conclusive in any positive way, other

THE STALEMATE

NEW YEAR'S DAY 1917

☐ NEUTRAL   ▨ ALLIED POWERS

▨ CENTRAL POWERS

than to keep Austria and Italy in the war. The Italian front was a sink-hole for both sides, but each of the protagonists believed support was essential. Otherwise the opponent might actually win in Italy, freeing substantial numbers of troops for use elsewhere.

On the first day of 1917, the war on the Eastern Front had also reached the stage of hopeless stalemate. The bright Allied prospects of the previous year had collapsed in a sea of blood and futility. London and Paris had persuaded Romania to join their cause, then had to watch helplessly as the small nation was crushed by German and Austrian troops. But Ludendorff could gain little satisfaction from his victory there. The effort in Romania had cost the Central Powers thousands of troops, who had hurried east from the Western Front. To Berlin the Romanian adventure had been a classic exercise in "robbing Peter to pay Paul."

In a similar way, the Allies' optimism over the great Russian offensive of 1916 had been destroyed. British, French, and Italian dreams of the Russian "steamroller"—an overwhelming, massive use of Moscow's manpower against the Austrian and German armies—were now at an end. The courageous campaign of the year past had cost Russia one million casualties, with no results to speak of. On this New Year's Day, the Allies now spoke of the Eastern Front in the same way they referred to the Italian front: keeping their friends, in this case the Russians, in the war so that the forces of the Central Powers could not be transferred somewhere else. The fact that Russian society was unraveling and would fail to prosecute the war was not yet fully realized by the participants. Ludendorff certainly did not expect a Russian withdrawal from the war in the coming year, so he could not be too optimistic. The Eastern Front was simply another area of endless death, endless stagnation, and endless despair.

If a solution to this global tragedy was possible, it was becoming increasingly evident to many that it would have to come on the Western Front. The battlefields of France and Belgium held the key to the end of the war. Of all foreign soil occupied by the Central Powers in January of 1917, the most valuable was in France and Belgium. It would bring the highest price at the bargaining table, if the war were to result in a negotiated conclusion. To Germany, Russia was endless, and her prime enemies, Britain and France, would not pay dearly for regained Italian territory. In the same way, Berlin was not terribly enthusiastic about protection of Turkish claims. Not only was Ludendorff interested in protecting his gains on the Western Front, he also knew that the western theater of operations offered almost the only real opportunity for offensive measures. A major German advance could push the British back on their line of communications, the French coast. The same attack, if delivered at the right point, could push the French armies back to protect Paris. Separating the French and British physically would force the Allies to reconsider their war aims in the light of more basic interests. For Berlin, the battlefields of France and Belgium presented an opportunity for a satisfactory resolution of the conflict that no other area could promise.

Similar reasoning governed the war leaders in Paris and London. France was the strongest ally of Britain, but since French soil was occupied by the German army, the French leadership could hardly be expected to pour significant military resources into any theater of operations outside of France. The main effort would have to be made there and in Belgium, where the battlefields were closest to the locus of French and British power. This location would also have the advantage of the shortest line of communication and supply, an important feature in the achievement of maximum combat power. Moreover, the western battlefields were not too far from German soil. If the Allies were to conquer part of Germany, their strongest adversary would have to bargain at a distinct disadvantage. Destruction of the Turkish, Bulgarian, or Austrian armies would not necessarily end the war. The linchpin of the Central Powers was the German army. If that army could be defeated or badly mauled, the war could end on favorable terms for Britain and France.

For both sides, the question was therefore not whether the Western Front was the decisive front, but how to reach a decision there, for it too was frozen in a deadly stalemate of agonizing attrition. Indeed, the Western Front was the most stagnant of all World War I battlefields. Throughout the previous two years, 1915 and 1916, an advance of as little as four miles by either side was considered to be a major achievement. The costs were appalling. In 1914 and 1915 the French managed to lose 2.4 million casualties, the British lost 381,000, and the German total came to about 1.5 million. The situation in 1916 was little better. The German-initiated campaign in the Verdun sector raged from February to December of that year, and the butcher's bill was high. The French defenders—later the attackers—lost about 362,000 men, including killed, wounded, and captured. The Germans came out with 337,000 casualties. From June to November of 1916, the British, under their leader Sir Douglas Haig, staged a massive offensive to relieve pressure on the French. In that campaign, later known as the Battle of the Somme, British losses amounted to approximately 420,000. On the right flank the French lost another 194,000. The German totals amounted to some 650,000. Each nation counted casualties with different criteria, and the official figures are still highly suspect, so comparisons are hazardous. But by any line of reasoning, what was happening on the Western Front amounted to nothing short of the systematic genocide of the flower of Western youth.

The prewar male population of the British Isles had been about 22.4 million, that of France 19.5 million, and the German total approximately 32 million. Discounting those who were too young, too old, or otherwise ineligible, the maximum prewar troop strength would be about 8.4 million for the British, 7.3 million for the French, and 12 million for the Germans. In essence, the bloody fighting on the Western Front alone had cost the French about 47 percent of their prewar military manpower. The German figures came to somewhere between 20 and 25 percent of their prewar manpower potential. British losses amounted to about 15 percent of their prewar maximum military strength. True, some of the wounded had returned to battle, and more young men became eligible for service each year, but there is every indication that the "official" casualty figures had been minimized, and the leaders of Germany, France, and Britain knew they were dealing with an almost impossible situation. An age-old soldier's rule of thumb held a 25 percent casualty rate to be the turning point in a combat unit's effectiveness. A rough but objective evaluation might well yield a projection that in January of 1917 France, as a nation, could no longer prosecute the war, that Germany was rapidly reaching the same status, and that only Britain possessed the capacity to continue military operations. So if the Western Front held the promise for decisive results, it also held the potential for national ruin.

How had it happened, and why did warfare differ so markedly from previous experience? Much was made of two American innovations— the machine gun and barbed wire—to explain the static lethality of the Western Front. These, along with the increased efficiency of artillery, provided the accepted rationale for the front's characterization as an area of "tactical deadlock." But the term "tactical deadlock" does not fully describe the actual conditions of the 1917 battlefields in France and Belgium. Tactical deadlocks had been experienced before. Complicated trench systems, extensive barriers to infantry assaults, and the massive use of artillery had characterized the lines of U. S. Grant and Robert E. Lee during the Petersburg campaign of late 1864 and early 1865 in the American Civil War. The fundamental factor that made the Western Front so remarkable was that the trenches stretched *in an unbroken line* from Switzerland to the English Channel—and that had little to do with tactics.

On that New Year's Day in 1917, the Allies were manning their almost continental-length ditches with 3.9 million soldiers organized into 169 divisions. The French supplied the bulk of the troops, about 2.6 million. British totals were at 1.2 million and growing. The Belgian contribution to the Allies amounted to approximately 100,000 men. And that was not all. The Allied leadership was reinforcing the Western Front. During 1917 it was expected that the total available divisions would grow from 169 to 184. Ludendorff's numbers were somewhat smaller. He had 129 divisions on the Western Front, and about 2.5 million soldiers. German plans in January included the creation of 30 wholly new divisions, and German officers in France and Belgium were hoping for their share.

These astounding numbers, the sheer magnitude of the size of the armies, created a situation that had never before been experienced. Barbed wire, machine guns, and artillery may have been the instruments that caused the casualties, but it was efficient modern mobilization procedures that got the soldiers to the battlefield. Never had Western society exposed so much of its youth to battle. The numbers enabled the generals to fill the trenches that extended from the Channel to the Alps.

Each man became a target for someone's weapon, and the more targets that became available, the greater were the chances actually to alter the nature, attitudes, and future of entire nations. The generals and politicians had devised the mobilization schemes prior to the war, but had never fully understood the implications of what they were doing. If technology was to be singled out as the culprit in the creation of huge casualty lists, the telephone and typewriter had as much to do with the length of these lists as did the machine gun and barbed wire. Unprecedented, massive mobilization had produced a situation on the Western Front that had hitherto been unthinkable.

A principal reason for the unprecedented nature of the Western Front was that a prime tool of the soldier had vanished. Since the days of Napoleon, European and North American officers had been schooled in the advantages of the envelopment. Tactically, placing troops on your opponent's flank not only diminished the amount of firepower he could confront you with, but also robbed the enemy of his natural or artificial defenses. A flank attack was almost invariably less costly than a frontal attack, and a fundamental tenet of the military art was to preserve one's own force while destroying that of the adversary. Strategically, envelopment offered the opportunity to place forces on the enemy line of communications, ideally without fighting. The opponent would then have to fight without the benefit of supplies or reinforcements. If he chose not to give battle he could be isolated, defeated in detail, or starved into submission. Western officers were constantly reminded of the superiority of envelopment, instructed on the disadvantages of frontal attacks, and given endless historical examples of situations where an inferior force had defeated a more numerous opponent by the use of envelopment. At the outset of the Great War, these officers had been intellectually ready to use envelopments, but were not mentally prepared for the Western Front of 1917.

At the strategic level, an envelopment of the trench lines in France and Belgium was not a realistic option for either side. The German High Seas Fleet was no match for the Royal Navy, and an amphibious operation would require naval protection of a specific point, the landing beach. If the Germans chose to attempt an envelopment by sea, the High Seas Fleet would surely be destroyed and Ludendorff's troops would perish for lack of support. An envelopment through Switzerland could not be done in secrecy, and the precarious supply line through that rugged terrain would not support the tonnages essential for a major operation. For the Allies, the Swiss route presented the same obstacles that faced the Germans. That left an Allied amphibious option, which, given the superiority of the Royal Navy, was a distinct possibility. What discouraged such an attempt, however, was the example set by the failed Dardanelles campaign of 1915. That British amphibious operation turned out to be an Allied disaster of major proportions. There were many reasons for it, among them an inability to build up British combat power at a rate that overwhelmed the Turkish defenders. The initial phases of the operation had looked rather promising, but in the end the British had to withdraw. A similar attempt behind the German lines in 1917 would be staged against first-line forces, not ill-armed and poorly equipped Turkish conscripts. Ludendorff would have a great transportation network in Northern Europe at his disposal to rush in a counterattack, something the Turks had lacked. The Allies also had more than enough secondary fronts, peripheral operations, and "sideshows" that demanded attention and resources. These had given no promise of ending the war. An Allied landing in German-occupied Belgium would certainly be difficult, but maybe not impossible.

Tactically the same situation prevailed. The defenders on both sides had ensured that no flank was exposed or vulnerable. There were certainly some soft points in the extensive trench systems, but those areas were "soft" for good reason. Some sectors of the Western Front were lightly held because they presented no real opportunities for the attacker. The terrain in these regions would not permit the rapid advance of an offensive, would not support the logistical structure essential to sustain one, or offered no tactical advantage in the immediate rear of the defender. Other regions were lightly held because the defender could rapidly reinforce them, the attacker's preparations could easily be observed by the defender, or both. Two years of daily scrutiny, careful calculations, and considerable construction made the front an area where a tactical envelopment was impossible.

The Western Front was something beyond man's previous experience: two giant systems of inverted, subsurface walls that faced each other, each carefully designed to observe, delay, trap, and kill any intruder.

TO RESOLVE THE IMPASSE ON THE Western Front, three basic approaches could be used. Each offered an end to the war. The first was well within the realm of the politician, the other two were clearly the business of soldiers. The political solution would be to negotiate a termination of the conflict by establishing the war aims of both sides and reaching a compromise through arbitration or mutual agreement. The military options were (1) to defeat the opponent by continued attrition of his forces, or (2) to devise an offensive scheme that would destroy the opponent's defensive system. Since envelopment was out of the question, the offensive scheme would have to involve some sort of penetration method, a new kind of attack that would put enough combat power in the enemy rear to allow the use of what soldiers knew best: envelopments. In the final analysis, it all came down to negotiation, attrition, or penetration. Clearly the most sensible approach would be to negotiate an end to this global catastrophe.

On New Year's Day two peace initiatives were being analyzed. The first had come less than three weeks before from the German government. A reading of the text left no doubt that Germany's leaders regarded their cause as just and the military situation of the Central Powers as unshakable. The timing of the German note corresponded with the fall of the Romanian capital, an event that emphasized the strength of Berlin and Vienna and the Allies' inability to influence events on the Eastern Front. The key element of the note was what it did not say. No terms were offered, and no specifics were addressed.

To the uninformed reader, the German note might indicate a willingness to talk and a possible reason for hope. The leaders of all the belligerents knew otherwise. Several previous peace initiatives—the more serious ones conducted in secret—had been based on the premise that war aims had to be announced by both sides before rational negotiations could take place. The absence of those aims and the absence of specifics meant that Germany was actually not ready to deal with the Allies in peace talks. The truth was that the German leadership fully expected a rejection of the note. This would provide the prime ingredient in the rationale for the forthcoming unrestricted submarine warfare campaign, which would destroy neutral shipping. Berlin was looking for as much support as it could get from its own citizens and from world public opinion. When the expected public outcry arose in February, Germany could then point to her attempt to secure a negotiated solution, its rejection by the Allies, and the understandable need to break the naval blockade. The first of the peace initiatives was more cynical than serious.

The second initiative had actually provoked the first and was the product of the newest of the great world powers. The American president, Woodrow Wilson, had been using the neutral status of the United States for some time to try to bring the World War to an end. His most serious efforts had been conducted in secret, hidden from the American public. At one point, he had even authorized an arrangement whereby the United States would join the Allies with its military forces and abandon neutrality, provided that some accommodations could be made. The Allies had ignored this offer, in part because America's military power was so slight that its addition to the Allied ranks would not be worth the political compromise.

On December 18, 1916, six days after publication of the German note, Wilson abandoned secrecy and called on the belligerents to state their specific terms. The Allies accommodated the American president almost as quickly as they had rejected the German initiative. Their response, orchestrated in Paris and London, had an even greater tone of confidence and self-assurance than Berlin's note. And this communiqué had specifics. Analysis of the Allied position yielded a clear message. Among other things, Germany would have to give up all of the bloody ground of the Western Front for which she had paid so dearly.

Like the earlier announcement of the Central Powers, the Allied note was an offer meant to be refused, but with a difference. The note from Berlin had contained no specifics, because there was a growing separation between Berlin and Vienna. The Austro-Hungarian emperor had died in December, and a drift toward a negotiated peace was under way in the latter capital. Furthermore, there was growing discontent in

Germany. These factors prevented the German leadership from citing specific war objectives in the way that the Allies had.

It was a curious situation. The political system of the Central Powers appeared to be an autocracy. In reality, both Germany and Austria were controlled by oligarchies, with actual power held by a handful of men. In both cases the prime actors were the respective emperors, generals, and a small group of appointed civil administrators. The same could be said of wartime France and England, for these democracies had suspended many civil rights, suppressed public information, and dealt in secrecy. The essential difference was not how power was held, but where that power came from. The governments in London and Paris were given power by their people through complex, sophisticated political arrangements. Power in Berlin and Vienna came from the oligarchies themselves.

If the stress of the war became too much to bear, the people of the Allied nations had the ballot box as a remedy for the changing of their "oligarchies." The people of the Central Powers had only the streets and revolution. Thus, as the war became more intolerable, the leaders of Germany and Austria became less secure. They could not risk a public discussion of war aims. The Allies could, for they risked only their jobs, not their necks.

The major reason that neither side would make a serious attempt to negotiate the end of the war was that both had become victims of their own propaganda. The great and unexpected losses on the Western Front had required each of the belligerents to call for heretofore unprecedented sacrifices from their citizens. The democracies had suspended many liberties, and had forced huge levies of manpower to fill the trenches in France and Belgium. Germany had done the same to an even greater extent. Because of the Allied naval blockade, the failure to ration intelligently at the beginning of the war, and the loss of so much domestic male labor, Berlin had been forced to limit both her citizens and her army to a marginal diet and inadequate clothing.

The explanations for these extreme measures were the same on both sides. The opponent was evil, the government was doing its best in a just cause, and national salvation was at risk. On the propaganda front all stops were pulled. Over the course of two years of warfare, the politicians had backed themselves into identical corners. They had raised the stakes to such heights that only blood might suffice to pay for the cause. By 1917 so many youths had been sacrificed that any kind of compromise would appear unworthy and even dishonorable.

By the beginning of the new year, it was evident that the peace initiatives had failed. The positions of the belligerents were so far apart that further efforts at a negotiated solution would be futile. The three options—penetration, attrition, and negotiation—had been reduced to two. Both were the costly and dreaded solutions of soldiers. Not only would the war continue, it would be fought to its yet-undetermined conclusion on the most fearful of all battlefields: the Western Front. Final resolution, and the nature of the outcome, would hinge on the character and strengths of the military leaders and the armies they led.

THE FORCES OF THE BRITISH EMPIRE on the Western Front were commanded by Sir Douglas Haig, a fifty-six-year-old former cavalryman. Few British officers had more experience on the Western Front, and fewer had more experience in the profession of arms. Haig had served in India and had fought in the Sudan and the Boer War. At the outset of the British deployment, he had gone to France in command of a corps. When the war broke out, Haig had already been a lieutenant general for four years. After he replaced Sir John French, who had resigned in 1915, Haig would lead his nation's forces in France and Belgium until the end of the conflict. He received the accolades of the public for his leadership, but in the late 1920s and early 1930s, his image would be tarnished when critics began to place the blame for the British Empire's Western Front casualties at his feet.

Douglas Haig expressed himself well in written communications, but was somewhat inarticulate verbally. He was already becoming controversial by the beginning of 1917. Haig's first action against the Germans had been in August of 1914 near Mons, Belgium. The British Expeditionary Force had arrived on the Continent in great secrecy and managed to surprise the advancing Germans. It had been little more than a delaying action by two corps—90,000 troops in all, organized into five divisions. Haig's corps acquitted itself so well that the German commander later described the British performance in the operation as the handiwork of "an incomparable army." Since then, that professional army, the initial British contribution to its allies, had simply dissolved. The casualties in that rather small event on the Western Front cost the British more men than had been lost in the entire Boer War. Haig's next significant action against his German enemies occurred at Ypres (pronounced "eeps"), Belgium, in October and November of 1914 and resulted in the Ypres salient, which thrust well into German lines. It also featured splendid cooperation between the French and British, produced terrific losses in German ranks, and essentially destroyed what was left of Britain's professional army.

As an army commander in 1915, Haig had performed well during the British attack at Neuve-Chapelle, France, gaining a reputation for thorough preparations and plans. Later that year he demonstrated an ability to protest orders he thought to be unwise, and even risked his career by going over his superior's head to voice his opinion.

By January 1917 Haig had been the senior British commander on the Western Front for over a year. The army that Haig commanded bore little resemblance to the professional force that he had brought across the English Channel in 1914. Of all the nations represented on the Western Front, the British had been the least prepared for the size of the effort required. Their prewar planning envisioned an army of only about 60 battalions and, as with all of the participants, a short war. The actual conditions of protracted conflict dictated the use of about 540 battalions. Available prewar ammunition stocks were vastly smaller than those needed for the real war. The prewar maneuver doctrine was completely inadequate for trench fighting. The tiny British General Staff in London, organized some ten years before, was overwhelmed by the management tasks of the war. The magnitude of the difference between what was planned and what was actually needed amounted to a tenfold miscalculation.

The failed estimate had been costly. The lack of ammunition had caused the British to be cautious in some instances and foolish in others. By 1917 that shortage had largely been alleviated, but the French had borne the burden in the interim. At the outset the inadequate British staff could not be expected to handle industrial mobilization, revision of doctrine, the training of a huge army, and supervision of a research-and-development effort that would bring the power of technology to the Western Front. By January of 1917 the British were coping with all these problems and more, but their solutions were necessarily hastily assembled and inefficient. The cost of the prewar miscalculation could be measured not only in money and time but in the numbers of lives needlessly lost.

The largest single deficiency of Britain's New Army, the successor to the small professional force that had been destroyed in 1915, was the lack of veteran cadre. Those professionals who had survived knew how to raise an army, train it, supply it, and employ it with some degree of wisdom. These soldiers had seen the mistakes. They knew what was worth keeping from the old army and what should be discarded. They knew each other and could assign the adept to positions of responsibility and the mediocre to mundane tasks, thereby avoiding disastrous leadership selections. But the ranks of the remaining veteran professionals were terribly thin. Thus the New Army, a conscript force and a rarity in the British tradition, had to train itself. It had to develop its own doctrine.

The New Army was learning how to use technology; it was selecting apparent talent for leadership positions and living or dying with the choices. All during 1916 it had groped for solutions. It was now becoming a veteran formation, but the process was a bloody business. The New Army was busy with fundamentals and could not adapt to change quickly. Since it could not draw on experience before the last few months, its reference point was the previous campaign. This army had little finesse and too much confusion. Its talent lay in its ability to absorb huge losses and continue the fight. It was an army of great determination, marvelous courage, and comparatively little skill. Sir Douglas Haig possessed an awesome force, but it was a blunt instrument indeed.

WHILE BRITAIN'S NEW ARMY WAS GAINING competence and confidence in 1915 and 1916, the French army had carried the bulk of the fighting against Germany's legions on the Western Front. Now, in January 1917, the French had a new leader. Compared to Haig, General Robert Nivelle appeared to be an entirely different type of soldier. Where Haig had started the war as a lieutenant general in command of a corps, Nivelle had begun as a brigade commander and was famous for his personal bravery. In contrast to Haig he was very articulate; he spoke English fluently, and had a well-founded reputation for being able to persuade politicans to do what he wanted. Many of them became his strongest advocates. He rose to the command of a division in 1915, and in the spring of 1916 he became an army commander.

It was in this position that Nivelle first gained international recognition. It was not so much his rank as the location of his command that brought the notoriety. He had inherited the Verdun sector after the initial German thrust had been contained. His job was to hold and regain as much ground as possible. He had done both admirably. In defense, the Nivelle technique was little more than that of using what his predecessor had already arranged: massive artillery bombardments. It was the Nivelle offensive methods that attracted attention.

His attack scheme involved pulling selected units off line for rest and reinforcement. Then began weeks of intense training directed at specific well-identified objectives. This was not difficult to do because almost all of the targets were former French fortifications that had been seized by the Germans in the first phases of the Verdun campaign. The infantry attack that Nivelle employed was a major departure from British or French doctrine. There was no wave of aligned riflemen assaulting the opposing trench. The attack was composed of small groups of infantrymen who followed an advancing artillery barrage, avoiding contact with the enemy until the designated objective was reached. Furthermore, Nivelle's concept involved the use of deception. At a specific time all of the pre-attack artillery preparation was fired, including the rolling barrage, the telltale sign of a forthcoming French assault. But no infantry advance was made. The Germans were thus provoked to reveal all of their previously hidden weapons emplacements and concealed artillery positions. The real attack was then launched soon after the deception operation, normally with great success.

In contrast to Haig, Nivelle seemed to offer a refreshing, long-awaited alternative. Articulate, enthusiastic, optimistic, and persuasive, Nivelle was coming to represent the solution on both sides of the English Channel. Haig for his part embodied the status quo: continued bleeding and unimaginative plodding. Curiously, Nivelle was often referred to as youthful, but in reality he was four years older than Haig.

Nivelle's forces had borne the majority of the fighting on the Western Front over the past two years with magnificent courage and growing skill. The French had begun large-scale mobilization of its young men much earlier than the British and possessed an army of great strength. Its most glaring prewar deficiency was its schooling before the war in a concept of all-out attack, during an age that favored the defender. By January of 1917 the French army was becoming jaded, fatigued, and discouraged. The huge losses it had suffered, without compensating gains of recaptured French soil, contributed to a growing loss of morale in its ranks.

But there were strengths. Overall, French artillery was unmatched by allies or enemies. The Germans did possess better heavy artillery, but the French 75-mm howitzer delivered what was needed in this kind of war: volume of fire. Produced before the conflict with the notion of being used in mobile warfare, this weapon had been considered complex, but had proved its worth in the static situation of 1916. The crews and leadership that served in French artillery units were competent and had saved the day on many occasions since fall of 1914. The drawback of the weapon was its short range. The need to place it close to the front ensured that French batteries would be exposed to enemy artillery and mortar fire.

In this the German artillerymen had the advantage, because their heavy, large-caliber pieces could be placed far enough back so that the crews were relatively safe. In an overall sense, however, the French army had the best artillery service at the front on this New Year's Day.

Another strength of the French army was its engineers. Trained like their sister branch, the artillery, in the concept of rapid advance for offensive warfare, the engineers had also made the transition to trench fighting rather well. Their talents were now turned to constructing road nets behind their own lines, as opposed to building routes of communications to support an attack into enemy territory. Melding their energies with those of French civil engineers, the French army engineers quickly provided the means to transfer infantry and artillery units laterally from one sector to another so that reinforcement for a threatened area of the front was made with speed and efficiency. They had also been able to revise their notions of fixed defenses, making a dramatic change from the construction of concrete fortresses to the building of trenches, barriers, and supporting facilities buried in the earth.

The prime arm of the French army was its infantry, and that branch was arriving at a turning point by early 1917. There were both positive and negative aspects. The French infantryman could point with some pride to the undeniable fact that he had been the supreme factor in preventing a German victory thus far in the war. He could also compare his recent actions in 1916 with those of both the German and British armies, and claim a considerable degree of superiority. At the Battle of the Somme, French infantry had not only outpaced their British counterparts initially, but had also managed to contribute to Haig's offensive without the high casualty rates per unit that British units had suffered. This situation had been achieved by the use of new tactics. Where the British infantry advanced from their trenches in waves of riflemen on line, the French technique had been to go forward in small groups, zigzagging from one point of cover to the next and avoiding the advanced strongpoints the Germans favored in front of their main lines.

The French were learning—or more accurately, benefiting—from their previous mistakes. French infantry had what the British lacked, a veteran cadre. A larger, earlier, full-scale French mobilization had meant that each French division was likely to have a number of experienced survivors ready and willing to accept new techniques. Thus the French infantry divisions had an advantage over the largely amateur ranks of Britain's New Army divisions. The German-initiated Verdun campaign had been designed to subject the French to intolerable casualties, but in the end the Germans suffered almost as much as the French.

The morale of the French infantry was not helped by reports that it was nearing exhaustion. Verdun had reaped a terrible toll in maimed and killed, but there was justifiable pride in the stout French defense. But there was another perception gaining currency among these soldiers. French troops were being exposed to literature that depicted their plight as unnecessary and hopeless. Although both France and Britain had imposed strict censorship rules during the conduct of the war, the French censorship office had failed to vigorously pursue its charter and responsibilities. As a result, leftist and pacifist tracts were finding their way into the trenches. The message was clear. The war would simply go away, and happiness and justice would prevail, with the elevation of socialism. Fighting was not essential, and those who had given their lives for France had died in vain. This morale-sapping activity was beginning to cut into the effectiveness of French infantry. The British kept a much tighter rein on their censorship, with better troop morale as a result.

The French General Staff was about on a par with its British counterpart. Although the French staff was larger and perhaps better trained, it had the legacy of a failed offensive at the beginning of the war, and had lost the confidence of the French body politic. The proximity of Paris to the front had the effect of encouraging French politicians to tinker with the conduct of the war. Additionally, the choice of leaders for the French army had very much become a political process, in which the General Staff was circumvented. Although some individual French officers were very imaginative, the staff had as little talent for putting technology to work as its British counterpart did, and it was not noted for innovative doctrine. It had become a tool for handling technical details and replenishment of units, and for doing the bidding of the next general that the politicians found acceptable. In January of 1917 it was busy at work for Robert Nivelle.

NIVELLE'S REAL ADVERSARY ON THE OTHER SIDE of the trench lines was not a commander but a staff officer. The German military system was quite different from that of the Allies. Erich Frederich Wilhelm Ludendorff was eight years younger than Nivelle and four years junior to Haig. He was first and foremost a product of the German General Staff, an institution that thrived on careful study, selection, and elevation of talent, and the encouragement of practical innovation, all in dramatic contrast to the French and British general staffs. Although as a nation Germany was certainly more autocratic than its Western enemies, there were aspects of its staff system that were more "democratic" in nature. Although the French and British were quite prone to assign responsibilities on the basis of seniority, it was not uncommon for very junior members of the German staff to assume duties that resulted in major changes on the battlefield. At heart, the German General Staff was an unabashed meritocracy. In 1917 Ludendorff was its most celebrated product.

As a young officer Ludendorff had a very brief experience as a company commander, then joined the General Staff as a junior member. He almost immediately became controversial over his advocacy of a greatly expanded army. His views were rejected by the War Ministry, but it was typical of the General Staff that this young hothead would be promoted, transferred, and protected when his continued presence became an embarrassment. The organization placed a premium on intelligence and foresight, not on past glories or temporary political discomfort. As the war opened, Ludendorff's projection proved to be the correct one, because the size of peacetime military establishments had much to do with initial advantages and disadvantages, capacities for expanding the armies, and the ultimate number of veteran cadre available to implement changes and to train new units.

Ludendorff's professional judgment was recalled when German forces appeared to be in trouble in the initial phase of the war. Operations against Russia had faltered and the staff chose Ludendorff, fresh from a highly successful assignment as chief of staff for one of the Western Front units, to solve the problem. Almost as an afterthought, a new commander for the Eighth Army enterprise, General Paul von Hindenburg, was added to the General Staff's solution to the problem. It worked, and Ludendorff was promoted to lieutenant general in November 1914. Hindenburg, supposedly Ludendorff's immediate superior, was given increased responsibilities and followed his chief of staff to greater vistas. By August of 1916 this pair was elevated to new heights of authority, and in reality assumed control of the Central Powers' war effort, at least the part that was capable of being coordinated. On the basis of war performance, the German General Staff had chosen well. By January of 1917 everything that Ludendorff had done was either considered successful or was believed to have produced the best obtainable results given the circumstances. The Verdun campaign had not been Ludendorff's idea, and there was every reason to expect that under his careful planning and supervision Germany would triumph.

Ludendorff had looked at his army on the Western Front and was not optimistic. As he traveled from one unit to the next during the fall of 1916, he had demanded the truth from staff officers, and their views were sobering. First, there was the hunger of the troops. Germany, another victim of the preconflict short-war theory, had been unprepared for the actual protracted nature of this war. An efficient early mobilization had robbed the farms of labor; livestock were indiscriminately slaughtered, resulting in a lack of breeding stock. Second, there was the growing problem of numbers. Germany's prewar military strength was twice that of Britain and 25 percent larger than that of France, but Germany had to fight on many fronts. The recent victory in Romania would give Ludendorff only four additional divisions. With more of its youth exposed to battle for longer periods than the Allies, the casualties were more damaging to German future prospects than to those of the Allies. Germany had managed to outfight its enemies during the initial phases of the war, often by placing more of its troops in a situation at the right place and time. However, it had not assembled quite enough strength to win at any particular point, other than the victory against the small Romanian force. In the fall of 1916, Ludendorff must have often thought back with anger on the failure of his prewar recommendation. The peacetime notion of a short, clean war had been a recipe for near failure for each of the participants, but in January of 1917 it had hurt Berlin most of all.

Despite his previous successes, Ludendorff decided to evaluate the situation of the Western Front on its own merits, carrying no preconceived ideas in his baggage. When the subordinate staff officers described the massive use of artillery that the Allies had employed during the Somme and Verdun campaigns, he put a new industrial program into effect that was coming to fruition by January 1917. When he found that the Western Front leaders had become despondent over the losses of 1916, he sought out new ideas—and actively solicited advice from very young officers. Fundamentally, Ludendorff had imbued his Western Front organization with the concept of change. By January there was a promise of improvement in the German army.

The month before, in December 1916, the first of Ludendorff's major changes for the Western Front surfaced in the form of a radical departure in defensive doctrine. Based in part on a captured French document, the new German doctrine stated that ground was no longer to be held at all costs. Every effort was to be made to save lives while conducting a successful defense. The idea was to withdraw as many troops as possible from the forward trenches, thus removing them from the reach of the

Allies' high-volume artillery fires. The forward edge of the German defense was to be composed of well-constructed concrete emplacements, not simply earthen trenches. The construction of these outpost positions as well as the defensive lines in the rear were to take into account troop comfort and sanitation. German commanders were told to rely primarily on firepower, not manpower, to conduct the defense.

The key to this concept was the basic idea that ground could be re-taken by the use of immediate counterattacks after the Allies overran the outposts. If the outposts were constructed well enough, they might hold out in the interim. The vast majority of the troops were not to be subjected to enemy artillery if there was another way to defend. The doctrine had the added benefit of rehabilitating the spirit of attack in the infantry units. The problem with this wave of rationality, however, was how to implement it in the midst of battle.

Of all the armies on the Western Front, none was better prepared to accept change than the Germans. Ludendorff's organization pos-sessed three great assets that were either missing or in small supply in the French and British armies. The first was the General Staff. Com-manders and troops were accustomed to accepting and supervising the execution of staff guidance. There was some degree of insubordination and indiscipline in this army—resentment of the status of staff officers, particularly the young ones, and an understandable proclivity to recog-nize the prerogatives of those officers who had royal bloodlines. But, on the whole, the staff was respected and obeyed. Much of its power came from a great devotion to truth. If the situation was bleak, it would be so painted. If incompetence was found, action would usually be taken, no matter whose reputation was at stake. The second great strength of the German army lay in its veteran cadre. They were thoroughgoing profes-sionals who had seen every mistake of the war and knew how to effect change. Finally, this army communicated with itself. Staff visits to front-line units were the norm. Honest, painful appraisals, often delivered with some humor, bounced back and forth with regularity. The Allies' propa-ganda that depicted the German army as an unfeeling, unthinking robot at the command of Prussian royalty was just that—propaganda.

Despite the fact that a product of a family of merchants, Ludendorff, was at the head of an effective, vibrant military organization, there were flaws in Germany's overall posture. The management of a global conflict requires skill in diplomacy, and even with the focus on trench warfare, naval matters certainly counted. Germany's best effort at sea had to be the use of submarines; there was little other choice. But how the forthcoming

U-boat campaign was waged would determine subsequent events. An all-out, unrestricted campaign would possibly bring the United States into the war on the side of the Allies. A selective, graduated campaign, conducted in close harmony with a vigorous diplomatic effort, might delay or even forestall American entry. All of this was considered at various levels in Berlin. When Ludendorff sided with the navy's proposal to begin an unrestricted, maximum effort, a stamp of approval might well have been affixed, because no other segment of the German government had the strength to obstruct such a powerful endorsement. It was now up to German diplomacy to encourage the substantial antiwar lobby in the United States in an effort to negate what was certain to be an intensified drive for a U.S. declaration of war.

The German Foreign Ministry was not noted for its brilliance, nor, in some circumstances, for an overabundance of common sense. The ministry was headed by the newly appointed Arthur Zimmermann, an enthusiastic supporter of Germany's generals and admirals, particularly the latter. Zimmermann's handling of the unrestricted submarine campaign brought the ministry to a new zenith of doubtful performance. The plot he hatched to handle the Americans centered on persuading Mexico to launch its army northward in an offensive aimed at the reconquest of Texas, Arizona, and New Mexico. California was not mentioned, possibly because the Berlin diplomat was banking on his Mexican counterpart to attract Japan into this novel enterprise; there was a notion that Tokyo should have some part of the action. All of this would have been bad enough, but in another stroke of idiocy the zany scheme was transmitted to Mexico over British-owned telegraph cables. German approval of the unrestricted submarine campaign that would target all shipping, neutral and belligerent, the creative piece of diplomatic planning, the transmission of the plan to Mexico, and the subsequent British interception and decoding of the "Zimmermann telegram"—all took place in the month of January. Thus, at the outset of the new year, events were in train to bring yet another army to the Western Front.

WHILE THE EUROPEAN ARMIES WERE STALEMATED in France and Belgium, the U.S. Army was stalemated in the Mexican desert. Publicly ordered to capture Pancho Villa in March of 1916, Major General John Pershing and his command were both politically and militarily stymied on New Year's Day in 1917. Villa's strength had grown during the interim. Pershing's actual orders were worded in a more restrained form than was commonly known at the time, and the punitive expedition had brought about some stability on the border. The U.S. deployment had given American diplomats a bargaining chip with a recalcitrant Mexican government. However, the international perception of American ground forces was justifiably that of a rather minor military organization. In 1911 the first attempt to put together a modern division had taken ninety days, and the results had been singularly unimpressive to European military observers. The United States had always possessed a strong and well-respected navy but its army drew mixed reviews at best. On the basis of recent demonstrated performance, it could well be said that the U.S. Army was as much a threat to itself as to an adversary. It had been the victor in the Spanish-American War, but had suffered large numbers of casualties because of a lack of fundamental sanitation measures. The United States had yet to show that it could mobilize and field a large army overseas. In January 1917 it had yet to prove that it could even catch a bandit.

There were, however, several strong points to the U.S. Army, although these factors were largely unknown to European military leaders. First, it had organized a progressive system of education for its leadership. The process culminated in the Army War College, whose graduates had been introduced to the best available literature on the subject of war, by recognized European authors. Second, the glaring deficiencies of the Spanish-American War had been taken to heart, and the U.S. Army leadership had been disciplined to new methods. The Americans had the benefit of observer status during the first two and a half years of the Great War, and could see that small, professional armies were wholly inadequate to modern European battlefields. While they might not have grasped the real nature of Western Front combat, they saw what their European counterparts had not seen at the beginning of the war— the need for a large, national army, organized and equipped to fight a protracted war. A fourth factor of strength at this juncture in the war was that a potential American army entering the war at this point would not have the fatigue, underlying discontent, and debilitating effect of several years of casualties to carry into battle.

A final strength of the U.S. Army lay in its commander-in-chief. Few American presidents have entered office with less military experience than Woodrow Wilson, and his introduction to military operations had been somewhat bruising. By New Year's Day 1917, however, he knew all too well that overly restrictive orders, close supervision, and rigid control from Washington, D.C., resulted in press sympathy for a field commander at the expense of the presidency. Wilson had fared badly with his ventures into the revolutionary maze of Mexico. In the end the failed commander, Pershing, had managed to gain a substantial newspaper and political following. As a result, Wilson was likely to provide his army and its leadership with consent and support without attempting to interfere in its handling of military affairs.

In 1917 John Joseph Pershing was fifty-seven years old, a little younger than Haig and Nivelle, but four years older than Ludendorff. Having married well, Pershing had been able to subvert the seniority system and had been advanced past 800 more experienced officers to reach the rank of brigadier general in 1906. In comparison to other American generals he was therefore rather young and still junior to any number of U.S. Army leaders. A West Pointer, Pershing held a law degree and was considered somewhat formal, stern, and distant. Although he had been an on-site observer during the Russo-Japanese War, his firsthand experience in combat was limited to the pacification campaigns in the Philippines and Mexico. In his lack of experience in large-scale ground combat, he was representative of the army he served.

When the United States eventually became a belligerent in April of 1917, it would enter the war less prepared than it had ever been at the eve of a conflict. The total uniformed ground strength of its army, counting both national guard and regulars, amounted to fewer than 310,000 troops. That figure was less than the British losses at the Somme, the French losses at Verdun, or the German losses in the same battle. The nation that created powered flight had managed to crash all six of its initial army airplanes during the abortive punitive expedition. Machine guns, another American invention, were in short supply, and there was not enough artillery ammunition for war with Mexico, much less the demands of the Western Front. Tanks were increasingly being used on European battlefields and were based on the U.S.-designed Holt tractor, but the American army had none. Only twenty-three officers had been through the new education system, having graduated from both the school at Fort Leavenworth and the new Army War College. The U.S. Army's General Staff consisted of nineteen souls in Washington, who had recently been chastised for having the audacity to prepare a contingency plan to be used in the event of a war with Germany. All in all, the entry of the United States into the war offered little promise of breaking the stalemate that existed in Europe.

FOR WESTERN CIVILIZATION, THE FIRST day of 1917 appeared to offer little hope. A strange series of events had led to an unprecedented bloodbath that seemed to have no logical end. Peace initiatives had failed, while the lethality of combat grew. A rational projection as to the probable end to combat on the Western Front would, on this day, point to an inevitable victory—for the last man still able to fight. Cold logic could foresee only the grim arithmetic of attrition. In that calculation, one counts not the dead, not the current combatants, but those who are left to kill. For this gruesome reason, attrition is rarely referred to by either politicians or generals. Those two professions are linked by the common characteristic of optimism; generals and politicians must either profess optimism or step aside for those who do. Generals and politicians are expected to have a solution, and on New Year's Day of 1917 there was more than one plan for ending the war on the Western Front.

TWO

Maneuver in Mass:
The 1917 Allied Offensive

THE NEXT DAY, JANUARY 2, 1917, General Nivelle ordered the French aviators to conduct reconnaissance of the German rear in close cooperation with Haig's pilots. There had been a number of reports from German prisoners, escaped Russian laborers, and British aviators that the Germans were hard at work on a new defensive line, situated well to the rear of their current positions. The first such report had come in as early as October of 1916. In early 1917 ordering pilots to conduct a deep reconnaissance of the German rear was not a matter to be taken lightly. The German air arm was sporting twin-gun Albatross and Halberstadt fighter planes and taking a toll of the lesser-armed Allied aircraft. The returning French pilots reported no signs of a new line of trenches. Still, throughout the next three months reports of a new German line persisted.

On the other side of the trenches, Ludendorff had a far greater insight into his enemy's activities than they did into his. Although he did not know that German diplomatic messages to Mexico City were routinely deciphered by British intelligence officers, he was aware that the German intelligence apparatus was reading Italian diplomatic traffic going to Russia. During the first week of February, the Germans would discover through this link that the Allies were planning a great offensive on the Western Front involving some one hundred divisions, and that the attack would be in April. The news brought relief in Berlin, where an Allied offensive had been expected. What the Germans feared was an early date for the attack. By April the new industrial effort would have provided enough ammunition so that intensive combat could be supported. The ninety-day interval would also provide time to put the new defensive doctrine into effect. There would also be time for the unrestricted submarine campaign to wreak its havoc on Allied shipping. Finally, knowledge of the date of the Allied offensive would give Ludendorff the chance to launch a preemptive attack. All told, in the critical field of military intelligence, Ludendorff had the better of his adversaries.

The German general may have been surprised at the date of the forthcoming Allied offensive, but he could not have expected his opponents to elect a defensive posture during 1917, because the conditions and advantages that promoted an attack decision were all in their favor. Allied forces on the Western Front outnumbered the Germans. Russia and Italy were not likely to tolerate a French and British relaxation of pressure in the west that would allow Germany to shift forces south or east. Moreover, German forces were occupying French and Belgian soil. This latter condition made it imperative for the Allies to attempt reconquest in the event that serious peace negotiations might finally begin. Realistic Allied options in early 1917 did not include defense in the west. The Allies must attack. But where and how? What would be the objective of the Allied campaign? Would it be an all-out offensive, aimed at retaking specific pieces of territory? Or would the Allied attack be designed to use superior numbers to wear down the German army, a campaign of protracted attrition?

The Allies had many options, and so did Ludendorff. Knowing the date of the Allied offensive, he could launch an attack, perhaps in late March. Such a German offensive could have the effect of absorbing Allied reserves, since they would have to be rushed to the point of attack. It would deplete the Allied artillery ammunition stocks planned for the support of their April offensive. And a German offensive in March would preempt the attention and time of the Allied command and control apparatus.

A late March offensive—a spoiling attack—had much to offer Ludendorff. It was an attractive option. Another German option was to defend. That decision would not require the massing of additional troops from other fronts to support an effective spoiling attack. Defending would probably ensure a lower casualty rate for 1917—a serious consideration at this point in the war. It would allow time and opportunity for the new defensive doctrine to be learned by Western Front units. And defense in the west would permit Ludendorff to continue his offensive pressure on the Eastern Front against a weakening Russian army, reinforcing the German and Austrian success that had been gained in Romania. It has always been judged better to reinforce success. The choice between an offensive campaign or a season of defense in the west was not an easy one for the German General Staff.

Allied offensive options also amounted to two fundamental choices. It was essential that the 1917 attack be conducted in both the French and British sectors, since otherwise one nation's army would have the unfair advantage of the lower combat death toll normally associated with a mission of defense. Knowing this, none of the Allied military and political leaders wanted to endanger the bonds of the alliance by suggesting that his nation's forces remain passive in the upcoming campaign. The prime options were, therefore, a French main attack with a supporting action by the British, or a British primary effort with the French supplying the secondary action. If the British staged the larger attack, it was understood that their desires for the location of the major effort would predominate. It was further known that the British preference for an area would be near the coastline, in order to facilitate the reconquest of the lowland ports—a prime concern of the politically powerful and essential Royal Navy. A choice of that area for the attack would also ensure the enthusiastic cooperation of the small Belgian army and clearly contribute to one of England's heavily advertised moral aims in the war: the eventual liberation of German-occupied Belgium.

The British preference for a lowland offensive was not in concert with what the French wanted to do. If the French were to make the primary attack, their desire would understandably center on pushing the Germans back from the area near Paris. The choice was not simply a political matter. French industry, the communications network, and the bulge in the German lines all pointed to the wisdom of a Paris-based offensive. Thus the two basic Allied offensive options on the Western Front boiled down to a British attack in the lowlands supported by the French, or a major French effort east of Paris supported by a British secondary attack.

Each side, therefore, had to choose between two fundamental options for the forthcoming campaign of 1917. For Ludendorff it was simply whether to attack or defend. For Nivelle, Haig, and their political masters, it was between a French- or British-led offensive. On the surface the decision-making process seemed to be a relatively simple matter for the Germans: Ludendorff could decide. A one-man decision, however, was not a true reflection of fact. Ludendorff himself insisted on obtaining the views of others. While he would not place great weight on the opinion of the German diplomatic service, he did listen to what the diplomats had to say. With the new U-boat campaign under way, naval thinking also had to be increasingly considered. Nor did Germany fight alone; Austrian and Bulgarian opinions, as well as the views of German officers with the Turkish army, contributed to a complex decision-making mechanism in Berlin. Finally, the effective use of German power was centered on the talents, labor, and resolve of the German people. Although Berlin's political apparatus was certainly autocratic in comparison to that of its enemies, it was not devoid of concern for the well-being and desires of the German population.

The Allied decision-making system was, of course, somewhat more complicated. Yet there was an unwritten but well-understood tenet: the side that supplied the most resources on any front had the strongest voice. The Allies had not appointed an overall military commander on the Western Front. The stakes were so high that no nation would be willing to commit troops to a foolish or unreasonable endeavor, but a spirit of cooperation, though sometimes grudgingly given, existed in the councils of the Western Allies. It was this cooperation, perhaps the result of a culture that had been disciplined to democratic compromise, that provided the cement for the alliance. The cohesion of the Allies was always shifting, subject to the whims of political and military personalities, and constantly tested. But it had weathered over two years of blood and tragedy, and it promoted an ability for men of diverse opinions to stand behind and support even controversial solutions. Fear of the consequences of noncooperation often outweighed the logic of one's own views. Mutual Allied decision-making was not easy, but it was never impossible.

Both sides had reached their decisions in the waning days of 1916. The Germans opted for defense in the west and continued offensive pressure in the east. Ludendorff's thinking hinged more on his new defensive scheme for the Western Front than on the prospects for ultimate success against Russia. An ability to thwart French and British offensive action with minimal cost might drive the Allies to negotiations. But the new doctrine and the new positions required time to be implemented. That time could best be gained by remaining on the defensive in the west. Ludendorff calculated that the Allies would have some seventy-five divisions in reserve for 1917, whereas he could only muster about forty. That alone was a powerful argument against a German offensive.

The Allies decided on a French attack along and north of the river Aisne, near Reims. The supporting and secondary Allied effort was to be conducted by Haig's New Army east of the French city of Arras, south of the Belgian border. The British were to strike first, in the hope that they would thereby draw off German reserves from Nivelle's main Aisne offensive. British hopes for clearing the lowlands had to be shelved. The British acquiesced in Nivelle's request for British occupation of a considerable extent of the French defense sector. Freeing up a number of French divisions while increasingly tying down his own, Haig conformed to the plan and contributed to Nivelle's gathering offensive force. The French commander had been extremely persuasive with British politicians.

The remarkable quality of Nivelle's scheme was not his insistence on the French carrying the main burden of the offensive. After all, France had more than twice the troops that Britain had contributed to the front. What made Nivelle's plan unique was its objective, and the way it was presented. The French general's aim was nothing short of the total destruction of the German army and the end of the war. He estimated that Berlin's Western Front forces had been so depleted during the 1916 battles of Verdun and the Somme that they could not stand up to a similar bloodletting in 1917. His plan was to employ both his own and Haig's troops to completely absorb German reserves in two great offensives. Then would come a massive attack in the French sector that would break the reserve-starved German lines. At that time, Nivelle would unleash the large, fresh force that he had been gathering. He called it the "mass of maneuver," twenty-seven divisions of French infantry and cavalry. It was portrayed as the technique he had used so successfully during his counterattacks at Verdun, but upscaled, involving the entire front rather than a sector. To war-weary politicians, the enthusiastic French general's plan was welcome.

The British offensive was scheduled for April 8, with an enormous artillery preparation that would begin on April 4. Nivelle's main infantry assault was scheduled for April 12, with an even more massive artillery preparation. All during January and early February Allied quartermasters, engineers, artillerymen, staff officers, commanders, and troops labored to prepare for the scheduled offensive. In the British sector alone, water supplies for the attacking forces required the construction of six pipelines totaling 1,500 tons of water mains. Twelve plank roads had to be built over the mud, requiring 50,000 tons of timber and 206 trainloads of crushed rock. Millions of artillery shells were stocked in convenient depots. All of this and much more had to be done under the noses of the Germans, but without their knowledge. Hence there was much feverish activity, planning, and detailed supervision.

In late February, however, the attention of logisticians, staff officers,

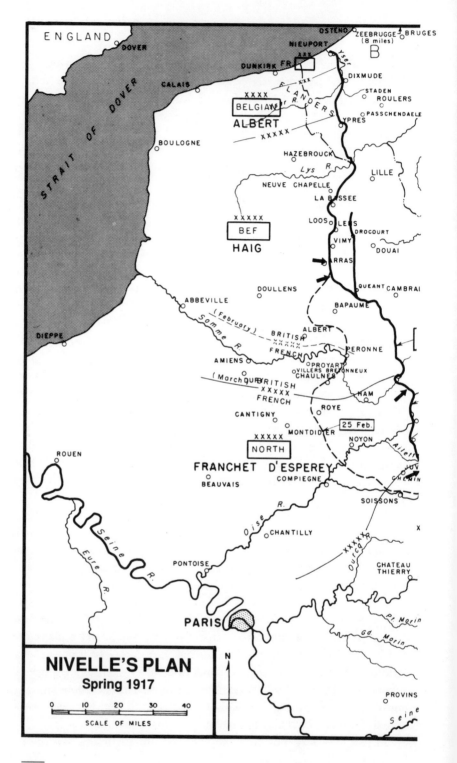

ENGLAND

DOVER

STRAIT OF DOVER

CALAIS

BOULOGNE

DIEPPE

ABBEVILLE

DOULLENS

ROUEN

PONTOISE

Seine R.

Eure R.

PARIS

OSTEND

ZEEBRUGGE
(8 miles)

BRUGES

NIEUPORT

DUNKIRK FR. xxx

DIXMUDE

STADEN

ROULERS

XXXX

BELGIAN

ALBERT

XXXXX

HAZEBROUCK

Lys R.

NEUVE CHAPELLE

XXXXX

BEF

HAIG

YPRES

PASSCHENDAELE

LILLE

LA BASSEE

LOOS LENS

DROCOURT

VIMY

DOUAI

ARRAS

QUEANT CAMBRAI

BAPAUME

(February)

Somme R.

BRITISH
XXXXX
FRENCH

ALBERT

PERONNE

AMIENS

(March)

BRITISH
XXXXX
FRENCH

PROYART
VILLERS BRETONNEUX
CHAULNES

HAM

CANTIGNY

ROYE

MONTDIDIER

25 Feb.

NOYON

XXXXX

NORTH

FRANCHET D'ESPEREY

BEAUVAIS

COMPIEGNE

Ailette

CHEMIN

SOISSONS

Oise R.

CHANTILLY

XXXXX

Ourcq R.

X

CHATEAU
THIERRY

Pt. Morin

Gd. Morin

PROVINS

Seine

NIVELLE'S PLAN
Spring 1917

0 10 20 30 40
SCALE OF MILES

N

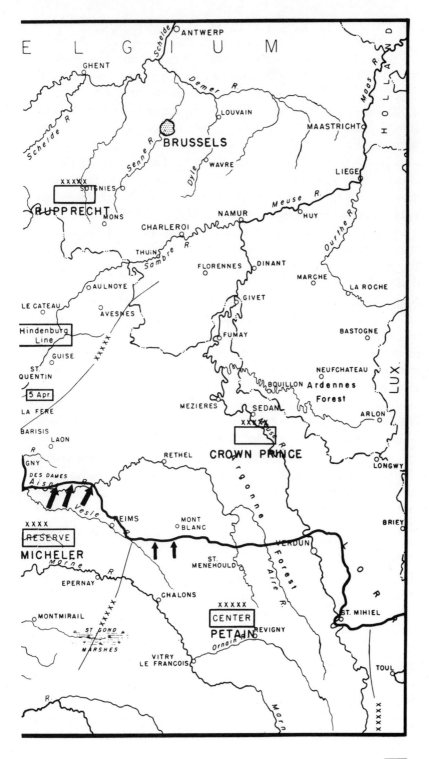

and commanders began to shift from their own concerns to a growing change taking place on the other side of the trenches. The Germans were pulling back. Not in every sector and certainly not all at one time, but they were leaving forward positions that only recently had been bitterly contested. Throughout late February and all through March it slowly dawned on Allied officers that in many places they faced not only a new defense line, but a new German defense system. The first thing that drew attention was the wire. Barbed wire in front of trench lines was a standard feature on both sides, but what the Allies saw was different. Rows and rows of coiled concertina, some stacked as high as eight feet, were being carefully emplaced to channel attacking infantrymen into killing zones. In many sectors the new wire entanglements could be seen only from the air, because the forward German trench line was placed on the other side of the hill, on the reverse slope.

Night reconnaissance patrols reported that the forward slope was protected by a checkerboard arrangement of buried and camouflaged concrete machine-gun bunkers, used as outposts. They would obviously be used to break up the Allied infantry assault before it reached the German trenches, and it appeared likely that these outposts would survive a heavy artillery bombardment. The next feature, also discovered by air reconnaissance, was the distance between the successive trench lines. The Germans had increased the gaps between their lines. It appeared that they had done this in order to put their second line beyond the range of the most common pieces of Allied artillery. French and British staff officers and their commanders surmised that this defensive technique had been employed so that after the Allies successfully seized the forward trench they would have to pause long enough to displace their artillery forward before they assaulted the second German line. The interim would give the defender time, but for what the Allies were not entirely certain.

The new German positions caused growing doubt among French officers about the wisdom of Nivelle's plans for a major offensive. This was particularly true of his subordinate commanders. Their sectors had been heavily affected by the surprise withdrawal. The British were less concerned because much of their area of responsibility seemed to be relatively unchanged. French fears loomed larger when it was learned that a sergeant carrying an important plan describing the forthcoming offensive was missing in the midst of a tactical action. Their fears were well founded. The Germans had both the hapless sergeant and the plan.

After a hurried council of war, Nivelle's plan was allowed to remain intact. There were many factors that influenced French deliberations, but two stood out. Pressure on Germany could not be relaxed because its occupation of French and Belgian soil could not be tolerated, and Russia and Italy could not bear the brunt of German reinforcements alone. Moreover, while Ludendorff had picked up about thirteen or fourteen divisions from his now-shortened lines after the withdrawal, the French reserve strength had also grown from the same process. Nivelle's "mass of maneuver," the exploitation force, had become stronger. The northern French sector alone had been able to release thirteen divisions. True, Ludendorff possibly now knew the date of the offensive and where it was to be made. But the full details of Haig's secondary and supporting attack may not have been discovered by the Germans, and they might well believe the French attack would be the sole effort.

The British were to attack to the east, on a front of about twelve miles. The attack sector was divided roughly in half by the Scarpe River, which ran in an east-west direction. To the north of the river the terrain was dominated by Vimy Ridge, facing west. This was a strong German position that overlooked the Canadians, who were waiting to commence the assault. To the south of the Scarpe River, the corridor chosen for the attack was overlooked by a village on a rise in the ground, Monchy-le-Preux. The river itself was rather shallow and small, but its flood plain was habitually wide, muddy, and dotted with marshes. Although the British forces south of the Scarpe faced what appeared to be the new German defense system, the Canadians to the north of the river were pitted against positions that seemed to be little changed. The war-torn city of Arras, in the middle of the Allied lines, presented Haig's troops with a choke point, since its narrow streets would obstruct the rapid movement of forces to exploit a breach in the German lines.

In part, this obstacle had been overcome by dint of a massive subterranean engineering effort. Arras, and the area surrounding the city, were situated over a veritable labyrinth of elongated caves and sewer lines. The British and Canadians had spent months connecting the caves and sewers so that their troops could approach their attack positions underground, protected from German artillery. The tunneling effort had resulted in accommodations for 30,000 men, an underground hospital, and an administration center. Many of the tunnels had lighting, ventilation, and drainage systems. Not only did this sophisticated system provide safety and relief for the congested road net, it also provided a measure of surprise, because, if it were properly used, the approach march for the attack could be hidden from German observation.

All of this activity and the responsibility of command fell on the shoulders of General Edmund Allenby, a descendent of Oliver Cromwell and veteran of the Boer War. Allenby had begun the war as a cavalry division commander. By 1917 he commanded the Third Army. The fifty-six-year-old general had a reputation for a bad temper and explosive outbursts of anger; he was referred to as "The Bull." Allenby's basic scheme to carry out the Allied secondary attack involved an initial assault by eight infantry divisions of the Third Army in the central and southern portions of the attack corridor. On his left, four Canadian divisions of the First Army would seize Vimy Ridge. Altogether Allenby had sixteen divisions operating under five corps headquarters. One of these corps formations was composed of cavalry, and its horse-mounted troopers were expected to exploit the penetration gained by the infantry. Additionally, the attack would feature the use of forty tanks under Allenby's command. The Arras offensive, even in terms of the enormous forces employed in World War I, would be a gigantic effort.

To support this attack, destroy the German defenses, and pave the way for the infantry, the British and Canadians had massed 2,817 pieces of artillery and large-caliber mortars—an artillery weapon for every twelve yards of the attack sector. Preparation fire was to open up on April 4, four days prior to the infantry assault. Most of the firing was scheduled in daylight, so that there would be lull periods for air observation and adjustment. At night, the firing was carefully planned to occur at varied times, supplemented by heavy machine-gun fire where the terrain permitted, so as to prevent the German defenders from repairing the damage to wire entanglements. Two-inch mortars were employed to destroy German barbed wire in the extreme forward areas, and large-caliber artillery was targeted on the more distant coils of concertina. Special points such as road junctions were to be placed under continuous salvos, at the rate of about six per hour at random intervals. When the infantry was finally launched, it would be supported by a creeping barrage, carefully planned so as to match the advance. This was to be accomplished by artillery weapons spaced on an average of one every twenty yards, firing eight rounds every four minutes in front of the foot soldiers. After each four-minute interval, the artillery fire would be adjusted forward one hundred yards and the whole process would begin again. The infantry would thus be advancing closely behind a wall of explosions and flying shrapnel. All during the assault, enemy trench lines were to be kept under the fire of other guns, while still other long-range pieces were delivering gas shells

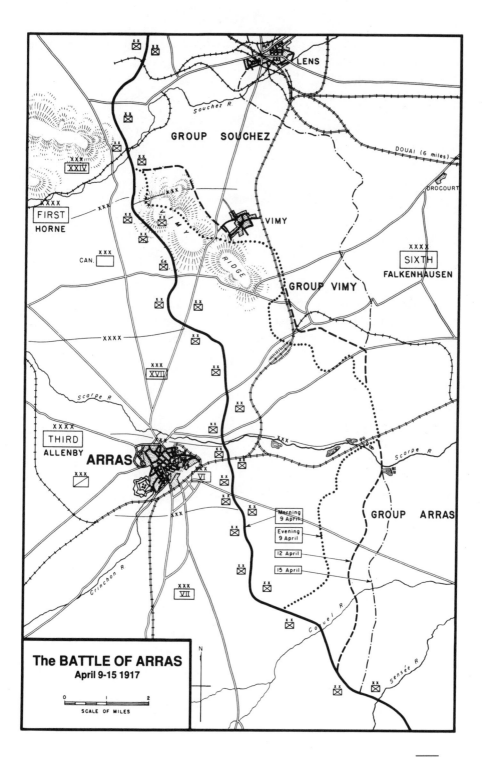

The BATTLE OF ARRAS
April 9-15 1917

0   1   2
SCALE OF MILES

LENS

GROUP SOUCHEZ

Souchez R.

DOUAI (6 miles)

DROCOURT

XXX
XXIV

XXXX
FIRST
HORNE

XXX

VIMY

GROUP VIMY

XXXX
SIXTH
FALKENHAUSEN

CAN.   XXX

V I M Y   R I D G E

XXXX

XXX
XVII

Scarpe R.

XXXX
THIRD
ALLENBY

ARRAS

XXX

VI

XXX

Scarpe R.

GROUP ARRAS

Morning
9 April

Evening
9 April

12 April

15 April

XXX
VII

Crinchon R.

Cojeul R.

Sensée R.

N

39

on German artillery positions. A German soldier would later describe the artillery at Arras as a storm of steel.

The forty tanks that Allenby was to employ were of a rather inferior model; the newer British machines were as yet unavailable. Tank crews were given carefully selected targets, usually positions where the Germans had constructed strongpoints containing bunkered machine-gun emplacements. Two or three of the tanks were allocated to reduce each of these positions, and would approach the enemy site over a carefully selected route in accordance with a schedule that was keyed to the infantry advance. It was hoped that in the latter phase of the assault, twenty of the tanks would be combined to lead the attack on the important position of Monchy-le-Preux. Not much faith had been placed in the performance of British armor, and it was well understood that mechanical difficulties could occur.

As the British artillery preparation roared to its climax, the news spread throughout the opposing trench lines that the United States had declared war against Germany on April 6. The sinking of American merchant vessels without warning by submarines, and the public disclosure of the German diplomatic initiative aimed at sparking war between Mexico and the United States, had produced the inevitable result. The news had little effect on either of the two armies facing each other at Arras, however. American participation on the side of the Allies would not necessarily mean the use of its land forces. The U.S. Army might never even see the Western Front. The American differences with Germany had centered on naval matters, and it was possible that the United States would confine her actions to the sea. To the British, Canadians, and Germans deployed in the basin of the Scarpe River, American entry into the war was of minor interest.

Of more importance to the Canadians and British was the announcement that the attack would be delayed. The reason for the delay was a French need for more time to prepare for the main attack. The delay was to be for twenty-four hours. British officers who felt that prolonged artillery preparations were counterproductive voiced their displeasure. Since the French were carrying the main burden, however, British plans had to conform to French needs. There were British leaders, too, who believed that the extra day was necessary to ensure that the German wire was cut. The counterargument was that a surprise bombardment of only a few hours could accomplish the same task without giving away the location of the attack and allowing the enemy time to position reserves. Both views were heatedly argued.

A technological solution was also being tested. The British were using a new instantaneous fuse that detonated the artillery round before it could sink into the mud for any appreciable distance. British officers who argued the merits of short or long artillery preparations did not know that the new fuse was working. In the first days of the now-prolonged British artillery preparation at Arras, the new German wire system was being systematically destroyed.

The climax of artillery preparation was actually a tapering off in the intensity of fire. The Germans would expect the massive bombardment to build to a crescendo heralding the infantry assault. Therefore the British planned a decrease in fire just before the attack to enhance the chances of surprise. It was a welcome respite to the German troops, who had been through what they later described as "the week of suffering." The devastating schedule of preparation firing had caused havoc in the German lines. Throughout the week, ration parties, when they got through at all, were taking six hours to make a trip to the front that normally took only fifteen minutes. Much of the trench line was totally demolished. Some of the German front-line troops had not had food for two or three days. Wire communications and messenger service had been badly disrupted. North of the Scarpe, in the Canadian sector of attack, the Germans were in deep trouble prior to the assault.

ON THE NIGHT OF APRIL 8, THE Canadians began to move stealthily forward to their assigned jump-off positions. Some went through tunnels that had exits within 150 yards of the German positions. Others moved by single file through breaks in the Canadian wire, silently dropping into shallow trenches or shell holes to await the signal to launch the attack. By 4:00 A.M. on the morning of April 9 they were ready. The first wave in this northern attack sector contained fifteen thousand Canadians. Behind them were still more thousands of Canadians and British under the command of the Canadian Corps.

At 5:30 A.M. the artillery firing schedule quickly kicked in the creeping barrage sequence, whistles were blown in the cold dark night, and the Canadian infantry began its long-awaited attack. The great Allied offensive of 1917 had begun.

Pressing their way forward through the churned-up French soil, the confident Canadians moved to their objectives in much the same way they had rehearsed weeks before over a to-scale terrain model in the rear areas. Some units employed the techniques that their officers had learned from visiting the Verdun sector during the successful French counterattacks the year before. Now, far to the north, Nivelle's concepts were taking root. Twenty-five battalions advanced behind a massive, moving storm of steel. It was an irresistible force of North American power, fortitude, skill, and cunning. For the most part, the Canadians caught the Germans still in their bunkers. In accordance with the Nivelle philosophy, they left small contingents to hold pockets of resistance while the rest of the tide of riflemen moved east into the darkness. Surprisingly some of the Canadians found a few Germans who were still unaware of the assault even in the second enemy trench system. The Germans were not communicating with each other.

At some of the heavily protected machine-gun emplacements, however, the Germans fought well. Canadians died, and their comrades worked their way to the very gun embrasures using grenades and in some cases bayonets. In one instance Lance Sergeant Sifton of the Second Division jumped into a German machine-gun position, bayoneted every member of the crew, and with his rifle used as a club, fought off a German rescue attempt until his fellow infantrymen came to assist him. Sifton was killed—the last act of one of the Germans who had briefly survived his one-man assault. The Canadians had a high reputation with the German soldiers, and that reputation was considerably enhanced after Arras.

The Canadian attack on Vimy Ridge had eight tanks assigned to it. All failed mechanically and were left behind, but the infantry continued to move forward through an early gray morning of sleet and snow. A sudden and all too brief burst of sunshine after 9:00 A.M. bathed the shell-pocked battlefield in light. Both the Germans and the Allies got an unexpected glimpse of the situation. Vimy Ridge was crawling with Canadians, with small packets of unarmed Germans being herded westward into captivity. One could also momentarily view crews of North Americans manhandling heavy machine guns to the new forward positions. The water-cooled guns and their tripod stands weighed as much as seventy-five pounds without their hefty belts of ammunition. With the required security and ammunition bearers, a machine-gun displacement and subsequent employment involved the services of twelve to fifteen men. The guns, however, were essential, for a German counterattack could be expected at any moment.

South of the Scarpe, in the British attack sector, Allenby's Third Army, numbering about 350,000 troops, put ten divisions into the initial assault, using 120 battalions. Forty-four of these battalions were Scottish. The scheme on the British right flank resembled the overall campaign plan. The Canadians to the north were expected to draw German attention with their early-morning assault on Vimy Ridge. The British on the extreme right of the attack sector were to delay their assault until the afternoon. This was thought necessary because the British faced the new German defense system, with its more formidable trenches, obstacles, bunkered outposts, and lines with wider separation. On the British left flank, near the Scarpe, the assault was keyed to begin slightly later than the Canadian attack. It was to be an attack in echelon.

The British right made progress against the new defenses, capturing parts of the first trench line of the defense system, referred to as the Hindenburg Line. In some areas, however, the British attack was stymied, particularly in those regions where the main German defenses were placed on the reverse slope. Arriving at the crest of the forward slope, British leaders found that the main defensive system on the reverse slope was still largely intact. Wire was only partially cut, machine-gun bunkers forward of the trench line were in full operation, and the trench lines themselves appeared to be little damaged by the five days of bombardment. The new German defense system also precluded direct observation and adjustment of artillery fire. British infantry on the right of the line had its work cut out for it.

Further to the center of the offensive the German defense was less sound, and their troops appeared to be demoralized. Some were found in bunkers, simply awaiting an opportunity to surrender. A few British tanks were performing well, but for the most part the results were disappointing. Of one group of ten tanks, seven became mired in the mud early on, and the remaining three were put out of action by the Germans, two by artillery fire and one by an enterprising and courageous German infantryman who threw a grenade under its track. Although the British center experienced success in moving forward as much as a mile and a half, it nonetheless carried the seeds of danger. The farther it pressed on, the more exposed its right flank became, due to the lack of British progress to the south.

As the cold darkness of evening settled in on the mud and wreckage of the Arras battlefield, the British experienced the grim satisfaction of some well-earned successes. Despite the prolonged artillery preparation that had actually started in the last weeks of March with assembly and registration of fires, a strong measure of surprise had been achieved. The handling of engineering, artillery, and transportation requirements demonstrated a much higher degree of professional competence than the "New Army" had shown in 1916. Troop performance had been nothing short of magnificent. Attacking troops normally exhibit more esprit than those who defend, but Allenby's forces and the Canadians had clearly revealed to the enemy and their own leaders an organization of high morale and determination. New techniques had been successfully used. British heavy machine guns had not only been used in direct fire support, holding the enemy's heads down as friendly infantry advanced, but had also been displaced forward immediately after the assault. Those heavy, bulky engines of death were now being used as offensive weapons. Finally, and of great importance, the German army clearly had some demoralized units. Allenby alone counted 5,600 captives on the evening of April 9, along with thirty-six enemy artillery pieces. To the British, Ludendorff's legions were beginning to show weakness.

The sobering downside of the day's actions included the failure of what had been considered a distinct Allied advantage: the tanks. On the whole, the tank was still a machine whose time had not yet come. It was simply too mechanically deficient. In the few instances of success, the infantry failed to coordinate the exploitation of their advance. There were many areas where the massive artillery preparation had not made a dent in the German defenses. The British leadership in these areas had called a halt to the advance and requested more fire. The new instantaneous artillery fuse had proved itself, but there were not enough of them. In the regions where the British had achieved success, there was no exploitation force available. Horse cavalry had been designated for this role, but its employment was slated for a planned sector, one that did not open until very late in the day. In the few areas where the cavalrymen were used, they and their horses were cut down by German machine guns and artillery. So the overall success had been uneven. An analysis of the attack would indicate that the Allies had succeeded in the parts of the German lines where Ludendorff's new methods had been only partially implemented, or in areas that were organized around the previous German defensive system. Not surprisingly, in precisely those regions involving the new system, German soldiers fought well.

DURING THE NIGHT BRITISH STAFF officers and commanders labored by candlelight and lanterns. Compiling reports from the front, adjusting situation maps, and receiving the results of prisoner interrogations, they worked out a new plan for the next day. Although there was some reason for optimism, they knew that continued success would be increasingly costly. The German command was now fully alert to the size and magnitude of Haig's offensive, and could be expected to react in a familiar way. The British were torn between an all-out offensive push, regard-

Top: Field Marshal Paul Von Hindenburg, (center) and Quartermaster General Erich Ludendorff (right).—*National Archives*
Bottom: German dispatch rider, Western Front, wearing gas mask and armed with a lance and a rifle.—*National Archives*

Top: More than any other single weapon, the machine gun served to revolutionize infantry tactics in the Great War. Here, an American gunner mans a British-made Lewis gun, somewhere in Belgium.
—*National Archives*

Bottom: The trenches in the Great War stretched from the English Channel eastward across the continent of Europe. Here, English infantrymen are photographed as they leap across a front-line trench.—*U.S. Army Military History Institute*

Top: German machine-gun crew in action.—*National Archives*
Bottom: Dead soldier, probably German. Note that his hand still clutches his
  rifle.—*U.S. Army Military History Institute*

Clockwise, from top left: Field Marshal Douglas Haig, General Edmund Allenby, General Herbert Plumer, General Hubert Gough.—*National Archives; U.S. Army Military History Institute*

Top: British lancers moving through Arras. Sir Douglas Haig continued
to designate horse cavalry as an exploitation force throughout 1917.
—*U.S. Army Military History Institute*
Bottom: German Albatross fighters, pictured above, almost cost the Allies
air superiority in early 1917.—*U.S. Army Military History Institute*

French infantry on the attack.—*U.S. Army Military History Institute*

French Schneider fourteen-ton tanks, armed with a 75-mm howitzer on the right front and two Hotchkiss machine guns on the sides. One hundred twenty-eight of these were employed in the Aisne offensive in April 1917.—*U.S. Army Military History Institute*

Crown Prince Ruprecht of Bavaria, German commander in Flanders (right), with General Sixt von Armin.
—*National Archives*

Colonel General Ludwig von Falkenhausen leaving a dugout at Namur.
—*National Archives*

British raiding party heading toward German trenches, near Arras.
—*National Archives*

In preparation for a cross-channel amphibious assault on German defenses planned for 1917, British tanks were modified to carry inclined-ways that would enable them to climb the coping of the sea wall at Middelkerke.—*from "The Consise Story of the Dover Patrol," by Admiral Sir R. H. Bacon*

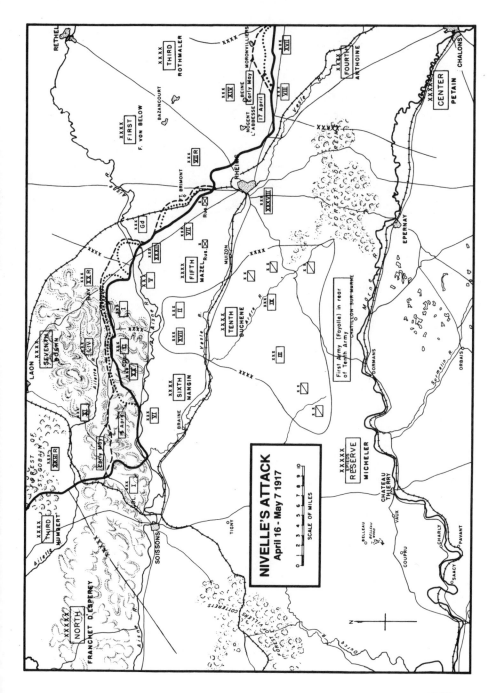

NIVELLE'S ATTACK
April 16 - May 7 1917

SCALE OF MILES
0 1 2 3 4 5 6 7 8 9 10

less of the conditions of exposed flanks, and a consolidation of gains, a straightening of their lines to better withstand the inevitable German counterattack. In the next few days, they would attempt a little of both.

When Ludendorff searched for the causes of the limited British success at Arras, he had little trouble discovering the reason. It was primarily a case of insubordination. Haig's attack had struck the forces of Colonel General Falkenhausen's Sixth Army. Falkenhausen had simply not implemented the new defense system throughout the area of his responsibility. Many of his units had been ordered to hold the forward trenches at all costs, and had thus been terribly wasted, mangled by the British preparation shelling. Ludendorff's new method, by contrast, required a forward area that was lightly manned, with a considerable distance of 1,200 to 2,000 yards between trench lines. The Sixth German Army had only partially adjusted its defenses to conform to the new doctrine. Particularly in the northern portion of the defenses astride the Scarpe, the two prime German trench systems were close together.

Then too, Ludendorff had insisted on reserves being kept within close proximity to the rear of the second main trench system. These forces were no longer to be fed into a line under assault. It was assumed that the first line, and possibly the second, would fall into enemy hands. Instead, "reserves" had now become counterattack elements. The idea was to weather the Allied artillery preparation in the concrete machine-gun outposts and lightly held trenches, then deliver a strong, immediate counterattack before the Allies had a chance to organize defenses. Falkenhausen, however, had kept his reserves as much as fifteen to twenty miles away. As a result of his failure to follow doctrine, German casualties at Arras were heavy, and the opportunity to exercise Ludendorff's elastic and life-saving defense plan was not utilized. Ludendorff determined that Falkenhausen could no longer be trusted with the lives of German soldiers and he was relieved.

Since Ludendorff fully expected a French offensive in the Aisne River area, thanks to the captured plan, the Germans were far better prepared in that sector than they had been at Arras. Facing generally south against Nivelle's fifty-three divisions, the German defenses were manned by twenty-one line divisions and seventeen counterattack divisions under the command of von Below's First German Army and Boehn's Seventh Army. The front-line French assault forces were oriented to the north, as part of General Mangin's Sixth French Army and General Mazel's Fifth Army. The Aisne River ran largely along the front lines in an east-west fashion, intersecting the array of opposing forces at several points.

Generally, more French than German units had the river to their rear. The "mass of maneuver" was poised in the rear of the French lines under General Duchene's Tenth Army, having five divisions of cavalry and three corps of infantry divisions. Since the German withdrawal had been more extensive in the French sector, the attack date was pushed back further, finally scheduled for April 16. The French took comfort in the fact that the battle in the north, at Arras, was still going on. They also had outdone the British in terms of tanks. Along the Aisne the French planned to use 128 of the new machines.

Promptly at 6:00 A.M. on the morning of April 16, French artillery-men switched from their protracted preparation schedule of firing to the creeping barrage. French infantry began the assault. North of the Aisne, success was almost immediate. Mazel's Forty-second and Sixty-ninth divisions quickly punched in some two and a half miles. Elsewhere, how-ever, reports of tragedy began to filter in. The problem was chiefly that the new German defenses had survived the artillery preparation quite well, and French infantrymen were being scythed down by the forward German machine-gun outposts. If the survivors bypassed these bunkers and topped the crest of the hill, they faced a reverse slope defense where wire had not been cut by the supporting artillery. Mechanical failures and enemy action rapidly reduced the French tanks to half their starting numbers. To make matters worse, in some areas the attackers were con-fronted with immediate and strong German counterattacks. By evening, most of Mazel's Fifth Army had made little progress since the early morning hours, and were barely clinging to objectives that should have been far behind them.

Mangin's Sixth Army had no tanks. One of his eight assault divi-sions, the 153rd, although immediately checked in its attack, paused to reorganize and pressed on, gaining a mile and a quarter. But his forces achieved little else. They too experienced prompt, powerful, and unex-pected counterattacks, and in some cases lost their small initial gains. Mazel's Fifth Army had done a little better than Mangin. The Fifth had taken 7,000 prisoners, with Mangin's Sixth netting only about half that number. The greatest disappointment to the French was the lack of a breach in the German lines sufficiently wide enough to push through the "mass of maneuver."

Undeterred by the modest results of the first day, and true to his philosophy, Nivelle ordered Mazel's Fifth Army to attack northeast on the next day, reinforcing the sector where the greatest success had been gained. The Sixth Army was assigned a mission that involved serving more as a flank security element than an attacking force. It did not work out. The Fifth Army was largely checked, and the Sixth Army achieved some advance only because the Germans in its sector withdrew to better positions. It was as if the defender, rather than the attacker, had assumed control of the initiative.

Day after day, Nivelle tried to make his offensive produce what he had promised. There was some progress. Through April 20, the French had captured 20,000 prisoners and 147 German artillery pieces, but the cost was high. On April 25, over 96,000 of Nivelle's troops had been killed, wounded, or were missing. The Germans had not gotten off lightly either; their losses to the French amounted to an estimated 83,000. During the last week of April, Nivelle began to be called to account by the French political leadership. There was little doubt that the Nivelle plan had failed; the grand design for the 1917 Allied offensive was a rapidly fading memory. The Tenth Army, the "mass of maneuver," was wedged between Mazel and Mangin's armies. The offensive, which had been conceived as a sudden rupture of German defenses and a fast-moving exploitation into open ground, had evolved into a grinding, bloody push, inching its way forward on a broad front.

While Nivelle was issuing his final orders for the Aisne advance, Haig's forces had been continuing their offensive at Arras. The day following their April 9 assault, the British made some slight gains, and by evening they had raised their total of German prisoners to 11,000 and the number of captured artillery pieces to 103. Although it was becoming obvious that they would probably not achieve a breakthrough, plans were made for another large-scale attempt on the next day, the eleventh. In a desperate and costly assault, British infantrymen slugged their way forward. The objective was the village on the rise of ground, Monchy-le-Preux. In a rare feat of cooperation between the infantry and a few tanks that had survived the first forty-eight hours of the offensive, the village fell to the British attack. Allenby then attempted exploitation—once more with horse cavalry. An enemy counterattack and devastating German artillery fire made short work of horses and horsemen.

By the evening of April 11, after three days of battle, the British and Canadians had suffered 13,000 casualties. British veterans of the Somme in 1916 viewed the losses as moderate. In the 1916 attack, made by approximately the same size force, the British had taken 57,000 casualties on the first day; the New Army was indeed becoming battle-wise. However, stiffening German resistance began to be felt all along the Arras sector, causing an additional two to three thousand casualties every day. By the end of April, totals from both the British First and Third armies at Arras amounted to about 78,000. The British fought on well into May, but like the French their attacks became fewer and farther between, each aimed at limited objectives.

By mid-May, however, the limited British actions assumed an importance that far outweighed their physical magnitude, because the French army was collapsing. It had begun on the night of April 21, a few days after Nivelle had begun the Aisne offensive. French soldiers advancing to the front were subjected to a most unusual display of unsoldierly conduct. As they moved forward, they encountered a convoy of colonial troops bouncing along in trucks on their way to the rear. These troops, of the First Colonial Infantry Division, were the elite of Mangin's Sixth Army, and were frequently charged with leading his attacks. Yet now, as they rode rearward, they were shouting, "We are through with killing— Long live peace!" while their officers simply stared forward in obvious and painful embarrassment. A week later, another unit was reported to be in a state of "indiscipline"—a more apt term would be mutiny. The Second Battalion of the Eighteenth Infantry Regiment had gone into the offensive on the first morning with six hundred men, and they had run head on into the new German defensive system. Not only were they cut to ribbons by the machine-gun outposts and reverse slope defense, but they were also subjected to the devastating assault of a full division of German counterattack forces. As a result, only two hundred of the battalion had survived. On April 29, the shattered remnants of this battalion were told that they must go back into the line. They were drunk, and they refused to go.

The response of the battalion commander was to bring in a platoon of military police, allow some time for the drunken troops to sober themselves, and then pick out those who were thought to be ringleaders. After a few hours the sullen soldiers were marched to the front, a few of their number remaining behind under arrest. Four of the purported leaders in the revolt were shot. News of the incident spread rapidly throughout the French army. By this time it was becoming obvious that the Nivelle offensive was failing and the spirit of the army was ebbing. With the leadership under question and the advance eroding into a series of unimaginative frontal attacks, all ranks of the French army began a reassessment.

A few days later, the next incident unfolded. The Second Colonial Division, like other French infantry divisions, was now composed of the very young and the very old. As an element in the previously designated "mass of maneuver" and part of the Tenth Army, the division and its sister units were ordered to the front on the third of May for the general offensive. When the division began to assemble, the officers saw that many of the men were drunk. They also noticed that some units had not brought their weapons with them into the ranks. All along the line of soldiers, officers were told by their men that they would not march to the front. Some of the troops began to shout, "Down with the war!"

When the dumbfounded officers queried the men about their behavior, many responded that they were no longer willing to attack uncut wire or unshelled German trenches. A quick investigation revealed that the division's bivouac areas were littered with political pamphlets, the messages of which extolled the virtues of socialism, the futility of the war, and the need to end the war at all costs in order to create a new form of government for all nations. Thus the efficacy of the new German defense system and the failure of the French censorship office were beginning to eat into the very core of the French army.

The leadership of the division selected a number of well-liked officers, who were sent out among the men. Meeting with the soldiers individually and in small groups, the officers listened, queried, and began a patient but persistent argument. They agreed that the hardships were difficult to bear, but pointed out that their comrades at the front were in an even more perilous situation. The forward units needed relief.

After a few hours, camaraderie, reason, and duty won out over politics, and the Second Colonial Infantry Division was put on the road to the front. The division's soldiers refused to attack, however; they would defend their trenches and themselves. Resuming the offensive was out of the question.

In early May, it was still possible to find a French unit here and there that would attack, but the mutinies were spreading. Along with the growing indiscipline, the themes of pacifist socialism worked their way deeper into the ranks of the once-proud army. Later it was found that skillful German agents in France had been responsible for some of the propaganda, but the great majority of the morale-sapping literature aimed at the troops was the product of the largely uncensored leftist press and a few opportunistic politicians.

The French held the greatest portion of the Western Front, and that sector of the line was quickly becoming an uneven rank of noncombatants. France was drifting into defeat. By the end of May, the French military bureaucracy had created a new term for the condition of its more troublesome units: "collective indiscipline." In actuality, France had an army in mutiny. In 1916 the number of desertions had been

8,924. By early June of 1917, the rate of desertion forecast a year-end total of 30,000. By mid-June, fully half of all French divisions on the Western Front were officially classed as being in a state of "collective indiscipline."

However, changes were in the air. Nivelle had been relieved of command. The chaotic situation was now the responsibility of a new leader, General Henri-Philippe Pétain. This veteran officer confronted a challenge as great as any faced by an army leader of a political democracy.

Pétain's first need was time. There were three conditions that could provide him with the required period he needed to rebuild the French army. The first was continued German ignorance of the true French situation. If the actual condition were known, Ludendorff would surely attack his weakened adversary, and would stand a good chance of taking Paris away from its dispirited defenders. But the Germans were defending, and not taking many French captives. The French prisoners falling into German hands were mostly taken by Ludendorff's counterattack elements from the ranks of French assault units. These units, the French offensive forces, were the most reliable and the least prone to mutiny. Although German interrogators did receive a few clues about the rapidly spreading French collapse, the evidence was not enough to be persuasive. There was little chance, either, that the Germans would learn of the low state of French troop morale through scanning the French press. While the Paris censorship office had failed to screen out subversive tracts destined for the soldiers, it did manage to suppress news accounts of actual conditions at the front.

The second condition that could give Pétain the time to mend his army was rapid American participation on the Western Front. On April 27, three weeks after the American entry into the war, General Joffre, the French hero of the Battle of the Marne in 1914, held a conference with the leadership of the U.S. Army in Washington. Joffre's appeal was for the immediate dispatch of a U.S. division and the ultimate deployment of a large, independent American army on the Western Front. Neither Joffre nor his listeners knew of the unfolding mutinies. On May 2 he repeated his requests to President Wilson. The president agreed to the French general's plea.

IN THE SPRING OF 1917, the United States Army had no divisions. One would have to be put together, transported to France, and trained there. The ability to produce a large American army was created with the approval of the Draft Act on May 18. Nine million U.S. male citizens registered on June 5, and selection began on July 20. Arrival at the yet-to-be-completed training centers was scheduled for September.

The question in the spring was, what would these American soldiers train with? In early 1917, the U.S. Army had 3,000 trucks. The need was for 85,000. It had 600,000 modern rifles on hand, but required 2,500,000. The army had less than 1,500 machine guns and would need hundreds of thousands. The nation that had introduced powered flight had no military aircraft suitable for Western Front combat. Despite the American origins of the basic components of the tank, the U.S. Army had none. The army had only 544 modern field artillery pieces and would have to have thousands more.

No one knew the inability to quickly field an American combat force in France better than the man chosen to lead it, John J. Pershing. Pershing had carefully selected a small staff, received President Wilson's promise of "full support," and departed for France on May 28. The American general had a difficult time becoming accustomed to the enthusiasm with which he was greeted by his new European allies. He also began to encounter the first of many suggestions that his soldiers should simply be integrated into existing British and French units, thus eliminating the time-consuming need to build a separate American army with its own staff, chain of command, logistics, and all the other trappings of an independent field force.

Holding to his instructions, Pershing continued to develop his plan for an independent American army, resisting suggestions of "amalgamation." On June 16 he met the officer with the biggest, and as yet largely unknown, problem on the Western Front. Pétain listened to Pershing's concept for American participation on the battlefield. After the American general finished explaining what the future would bring, the Frenchman made his own comment: "I hope it is not too late."

In the eyes of the officers who had the responsibility of leading armies of the democracies in the summer of 1917, there was only one realistic solution to the Allies' current situation. The forces of the British Empire must take the lead, the brunt, the cost, and the burden of the fight.

The empire's armies were no longer the "New Army." By the summer of 1917 they had demonstrated a considerable degree of competence and skill. The initial hours of the offensive at Arras had achieved so much success that hope had arisen that the British had somehow found the key to finally break the impasse on the Western Front. But the British and Canadian offensive had bogged down. There had been little success in the section of the line where the new German defensive system had been implemented. Then there was the matter of the tanks. This British innovation had borne little fruit. It was true that the model employed at Arras was recognized to be inferior to the new and as yet unavailable versions. But, in and of itself, there was little promise that the use of the tank could break the German defense.

Another consideration concerned artillery preparation. The new German defense system, particularly the provision for reverse slope defense, eliminated the attacker's ability to visually adjust artillery firing, and there was no assurance of destroying enemy wire prior to the assault. On the other hand, the new instantaneous fuse showed promise. That encouraging piece of technology, however, was more than offset by the fact that there would probably be no further French offensives in the near future, and the beginning of British preparatory firing would draw German counterattack forces as never before. Still, Sir Douglas Haig did have some reason for optimism. Arras was not a wholly unblemished success, but there was some indication that German will, morale, and staying power might be declining. The evidence lay in the large number of captives. For the first time in the war, British troops were seeing large numbers of German soldiers who clearly did not want to fight. By contrast, the morale, will, and abilities of British soldiers never seemed better.

In retrospect, the great Allied offensive of 1917 was a clash of two enormous forces in transition. On the Allied side, the British and their colonial legions were finally fighting their enemies with the immense resources of an industrial giant, a large population of talented people, and battle-tested leadership. At Arras the British had demonstrated cunning, skill, and no small measure of esprit. While the French had borne the great burden in the first year and a half of the war, the British had gathered, trained, and equipped a mighty army. For their part, the French were now showing the wear of that terrible bloodletting. The French soldier had been asked to do too much too often, with doubtful support.

French leadership in the spring offensive had been found wanting. General Nivelle had attempted to bring his successful tactical methods of Verdun in 1916 to the whole front, but had failed. The French did not have the staff system that could ensure implementation of Nivelle's concepts. Although the Canadians had studied his ideas and rehearsed their brilliant attack on Vimy Ridge prior to the assault, most French units failed to do the same. The morale and resolve of Nivelle's army were also being subverted by the lack of censorship, an activity the British pursued with vigor. Nivelle had also employed a mechanically inferior tank, and his artillery did not have the advantage of the British instantaneous fuse.

The greatest obstacle to Nivelle's success, however, lay in the actions of the Germans along the Aisne. Not only had Ludendorff's forces been well forewarned about the timing and location of the French attack, they had changed their defensive system. While Falkenhausen's compliance with the December 1916 defense directive had been half-hearted, to the south von Below and Boehn had obeyed instructions. The French had plowed into an elastic defense with a weak forward crust, a graduated casualty-producing interior, and a spring-loaded counterattack force. This system attracted the attacker, robbed him of his initial advantages, and then destroyed him when he was most vulnerable. The new German system was designed to strike Allied offensive elements when they were extended, beyond the range of much of their supporting artillery, and out of communication with their immediate headquarters. Against this previously unknown defense system, it is doubtful if any of the Allied generals could have done much better than Robert Nivelle.

Yet, in the face of mounting casualties and diminishing returns, both Haig and Nivelle had pressed their attacks. Hindsight makes their decisions seem stupid. In the spring of 1917, the Allied goal was to end the war. Since so much blood and treasure had already been lost, what did a few thousand more casualties matter if the prize would be victory and an end to the worldwide killing? As Allied casualties mounted, the stakes rose and the willingness to suffer increased. To stop the attack, to negotiate the dispute, or to temper the political demands was regarded as unworthy of the immense costs already paid. The Great War was now an event that fed on itself. Because it had consumed so much, it could not now be satisfied with less. Nivelle's "mass of maneuver" was a grand scheme that was accepted because its scale had seemed appropriate to the task. It had failed.

Now, in the summer of 1917, the task still remained. The Allies had only one real contender on the field: General Douglas Haig. The soldiers of the British Empire would have to carry the battle to the Germans. Canadians, Australians, Irish, South Africans, Indians, British, New Zealanders, and others must challenge Ludendorff and his German troops while the French rebuilt their army and the Americans prepared for war.

THREE

Maneuver by an Empire: The Lowlands Campaign

ON THE WESTERN FRONT, THE BRITISH EMPIRE, one of the greatest and unquestionably the largest of all empires, had not thus far controlled the timing, the nature, or the outcome of events. It had reacted to the actions of others. Initially the small size of its army had precluded an ability to dominate events in France and Belgium. In 1916 its growing army had been badly bloodied on the Somme, and in the early months of 1917 Haig's troops were playing their part in a French concept. Now the time had arrived for the British Empire's initiative.

The number of soldiers available to the empire in 1917 was potentially enormous. London could call on a rapidly expanding technological and industrial capacity. British financial strength was adding to the power of Haig's army by worldwide procurement of armaments and supplies. So complex a society as Britain's could also marshal the intellectual skills for innovative strategic planning. Britain had all of this available in 1917, and Douglas Haig set out to use it.

As early as 1915, Haig had worked with the Royal Navy on a plan that would take advantage of the superiority of the British surface fleet by landing and supporting a ground force behind the German lines on the Belgian coast. Together with a substantial Allied offensive on the Belgian portion of the Western Front, an amphibious operation might compel Germany to pull back from its northern lines near the Channel. If the two coordinated efforts were powerful enough, the Germans might well have to abandon coastal Belgium altogether, because their backs would be pushed to the borders of neutral Holland and they could not afford to violate Dutch soil. That might force Ludendorff to swing his northern lines away from the coast so that they would face an Allied-occupied northwestern Belgium. Haig and the naval planners calculated that a German disposition of that sort would lengthen Ludendorff's lines by about forty-five miles, further complicating the German numerical disadvantage on the Western Front. If the Germans could be forced to evacuate the Belgian coast under the pressure of an all-out British attack in the lowlands, complemented by an amphibious landing in their rear, subsequent German dispositions would form a giant, vulnerable salient. The amphibious enterprise and lowlands offensive was a strategic scheme that came naturally to the minds of a great naval power.

Of the many obstacles, the foremost was that the Germans had foreseen the eventuality and had placed heavy defenses along the Belgian coast. By early 1917, the Royal Navy faced eighty guns of over six inches along that coast. These weapons were concentrated within twenty-five miles behind the junction of the German lines and the beach. Despite this menace, Admiral Sir Reginald Bacon, the principal Royal Navy advocate of the amphibious operation, believed the task had to be undertaken. Bacon reasoned that if peace negotiations were to take place under the current situation, Germany might retain its new submarine and destroyer bases at Ostend and Zeebrugge, thus threatening British maritime dominance of the English Channel. He and Haig began arguing with those who favored delaying all further offensive operations until the United States could develop a substantial fighting force. When the Allies learned of the growing Russian Revolution in the spring of 1917, Bacon stepped up his efforts.

The energetic admiral had subverted British shipbuilding priorities in order to have three large and rather strange contraptions fabricated. He knew that the abortive Dardanelles operation had suffered from an inability to land substantial ground forces speedily. His goal was to have a thirteen-thousand-man British army division, equipped with tanks, ashore within twenty minutes. Such a feat would be hard enough to accomplish in the placid conditions of a friendly port. Bacon intended to do it in the teeth of a stout German defense, and without the benefit of existing port facilities.

Preceding the planners of the Normandy invasion by twenty-seven years, Bacon was going to have the troops and tanks already in place on his three 550-foot mobile steel piers when they touched the Belgian shore. The landing force would be bringing its own port with it. Using the awesome might of British seapower, Bacon planned a devastating and uneven slugging match with the German coastal batteries, followed by an artificial fog so that the 13,000 British troops running down the thirty-foot-wide mobile piers would be obscured from enemy guns during the period of maximum vulnerability. Each of the three piers was to be pushed by two old battleships armed with massive naval guns that would literally blow away Ludendorff's coastal defenses. The "fog" would be created by an oil spray injected into the exhaust stacks of specially designated destroyers. The engineering feasibility of the artificial fog and the piers was in hand in late 1916. Haig had given his concurrence and enthusiastic support.

By the spring of 1917, Bacon's work had progressed to the point where detailed planning and actual preparations were in order. Haig identified the First Infantry Division as his landing force, supplied it with reinforcements, augmented its strength, and sent it into an isolated secret area near Dunkerque. The division was put to work perfecting an operations plan. A landing beach behind the German lines was carefully chosen. Meanwhile, Bacon put the finishing touches on his mobile piers.

A critical element in the plan was the specific slope of the beach. The long, narrow floating piers were to be pushed into the sand by the heavily armed warships. The admiral knew that the troop-laden piers had to be nosed into place with a six-inch tolerance for the contour of the beach slope. Ordering an airplane to photograph the receding tide every twenty minutes under a hail of German antiaircraft fire, Bacon obtained exact data for the fabrication of the bows of the giant piers. With that essential problem solved, the army and navy planners moved to the tank and seawall problem.

The First Division wanted shock power ashore as early as possible. That could best be achieved by a rapid infantry attack led by tanks. But a concrete seawall on the chosen landing beach posed a problem. The task was to enable the tanks to climb the seawall. A replica of the barrier was built in England. The tanks were then fitted with a triangular, timbered extension of their bows; when this dropped, it provided an inclined ramp that allowed the ungainly machines to scale the wall.

By April this last problem of the seawall obstacle had been solved. The tanks had shown that they could climb the model wall and could negotiate to the other side. Haig was assured by Bacon and the First Division commander that the mobile piers and the landing force would be ready by August. Sailors, soldiers, tank crews, and planners were quarantined from the outside world and placed under heavy censorship rules. Success depended on secrecy. Haig determined that the invasion force would go ashore immediately after the seizure of the town of Roulers by the British

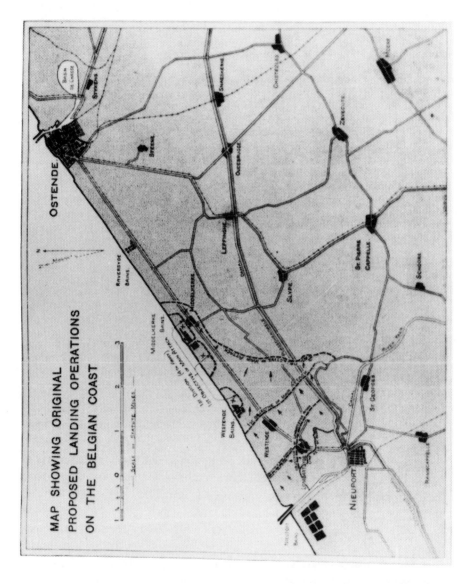

MAP SHOWING ORIGINAL
PROPOSED LANDING OPERATIONS
ON THE BELGIAN COAST

Scale in Statute Miles

lowlands offensive. The amphibious assault would ensure the further withdrawal of the German forces, provoking their ultimate abandonment of the Belgian coast.

The great British lowlands campaign of 1917 incorporated the imagination, skill, and resources of a great empire into its design. No other power on earth could undertake such a task. Yet this offensive was destined to erode the very foundations of the empire that created it. Decades later, official British historians would insist on naming the campaign "Third Ypres." The men who fought in this bloodbath of mud and despair, many of them Canadians and Australians, would refer to it by the emotion-burdened name: Passchendaele. That word, Passchendaele, would become synonymous with British callousness, and in some quarters it became a code word for incompetence. After this campaign British colonial subjects would again respond bravely to London's leadership, but their response would not be without questions or qualifications. The effects of the campaign would go far beyond the Great War, but few would stop to reflect that the road to Passchendaele was paved with good intentions.

Douglas Haig's immediate problem in the summer of 1917 was how to get the Germans pushed back to Roulers. His first decision was to appoint the youngest British army commander to lead the attack. Haig was looking for boldness and thus selected General Hubert Gough and his Fifth Army to carry the main burden of the offensive. Haig then decided to open the offensive with a move that would give him a terrain pivot, or hinge, to begin swinging back the enemy lines. Messines Ridge overlooked the dispositions of the British army in Flanders and was a critical bastion of the German defenses. If the ridge could be taken, the integrity of the enemy lines in the lowlands would be threatened. Haig would then have his hinge. Gough's task would be to press Ludendorff's forces north of the ridge back to Roulers. At that point the amphibious operation would be triggered, and the forces coming ashore would be placed under Gough's command.

The initial attack to get the Messines Ridge "pivot" was assigned to General Plumer's Second British Army. Plumer's troops not only knew the terrain of Messines Ridge well, but were also intimately familiar with the earth below the ridge. As early as the summer of 1916, the British had dug tunnels beneath the German positions to place explosive charges. British mining activity was known, or at least suspected, by the Germans, but their countermining effort had been dug too shallow. The British vertical shafts had gone down as much as eighty feet before the traverse sections underneath the lines had been excavated. The idea was simple. You simply loaded up the tunnel area immediately below the German positions with as much explosive material as possible, readied an infantry attack on the surface, kicked off the explosive charge, and occupied the resulting crater with your own troops. It was siege warfare of the most basic variety. The chosen date of the attack was June 7. It would all begin with no less than nineteen huge explosions that would literally blow up German defenses on Messines Ridge.

The five German divisions occupying the defenses of Messines Ridge were under the command of General Sixt von Armin's Fourth Army. Some of von Armin's officers, gaining information through the interrogation of British prisoners, recommended withdrawal from the position, citing British mining activity. General von Armin heard similar views from one of the most respected German officers on the Western Front, Colonel von Lossberg, chief of staff of the Sixth Army near Arras. Lossberg was becoming a favorite of Ludendorff, even though the younger officer often took exception to some of the details of Ludendorff's new defense system. Lossberg strongly advocated conducting defense with as little loss of life as possible. Von Armin could not dismiss the colonel's views lightly. However, the general had to consider the alternative. The next best terrain was six miles to the rear, and pulling back that far would necessitate a general withdrawal of the entire northern defense works. The commander of the Fourth Army decided to hold onto Messines Ridge.

General Haig had advised General Plumer, the British commander of the Messines attack, that the new German defensive system could best be defeated by a short advance. In a discussion with Plumer on May 10, Haig specified that the attacking forces should not overrun the range of their supporting artillery. Plumer was a firm believer in superiority of numbers. His plan involved an artillery preparation of over two weeks' duration, with 2,233 guns opposing about 630 German field pieces. Plumer's gunners would lob 3.5 million rounds of artillery ammunition on enemy positions. He also massed over 300 British aircraft to gain undisputed air superiority over the 50 or so German planes in the Messines sector. British airmen not only bombed and strafed the German defenders with impunity, but were able to adjust British artillery fire during the preparatory phases, thereby ensuring that the observed German defenses were reduced to rubble. So great was the British air superiority that Baron von Richthofen's famed "Flying Circus" squadron was chased from the skies over the objective. After the mines had

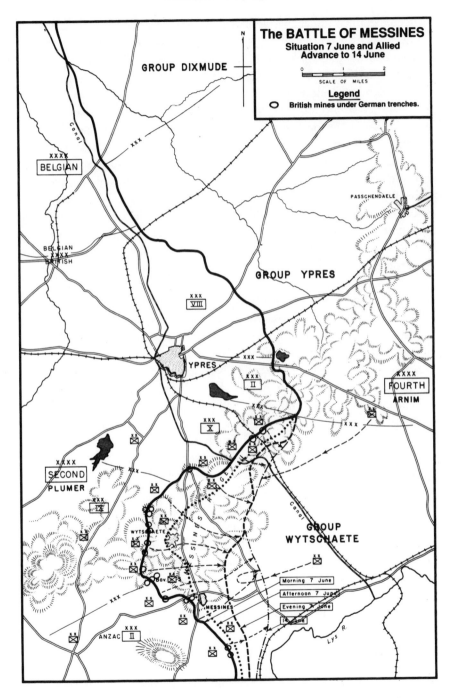

The BATTLE OF MESSINES
Situation 7 June and Allied Advance to 14 June

SCALE OF MILES
0   1   2

Legend

○ British mines under German trenches.

been exploded under the Germans, Plumer intended to push nine attack divisions over the remnants of the five German defending divisions. He was also holding three more divisions in reserve. The British Second Army certainly had the numbers, and they appeared to have an answer to Ludendorff's defense.

Shortly after 3:00 A.M. on June 7, nineteen brilliant flashes of light swept aside the darkness on Messines Ridge. Eyewitnesses later described a rush of air, trembling ground, and the unbearable roar of a mighty explosion. Others described a number of mushroom-shaped clouds in the light of artillery flares. Five hundred tons of ammonal had been successfully detonated under German positions along the ridge. German troops in bivouac fifteen miles away rushed into the streets in a state of panic. Australian, British, Irish, and New Zealand divisions moved forward, following closely upon one of the most powerful creeping barrages ever devised by man. In the morning hours, German opposition was light to nonexistent.

Not surprisingly, Plumer's siege warfare methods succeeded. The short, violent Battle of Messines Ridge was a unique event. The tunnels were more than a year in the making and were possible because of a peculiar type of soil. Much of the British success came because von Armin was without an adequate terrain alternative in the sector. Almost all of the attack objectives were in British hands before noon of the first day. A front about eight miles long had been moved forward three to four miles, and critical terrain had been secured. Haig had his "hinge." Ten thousand German soldiers had simply disappeared within the first few minutes. General von Armin's counterattack forces could not possibly react to such an attack with any degree of timeliness. In addition to the ten thousand missing, the Fourth German Army lost about fifteen thousand other casualties at Messines. Plumer's own loss was seventeen thousand, however; almost all of his casualties came during the consolidation phase in the afternoon of June 7. As the Allies were digging in, German artillery and machine-gun fire began taking a heavy toll. There was little that Haig could learn from this battle that he could apply elsewhere.

On the day of Plumer's success, General Pétain passed control of six French infantry divisions to Haig. These reinforcements were under the command of General Anthoine and were organized into the First French Army, to be employed by Haig on the left flank of his main offensive. Pétain had sent a staff officer to Haig five days prior to the transfer with a disturbing report on the French mutinies. However, the officer did not describe the full extent of French difficulties. It would take some time for the French reinforcements to prepare for their role, time that Haig needed, because he was becoming drastically short of infantrymen.

Although Haig had been informed in late May that the manpower problem was becoming increasingly difficult, he was not fully aware that David Lloyd George, the British prime minister, was withholding replacements to the Western Front. Lloyd George was looking for an alternative to the casualty-producing tactics of Western Front trench warfare. Thus Haig was undertaking a grand offensive without important facts he needed from his ally and his own political leadership. By late June, his army would be short by almost 100,000 infantrymen.

On June 14, with Messines Ridge in his hands, Haig laid out his plans for the lowlands offensive to his commanders. For the first time he briefed them on the amphibious operation then being prepared. He informed them that there was a good chance of restoring mobility to the Western Front, a battlefield that had been largely static for about thirty months. The officers departed, stepping up their preparations for an enormous undertaking. Five days later, Haig was recalled to London and a meeting of the Cabinet Committee on War Policy to defend his plan.

The meeting in London disclosed the growing reluctance of Lloyd George to commit the soldiers of the British Empire to yet another bloody Western Front offensive. The officers of the Royal Navy and Army stood firm in their support of an offensive in Belgium. It was argued that only the Western Front offered the chance for the decisive results that could end the war. Russia was leaving the war and an American army was far from ready. The politician tried to pin his general down on the subject of casualties. Haig repeated his original estimate, 100,000 per month for the lowlands campaign. He expected less but offered no lower figure. As the session broke up, the prime minister had not given his approval for the campaign, but preparations for the attack were to continue.

Returning to his headquarters, Haig found that his newly acquired French divisions needed more time to get ready for the offensive. The British general was surprised to discover that a significant part of all French combat units were at their homes, on leave. It was part of Pétain's comprehensive program to bring the French army back to fighting trim. Pétain and his officers were hard at work all during the summer. Although no proof of it exists, their program must have included the use of double agents, since the kaiser was informed on June 15 that the French were preparing for a substantial offensive, a story that had no basis in fact. During this fearfully uncertain period of French history, Pétain did not spare himself. Within thirty days the tireless general visited ninety of his divisions. He would gather soldiers around his car and then mount the hood of the vehicle. No appeal or threat was left unvoiced during these "cartop" talks. He promised leave time, better living conditions, the firing of incompetent officers, and the construction of rest camps.

Pétain's program also had a darker side, however. By official record twenty-three of his rebellious soldiers were executed. There were probably more. One hundred subversives were deported. The French government finally began backing their general by throwing over 1,700 troublemakers in jail and enforcing censorship regulations. One manager of a leftist newspaper was found with a large sum of money traced to a German agent, and a blanket of rigid surveillance settled over the French press. The government refused to allow French socialists to meet with their German counterparts in a June conference in neutral Sweden.

Pétain substituted his own "trench pamphlets" for the now disappearing pacifist tracts. He backed his officers when they imposed severe discipline on the soldiers and constantly held informal sessions with his younger officers, seeking ideas, recommendations, and solutions. He directed a change in tactics, insisting on the massive use of firepower prior to any new offensive. Of most importance, Pétain followed through on his promises. Leave was given, rest camps were built, marginal leaders were replaced, and discipline was enforced. The French army was not cured of its weaknesses yet, and nothing much could be expected of it during that long, sultry summer, but every effort was being made to put the French back in the war. Fortunately, Haig's First French Army was one of the least mutiny-plagued elements of Pétain's forces.

Haig believed he knew the lowlands well. He had fought there in the early part of the war. The area was separated from the two-mile-wide beach of the coast by a belt of marshes that was about six miles in width, a swamp that followed the contour of the coastline. Inland there was an artificial network of waterways, canals, dikes, and ditches. Designed in centuries past by the French engineer Vauban, the great defense genius, the network incorporated military, commercial, and agricultural purposes in its construction. It was a land that could not tolerate heavy precipitation. The water table was only three feet below the rich humus of the surface. Underneath that layer was a deep substratum made of a claylike material that resisted the absorption of water.

In the early part of the war, the lowlands had been relatively dry. The early summer of 1917 had seen little rain, and Haig had no reason to expect any significant change. The area's "high ground" was a series of ridges that were almost unidentifiable to the casual visitor, since they were rarely over 200 feet in height and had very gentle slopes. Yet these ridges were militarily important, for they provided excellent observation points over their flat surroundings. In a period of drought, the country-side offered the twentieth-century attacker a rather good ground for use. During a wet period, the terrain could well be an ideal region for defense.

One week after the successful June seizure of Messines Ridge by the British, General von Armin was directed to accept a new chief of staff for his Fourth Army. Ludendorff appointed Colonel von Lossberg to the position. With the German ability to observe British preparations in the lowlands from the commanding ridge lines, it was obvious that the next Allied blow would be projected from the Ypres area.

Ludendorff had to carry on a careful balancing act. The main Ger-man aim was to ensure the neutralization of Russia. That was not to be achieved by an all-out general offensive in the east, for such an operation might prove to be counterproductive, provoking Russian unity instead. Ludendorff's eastern efforts required carefully timed probes and a de-ployment of considerable forces there to coax the rapidly disintegrating Russian army into a peaceful accommodation. That meant a defense pos-ture on the Western Front for at least the remainder of 1917. Colonel von Lossberg's assignment was designed to ensure a successful defense on the Western Front while Germany closed out the war in the east.

The colonel set about improving the Fourth Army's dispositions and internal organization. He formed three defense zones, each of about two to three thousand yards in depth. The forward zone was already par-tially composed of the familiar concrete machine-gun bunkers, dubbed "pillboxes" by the British. More of these were added. The second zone contained regiment-sized counterattack forces, some in trenches, others dispersed in large bunkers holding twenty to fifty men each. The low-lands had some wooded areas, and these were made into obstacles by endless strands of barbed wire fixed to tree trunks and shattered stumps. The third zone was occupied by artillery, usually concealed in positions of two to three guns, and division-sized counterattack forces. Most Ger-man infantry elements completed reorganization during the month of July, so that the basic squad unit now numbered eleven members rather than the previous strength of seven. The new and larger group was more heavily armed. Each new squad had one of the new, reliable light ma-chine guns. Flamethrowers, rifle grenade launchers, and light mortars were also more available. The primary purpose of infantry reorganiza-tion was to make the counterattack more effective. These new groups of infantrymen were being trained to respond quickly to an Allied offensive by infiltrating the soft spots of the attackers when they were most vulnerable, immediately after they had seized an objective. By getting in behind the forward Allied units, the German leaders hoped that the newly won Allied ground could be quickly retaken at minimal cost.

German artillery was also experiencing change. As with the Allied armies, the Germans realized that protracted observation and adjustment of artillery preparatory fires, or "registration," alerted the enemy to a forthcoming attack. The prospective defender then went about his defense chores with increased enthusiasm and energy. The defender would also position artillery and infantry reserves behind the threatened sector. The new German methods involved keeping a detailed chart on the specific firing characteristics of each artillery piece, meteorological figures that influenced the flight of the shell, and precise ballistic data. The object was to improve the chances of accurate fire at the very beginning of an artillery bombardment, without registration. That would allow the Germans to move artillery secretly to a given area and suddenly deliver effective fire, using map data alone and foregoing the lengthy telltale registration firing. Effective surprise artillery fire, coupled with a more potent infantry counterattack force, enhanced the probability of a successful defense. Feverishly Lossberg worked to bring about these changes. By late July the new dispositions and infantry reorganization had been largely achieved. New artillery techniques were not quite perfected yet.

Although Haig did not have his government's approval for the offensive, his preparations had progressed to the point where a date for the first attack was established and the preliminaries had to begin. Learning from the experience of the Battle of Messines Ridge, the first combat initiative began in the air, with an Allied drive to secure superiority over the battlefield. Since the last few days of July would see the infantry assault, the air effort began on the eleventh of that month with 500 British and 200 French aircraft committed to the lowlands. Five days later, the artillery preparation commenced when 2,174 Allied weapons were pitted against enemy defenses and about 1,500 German artillery pieces. The air battle climaxed on the twenty-sixth of July with Allied pilots driving the heavily outnumbered German airmen from the sky. The French and British artillery poured 65,000 tons of ammunition into von Armin's Fourth Army during the preparation phase, easily gaining the upper hand. With no reasonable alternative and unrelenting arguments in favor of the operation, Lloyd George had given his approval for the lowlands campaign on July 20. The ground assault was scheduled for the early morning hours of July 31.

The prime effort of Haig's offensive would be carried by nine divisions of General Gough's Fifth British Army. Secondary and supporting attacks would be supplied by Plumer's Second Army in the Messines sector to the south and by the French First Army in the north. Awaiting the fall of Roulers, the British First Infantry Division and the invasion fleet were poised for embarkation along the coast. The plan called for the seizure of 6,000 yards of German-held territory on the first day. Haig had managed to mass 136 tanks for the assault. The leader of this armored force had complained during the preparation fire that the ground in the objective area was becoming so chewed up during bombardment that the terrain might be impassable for his machines. Nevertheless, the night before the assault, the British tanks lumbered forward to their attack positions. General Gough had directed each infantry company to leave a few officers and about thirty riflemen behind, so that when a unit took severe casualties, it could be immediately reinforced to regain effectiveness. Many British units also planned to use light machine guns in the assault. Altogether, Haig had the greatest assembly of combat power that the British Empire had ever fielded.

At 3:50 A.M. on July 31, the Allied infantry went over the top. In the southern sector, Plumer's riflemen found that German wire had been well cut by the artillery preparation, and good progress was made. The French made excellent gains as well. However, in the center Gough's main attack ran into a stubborn defense. The tank force had not improved on their general performance during past campaigns. The Thirtieth Division of Gough's Fifth Army had no less than fifty-two tanks in support of its assault, but nineteen of them were destroyed or disabled by enemy action, primarily at the hands of von Armin's artillery. Twenty-two more tanks experienced mechanical failure. Although the German forward outpost sector had been taken by the British, Gough's army began to encounter powerful counterattacks. The German Fourth Army seemed to be fighting with more fervor than the German defenders at Arras had shown. Yet the attackers did take a number of prisoners. As evening settled upon the battlefield, the British had advanced only about 3,500 yards at the deepest point. In one area, 500 yards marked the extent of the gain. By most accounts, the spirit of the attackers was rather high.

In the night, rain began to fall. The attack resumed the next morning but progress was difficult. German artillery became increasingly effective, and von Armin's troops seemed to pop out of the ground behind the

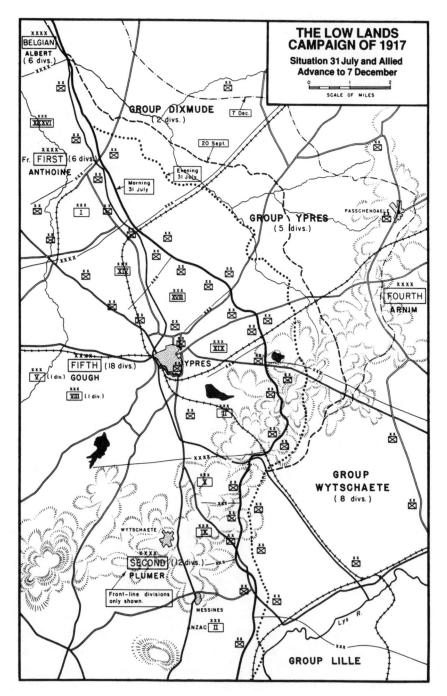

THE LOW LANDS
CAMPAIGN OF 1917

Situation 31 July and Allied
Advance to 7 December

SCALE OF MILES

advancing British infantrymen. British officers had to adjust their tactics, designating some units to mop up after their forward attack units had by-passed terrain previously considered secure. The German counterattacks were well supported by accurate artillery fire, which usually arrived on the top of exposed British units that had little chance to take cover. The rainy weather precluded Allied exploitation of the hard-won air superiority, and little was known about what was happening in the German rear.

Although von Armin's Fourth Army had not been completely successful in its defense, its July preparations and Colonel von Lossberg's energies and intellect had been put to good use. The detection of British preparations had led Ludendorff to transfer fourteen German divisions to the lowlands from other sectors of the Western Front. Lossberg had coached the leaders of the Fourth Army to abandon trench lines during the preparatory fires, and had encouraged the movement of troops forward—into shell holes. Lives had been saved by this technique, and General Gough's attacking elements found plenty of defenders left during the assault. Lossberg had also directed that each artillery battery within range of a British tank attack should dedicate one gun to fire at nothing but enemy tanks. By continuous adjustment, the German gunners were able to achieve repeated hits on the slow-moving machines.

The British tankers labored under several disadvantages. Tied to an infantry assault, restricted to the few areas in the increasingly muddy battlefield where they could move forward, and forced to avoid the wired tree-stump areas, the tanks often proceeded in single file. This line of tanks became perfect targets.

The Germans had yielded ground, but not as much as Haig had planned on taking. In a pouring rain that lasted for four days, Haig postponed the general offensive planned for the second of August. Local attacks continued so that exposed flanks of newly won ground could be protected, but the great lowlands offensive came to a temporary halt. The Germans had lost their first and second defense zones, but the British and French sustained about 23,000 casualties. Six thousand German prisoners had been taken, most of them in the first few hours of July 31. Many had simply given up when they saw British troops at the entrance of their bunkers. Not knowing the actual hour of the initial attack, von Armin's troops had not been able to discriminate between the preparation fire and the creeping barrage. The British attackers arrived hard on the heels of the last few rounds. It is estimated that the Germans lost upwards of 30,000 casualties during the preparation phase in July, while some of Gough's units had lost 30 to 60 percent of their numbers in the three days of the all-out offensive.

Haig began distributing the few replacements he had for a resumption of the offensive. Although he had made good only about half of his planned first day's gain in this initial part of his operation, he was well pleased and encouraged by the performance of the French and by the morale and confidence of his subordinates. The weather, however, seemed to be going against him.

Reassessing their situation, the British planners saw that the failure to control the line of planned advance for the first day prohibited them from bringing up their artillery, because too much high ground still rested under control of German infantry. If the artillery were to be displaced forward, it would be in clear view of the Germans, and could not survive their counterbattery fire. Clearly, the next phase of the offensive would be a limited one to secure the high ground immediately in front of Gough's Fifth Army. Some time was allowed for the ground to dry out, but the artillery preparation for this attack went into high gear. The effectiveness of the artillery fire was somewhat diminished, however, because the ground was so soft that explosions occurred well below the soupy surface, containing casualty-producing fragmentation and blast. Moreover, the resulting shell holes quickly filled with water. Soon the terrain began to resemble a moonscape, composed of well-defined craters with water in the bottom.

The new attack began on August 10. Some drying of the surface favored the assault, but there was simply not enough superiority achieved by British artillery. The inability to displace the lighter artillery forward meant that the volume of fire supporting the attackers was marginal. The most acute moment came in the now familiar German counterattack phase. At that time Gough's troops needed a lot of firepower, quickly. German artillery gained the upper hand during these situations because most of their weapons were within supporting distance of the fight, and because the German leadership knew when the counterattack would be launched and where it would go in. Another problem arose for the British. German gunners placed a considerable volume of fire directly behind the attackers, isolating them from reinforcements and cutting their communications with the rear.

As the end result of these conditions, the attack on August 10 was much like the first day of the offensive—only a partial success. Some of the high ground was taken, but not all of it. A new attack to get the remaining high ground was scheduled for August 14. Again it rained.

The third all-out assault was postponed for twenty-four hours. The rain continued, and another twenty-four-hour delay was ordered.

Finally, on August 16, four corps of Allied infantry stood ready to try again. The third attack was almost a carbon copy of the first two—limited progress in some sectors, none in others. Commanders of some of the Allied units began to report that their cumulative casualties prohibited designating enough "mopping-up parties," and that they were increasingly being attacked in the rear by small units of German infantry. Fewer and fewer German prisoners were being taken. Again Haig was encouraged by the skilled advance of his French First Army, but there were additional instances of a lack of gain in one sector inhibiting the chances of exploiting the success of other sectors. An advance element would find itself with an open flank, a situation that the Germans were quick to take advantage of.

Gough's instructions following the third try were to prepare for yet a fourth major effort. Local attacks continued, so the main offensive by the Fifth Army degenerated into a number of separate assaults that appeared to be uncoordinated. The Germans were paying a high cost in their defense, but they could deal with these separate actions.

On August 25 Haig had had enough. He decided to switch the main effort from Gough to General Plumer and his Second Army. The Fifth Army was ordered to continue its efforts in the center, but its sector was reduced. Plumer was given control of one of Gough's corps. The Second Army commander, now master of the set-piece attack, asked for and got three weeks for preparations.

With the shift of the main attack to the south, the offensive entered a new phase. The pause for Plumer's preparations did not mean that there was a lull in the fighting. Division-sized assaults were occurring throughout the battlefield, but there would be no all-out effort by the three Allied armies until late September.

The first phase, from July 31 until August 25, had seen twenty-eight of forty-two available Allied divisions employed in bitter fighting. The Germans had a total of thirty-seven divisions in the lowlands. Haig found it necessary to relieve fourteen of his divisions and the Germans had to relieve twenty-three of theirs. On both sides, some of the retiring divisions would receive only a brief respite from battle, but the Germans had fewer forces to employ and almost no units that had not recently been in serious combat. The British had suffered about 68,000 casualties, less than Haig's monthly estimate that projected about 84,000 for the twenty-five-day period of battle. They would, however, need to save every man they could, because the shortage in infantrymen was becoming severe. Replacements were few and far between. German casualties from this phase remain unknown, but about 6,000 German soldiers ended up in Allied prison camps. Later the Germans would characterize their losses in this phase of the campaign as "very heavy."

Thus far Haig's great offensive was a failure, and the miserable, muddy conditions of this battlefield were not improving. The best that could be claimed was about 4,000 yards of advance in over three weeks, far short of anyone's expectations. Seeing the lack of progress, on August 22 Haig and Admiral Bacon decided to postpone the planned amphibious operation. It would remain an available option, but the soldiers and sailors would be placed in a more relaxed state of readiness. Another disappointment for the British general was Pétain's failure to give requested assistance to the British in the early days of the offensive. Not knowing the full extent of the mutinies, Haig had reason for bitterness, since German reinforcements to the lowlands were largely coming from the French sector to the south. But on the twentieth of August, Haig and his officers were somewhat heartened by a bit of good news—eighteen French divisions were attacking at Verdun, and had captured 2,000 Germans in the early morning hours.

There was another reason for optimism. Haig had met the leader of the American forces, General Pershing, and was favorably impressed. Even more gratifying was the fact that American troops, which first arrived in June, had continued to land in France. American participation on the Western Front was not going to be a token effort. By July Pershing was talking about a million-man army. True, the soldiers who arrived were untrained, and no one was certain how much shipping was going to be available. The Americans were being readied for their combat role by a French cadre, and had to establish schools in France to train their inexperienced staff officers. Still, by the time that Plumer was ready for his main attack in the lowlands, the United States would have over 60,000 men in France, with more on the way. To Sir Douglas Haig, the American contribution meant some degree of future relief from his current desperate need for more infantrymen. As for Ludendorff, he had no new allies.

Plumer's concept for the renewal of the lowlands campaign was presented to Haig in late August. It took full advantage of the terrain won during the Battle of Messines Ridge to provide some cover for the British artillery that would support the attack. The idea of shifting the main effort to the south enhanced the probability of success. Moreover, Plumer had decided that his overall plan would be based on short punches of about 1,500 yards into the German defenses. This would keep his infantry under the range of most of his artillery, ease the problem of bringing up reserves to thwart German counterattacks, and ensure that command and control of the forward elements would be facilitated. The Second Army commander planned to execute these short attacks at approximately six-day intervals. The idea also included a very narrow attack front of about 1,000 yards for each division. This would allow a reserve element controlled by the division commander to stay close behind the cutting edge of forward units.

Plumer's scheme envisioned a use for artillery that had never before been seen on the front. The guns would number one for every 5.2 yards of attack front, the greatest density of artillery firepower ever assembled during the war. Five fire zones of about 200 yards in depth were assigned. The forward zone consisted of shrapnel fire, the next of high-explosive fire, the third, a belt of machine-gun fire. The fourth and fifth were also high-explosive zones. This 1,000-yard front of destruction was to move just forward of the advancing infantry. Plumer would also have twenty-six squadrons of aircraft to support his limited advance. Rather than blowing up the Germans as at Messines Ridge, the general had designed a plan to blow them away physically.

With a diversionary attack by Gough's Fifth Army to the north, the Second Army began its advance in the early morning hours of September 20. The preceding three weeks of relatively dry weather now provided good footing for the four divisions in the lead. In more ways than one, the Germans were taken by surprise. Plumer's high ground had shielded his preparations. When the objectives were largely taken by the early afternoon, the British quickly organized a defense, while their enemies were clearly expecting a further advance. Thus the inevitable German counterattack forces were not immediately released. The "short jab," rather than the attempt at a "knockout blow," failed to trigger German reaction. Not all of the objectives were initially taken by Plumer's forces and some fighting went on for three days. But altogether it had been a considerable success.

The sour note for the British was the heavy cost of fighting after the first day. By that time the Germans were fully alerted and gave ground only after a stubborn defense. Plumer had taken some 20,000 casualties, almost all of them occurring on September 21, 22, and 23.

On the first day, however, when most of the gains had been secured, losses had been light. For the first time in six months, it appeared that there was an answer to the German defensive system. Elated by their success, Haig and Plumer planned the next short attack. The weather continued to hold and it was decided to attack along an 8,000-yard front, hoping to punch into the German defenses at a depth of only about 1,000 to 1,200 yards. The artillery had been displaced forward and the offensive was scheduled for September 26. The main effort was to be made by the Australians, while units to the south and north would also move forward, covering the flanks of the lead attack.

The assault began at 5:50 A.M., and the Aussies quickly moved to their limited objectives behind the powerful artillery barrage. The Germans had been expecting an attack, but could do little to stop it. Their troubles were doubled by the Allied aviators. With good flying weather, the British and French airmen flew at altitudes of only 300 feet, using machine guns and bombs on the defenders. The Australians were in position to take on the inevitable counterattack shortly after noon, and had the full support of Plumer's artillery. The German response was halted in a hail of artillery shells. The "short jab" had worked once again. It was costly; Haig had taken 15,000 casualties. But the British had won—the Germans had lost.

On the next day, September 27, 1917, a turning point was reached on the Western Front. Tested once and proven on a second try, the British had devised an offensive system that could defeat Ludendorff's defensive methods. Haig was fully confident that the end was in sight and a breakthrough at hand. On the other side, Colonel von Lossberg knew that changes had to take place. Not only was the Fourth German Army losing ground, it was also losing large numbers of troops. Despite reinforcements, the German army was not matching Allied artillery, aircraft, or manpower. To Lossberg, the weakness in the defense doctrine was the assumption that the attacker would exploit the weak front, outrun his artillery support, and expose himself to a well-supported German counterattack. The doctrine collapsed when the attacker was satisfied with a short gain. There had only been two such British attacks, but it was clear that successive British assaults of this nature could not be stopped.

It was also clear that the answer lay in precluding the short gain, which could be accomplished by eliminating the concept of a weak-front defensive sector. The forward area would have to be strong, and that meant moving German infantry forward. In the next few days, the "outpost" zone became a crowded area as more and more German riflemen and machine-gun teams were rushed forward.

General Plumer, a rather unlikely-looking leader of men, had a quick mind and a firm grasp of the art of war. He suspected that his adversaries would revise their defense for his next attack. He knew that he had shown his hand and could not expect continued success. He would have to make some tactical changes so that his army could keep one step ahead and retain the initiative.

Whether by blind luck or design, Plumer hit on the very technique that would exploit a growing vulnerability now appearing in von Armin's defense. As the German infantrymen moved to the forward zone, they found little cover. Most of the pillboxes had long since been lost, and the short periods between British attacks did not permit the digging of adequate trenches. Plumer's revised technique involved foregoing the usual preparation bombardment and relying on surprise. The devastating creeping barrage and the infantry assault would be simultaneous and sudden. It would begin at 6:00 A.M. on October 4.

What happened could only be described as mass slaughter. The German defenders were wholly unprepared for a high-volume, rolling barrage, closely followed by a powerful infantry attack. In ground combat the attacker often has more casualties than the defender, but for this one-day offensive, the situation was reversed; the German army lost 30,000 men. What slim confidence remained in the top echelons of the German high command was swept away. To Ludendorff and von Lossberg, the British army appeared to be a force that could not be stopped. Within the councils of the British army, however, caution was much in evidence. The advance of October 4 had yielded only about 700 yards, and had begun in a drizzle. The light rain increased in intensity and became a downpour in the next few days. To the British army commanders, Gough and Plumer, a further attack was out of the question. They did not fully understand what they were doing to the German army, and could not find the replacements for their losses. The mud was making it almost impossible to displace artillery forward.

Haig listened to his subordinates, considered their negative recommendations, and ordered them even so to plan for resumption of the offensive. Douglas Haig was the sole optimist on the Western Front.

By now the German General Staff was in a state of alarm. Reinforcements had been sent to the Austrians on the Italian front. The war was winding down in the east and there was a chance to transfer German forces to the west. But that would take months and the British attacks kept coming. An offensive in another part of the Western Front, to take the pressure off the lowlands, would not be possible. A large part of the

German forces had been transferred to the lowlands since July, and as-
sembling an offensive capability in France could not be done in time to
take advantage of what little was left of campaigning weather.

Ludendorff considered an offensive of his own in the lowlands. He
needed badly to regain the initiative; dancing to Haig's tune was proving
too costly. An offensive would mask his inability to defend and require
the Allies to redispose their forces for defense. Again, however, time was
the enemy. It would take too much time to mass the artillery, plan the
attack, and move in divisions that were capable of attack.

In the end, Ludendorff's only realistic option was to defend. The German defense, however, would have to go back to the initial doctrine for
1917: a lightly held front and well-executed counterattacks. The choice
was not founded on any faith that a return to this system would stop the
British. In their short, successive attacks they seemed to have found a
solution. The basis for Ludendorff's decision lay in the sober fact that
the Germans could no longer afford heavy losses. The British would be
able to take ground, but they would be advancing with the least possible
cost to the defender.

Despite continuing bad weather, Haig pressed another attack for October 9. The objective now was the last piece of high ground in the offensive sector, Passchendaele Ridge. The battlefield, however, had been
transformed. There had been so much rain that the soil lost all semblance of solid material. So soft was the surface that one attacking unit
required over eleven hours to make an approach march that normally
would have taken about two hours. A lodgment was eventually made on
the high ground, but it had to be given up because the flanks were badly
exposed. A withdrawal was ordered. After a few days, another attempt
was made, but with similar results. The weather was not improving.

Haig now turned over the main offensive to the Canadians. The Canadian commander, Lieutenant General Sir Arthur Currie, told his superior that it would cost 16,000 casualties to secure the high ground.
Haig ordered the continuation of the offensive even so. Preparations
were almost impossible. At one point a mystified officer reported that
a light railway designed to carry ammunition forward had simply disappeared beneath the muck, with the locomotive buried up to the boiler.
Artillery pieces sank out of sight. Riflemen found it difficult to fire their
weapons because there was no solid place on which to stand, kneel, or
squat. Strangely, in a struggle characterized by the term "trench warfare," there were now no trenches; the ditches had simply filled with

The mud of Passchendaele: "Clapham Junction," near Sanctuary Wood, Ypres, 1917.—*U.S. Army Military History Institute*

Major General John J. Pershing, immediately after landing at Boulogne, 1917. —*National Archives*

Top: Italian troops in camp in the mountains.—*National Archives*
Bottom: Italian cannon, captured near Udine, Venezia, November 1917.
  —*National Archives*

Heavy Austro-Hungarian mortar firing, between Brenta and Piave, Italy.
—*National Archives*

Canadian troops inspecting German gun emplacement at Thelus, April
1917, during battle of Vimy Ridge.—*National Archives of Canada*

Clockwise, from top left: General Robert Nivelle; Lieutenant General Luigi Cadorna; the German crown prince (left) and General Max von Gallwitz; Baron Manfred von Richthofen, the "Red Knight of Germany."—*U.S. Army Military History Institute; National Archives*

Top: British SE 5As of the Royal Flying Corps. Note Lewis gun mounted above
  wings.—*U.S. Army Military History Institute*
Bottom: The British Sopwith Camel was the most agile Allied fighter of the
  Great War, but for an untrained pilot it was a dangerous ship to fly.—*U.S.
  Army Military History Institute*

German artillery laying a barrage, near Champagne.—*National Archives*

Captured Frenchmen on the road from Soissons to Fismes.—*National Archives*

German columns advance to the front for the great offensive in the west, 1918.
—*National Archives*

Heavy German mortar goes into position near Hams, 1918.—*National Archives*

Celebration of the thirtieth anniversary of Wilhelm III's reign, German army headquarters, June 21, 1918. The kaiser is at the left. At the right, Field Marshal von Hindenburg talks with the crown prince.—*National Archives*

The pilot of this Fokker D VII F fighter, photographed in August of 1918, is Hermann Goring, Adolf Hitler's future Reichsmarschal. —*U.S. Army Military History Institute*

a soupy mud. Cover was available only occasionally in the most recent shell holes, indentations in the liquid surface that were all too prevalent. To remove a wounded comrade, the Canadians had to organize parties of stretcher bearers of four men each. The trek through the mud was so exhausting that it required four such parties, one relieving another, to transport a wounded soldier 4,000 yards to the rear.

Day after day the Canadians slogged their way forward. Men were reduced to an animal-like existence. Horses drowned with regularity in the muck. The same fate awaited wounded men who were not found in time. Soldiers became afraid to sleep. Transportation was so difficult that the forward infantrymen rarely saw food or water. Many of the soldiers and their officers began to harbor an odd bitterness that would endure for the rest of their lives. It was a sort of proud contempt that they passed on to their families—a contempt for war, for the Germans, for British leadership. The veterans of Passchendaele would become a breed apart.

Eventually they succeeded in taking what their commander, General Currie, claimed was a worthless piece of ground. As he had predicted, casualties were severe, totaling 15,654 men. It ended on November 10. There was little fight left in the attackers, and precious little resistance left in the defenders. All of that had been left behind somewhere in the mud of the lowlands. The high ground was now in the hands of Haig. The Battle of Passchendaele was over, but the controversy over his decision to continue the offensive was just beginning.

THE FINAL PHASE OF THE BRITISH OFFENSIVE, Passchendaele, had been so arduous and difficult that its very character had an immediate impact on the subsequent prosecution of the war. The British prime minister, Lloyd George, was now convinced that he had been correct in withholding replacements from Haig. In the political leader's view, the high costs and slight gains of Western Front combat were undermining the British Empire's will to continue fighting. He redoubled his efforts to find another strategy, another front, or another method to defeat Germany. But logic and the continued arguments of his naval and military advisers did not support another solution. Having no real alternative to the battles of France and Belgium, Lloyd George chose a middle ground by refusing to replace Haig's massive infantry losses fully. Because of this conflict of attitudes in London, a growing number of well-trained, fit, and equipped soldiers began to accumulate in the British Isles. Haig would get labor troops, technical service personnel, and other support forces, but the shortage of infantrymen became acute. By December over 200,000 potential combatants were assigned to the "home defense" of Britain, while Haig's staff was searching for Western Front divisions that had retained enough rifle strength to manage an offensive.

Passchendaele also compelled the British military leadership on the Western Front to look for alternatives to another offensive such as the one they had just concluded. It could not be repeated. The nature of the shell-pocked mud and slime of the lowlands ruled out another large attack in that region. That condition also eliminated opportunities for a ground attack that could be coordinated with an amphibious operation. Haig had thus lost one of the advantages that the British Empire had over Germany. The unmatched power of the Royal Navy could not be used directly to enhance a ground offensive.

Another heavy offensive by infantry was no longer an option. No matter how much confidence Haig might bring to such a scheme, neither his superiors nor his subordinates could be counted on to support it fully. Not only was Lloyd George withholding the essential replacements for such an attack, but Haig's own army commanders were becoming increasingly skeptical. The very nature of the tactics that had been used to defeat the German defensive system precluded any likelihood of great results. The British success had been predicated on a series of short attacks, with five- to six-day intervals between assaults. The technique worked, but successive gains were small, and the intervals between them permitted German preparations and reinforcement. The British could move forward, but only at glacial speed.

The British attack had also damaged Ludendorff's forces, however. In the aftermath of the offensive, some inkling of the actual results began to emerge. British intelligence officers, specifically the order-of-battle experts who kept track of German units, reported that the lowlands offensive had absorbed much of the enemy force structure on the Western Front. Ludendorff had begun the defense of Flanders in July with eleven divisions. To prevent a breakthrough he had reinforced these eleven units with no less than seventy-seven other divisions. In comparison, the Allies had used forty-three British and Canadian divisions and six French divisions. Although at this period in the war the German divisions had about 80 percent of the strength of their French and British counterparts, there was little question that Ludendorff had been hard pressed. Not only had he lost the initiative in the west, he had been forced into emergency conditions, throwing every available unit into the fight. British intelligence officers could predict with confidence that the Germans did not have enough rested divisions in the west to mount any appreciable offensive for the next few months.

Neither side had any sort of precise figures for the losses inflicted on the other. Even with a distance of seventy years, the casualty totals of the lowlands campaign of 1917 are still in dispute. Perhaps the best guess for the British side of the ledger is provided in the report of Haig's staff shortly after the campaign, a period when it was desperately trying to justify the need for replacements. The estimate stood at 238,313 British and Canadian casualties from July 31 to November 10. The French reported the rather vague total of 50,000 casualties, certainly a high figure for the number of units they had committed. The total Allied estimate would thus be about 288,000 casualties.

German totals are even less certain. General von Armin reported to the kaiser that his Fourth Army had 84,000 casualties for the months of July and August alone. The best figure for the whole campaign is roughly 260,400 German casualties, although later Haig's defenders would claim 400,000. There is, however, one clear indication of the extent and seriousness of the effect of the Flanders offensive on the Germans. During the campaign the Allies took 23,000 German captives.

German leaders were now seeing indications of crumbling morale among their troops. When they came out of the front lines, the ranks of badly battered units in the lowlands suddenly swelled. Some German soldiers were dropping out of their organizations as they went to the front, hiding during combat, then rejoining their units when they were pulled out to rest. The German units that the British had faced at Arras were not considered to be equal in quality to the forces that Haig fought in Flanders, yet more prisoners had been taken in the lowlands than during the earlier spring offensive. Thus, while many British leaders were becoming distressed at the increasing costs of battle on the Western Front, their doubts and reluctance were more than matched on the other side of the line.

At both Messines and Flanders, the Germans had faced Allied air superiority, the overwhelming use of French and British artillery, and a steady offensive resolve in Haig's forces. Ludendorff had described the British lowlands offensive as "almost irresistible." He said, "The British had an extraordinarily stubborn will." By November the German soldiers in the west had little doubt who was dominating the skies and the artillery battle. It was also clear to them that their army was far behind the French and British in tank development and industrial production. To Ludendorff and his troops, the Allies appeared to be a force with unlimited material and fortitude. When that vision was coupled with Haig's proclivity for continuous attack, the future of the German army, as seen by both its officers and men, looked bleak indeed.

In the final analysis, the great British lowlands offensive in the fall of 1917 had three important effects. It had masked the weakness of the French army, providing Pétain with the time to rebuild his army and revise its doctrine. The loss in German confidence had been such that a continuation of their present defensive situation in the west was intolerable; the German defense system had been defeated, and their forces were overwhelmed. But the campaign had been so costly for the British that they could no longer stage such operations, and were thus seeking tactical alternatives.

In the waning weeks of 1917, the French were now preparing to resume their share of the fighting, while the Germans were convinced they could no longer remain on the defensive against the Allies in the west. Yet the British knew that they would not be able to attack in the same fashion that they had before—certainly not in the lowlands. November 1917 was therefore a time of change. The war would not be prosecuted as it had been in the past. The future conduct of this war would be determined by the army that could effect change in the least amount of time. But for the moment, the attention of the military leadership on both sides had been diverted to Italy.

FOUR

Mountain Maneuver: The Italian Front

IN THE MIDST OF HAIG'S LOWLANDS campaign, a British delegation was dispatched to Italy for a conference among allies fighting against the Central Powers. On September 11, 1917, Lord Derby, the British minister of war, and Major General Frederick Maurice, the British director of military operations, arrived at the headquarters of General Luigi Cadorna. The sixty-eight-year-old Italian commander's outpost was located at Udine, about twenty-five miles behind the front and ten to twelve miles short of the Italian-Austrian border. The headquarters had been at that location for some time, the Italian front being no more mobile than its western counterpart.

David Lloyd George, the British prime minister, would have welcomed any excuse to remove sizable numbers of British troops from the command of Douglas Haig so that they could escape the unending bloodbath on the Western Front, and General Cadorna provided his London visitors a perfect opportunity. The Italian commander laid out his situation, presenting a dark picture. Although he had just finished a somewhat successful campaign against the Austrians, he feared that Russia was nearing collapse, and to him that meant hordes of Austrian troops would be released from the Eastern Front. Cadorna foresaw an Austrian concentration against his front during the forthcoming winter, followed by a massive Austrian offensive in the spring of 1918. He stated that he could not withstand such an attack, given his current dispositions.

The Italian front was markedly different from the Western Front. In France and Belgium the terrain was relatively flat. Here the terrain was mountainous. Possession of a significant position on high ground along the Italian front not only offered great advantages, but usually spelled the difference between success and failure. The linear distance of front here was almost equal to that in the west, but the number of troops on opposing sides here was only one-third of the number in France and Belgium. This meant that there were gaps in defensive positions. In some areas not only were the defenders spread thin, but their ability to reinforce was impaired due to the time required to move troops along narrow mountain roads and trails and through the difficult terrain.

Cadorna was uneasy about his front-line position. It seemed that the recent Italian offensive had only partially achieved what had been set down as the desired result. Although most of his forces were well east of the Isonzo River and on Austrian soil, the Austrians still held a bridge-head west of the Isonzo near the fortress of Tolmino. Moreover, some of his units were now on terrain that did not favor defense. Cadorna saw no alternative to yet another Italian offensive aimed at taking better ground. To bring it off, his exhausted army would need assistance from its allies.

There were a number of reasons, however, why the Italian general's British visitors might not be sympathetically disposed to his request. The first had to do with the character of the general himself. Cadorna possessed a well-deserved reputation for autocratic, brutal leadership. While the French and British military leaders were struggling to revise their tactics so that infantry attacks could be less costly endeavors, Cadorna continued to press his soldiers forward at all costs. His response to long casualty lists and marginal gains was always the same; he relieved subordinates with wholesale abandon.

Cadorna's attitude toward discipline harkened back to the Roman Empire, an era he might have excelled in. He actually advocated the decimation of failing units: shooting every tenth soldier. His handling of civilians was closely akin to his views on military discipline. The general simply decreed that no Italian politician was authorized to visit his troops. The old fellow might have gotten away with such behavior if he had achieved a record of success in battle. Unfortunately, Italy's chosen commander had little to record on that score. His achievements at the front had been small, and the costs had been high. Understandably the British visitors were reluctant to forward any recommendation that would place British soldiers under the command of such an archaic mentality.

A second major reason that Lord Derby and General Maurice were reluctant to favor British support of Cadorna was the nature of Italy's strategic objective. The front here was much like the one in France and Belgium, oriented to the northeast. The extended line was merely interrupted by neutral Switzerland. One could envision a successful Italian drive pushing the Austrians into the arms of the Germans, an alternative to the Western Front, where the object was to push Germans back to Germany. The Italian view, however, was different. From 1915 on, Rome's focus had been on securing the Austrian port of Trieste. Essentially, the entire Italian endeavor had been directed at attacking north toward Vienna and then turning south to seize Trieste. Although that strategy might have been advantageous for Italy, such a goal did little or nothing for the larger Allied aims. Success would certainly gain undisputed Allied control of the Adriatic, but this control would have only a marginal impact on the progress of the war as a whole.

Lord Derby and General Maurice therefore recommended only a minimum response to Cadorna's request. Since the Italian general envisioned a limited offensive, the contribution of his allies could take the form of dispatching a small number of artillery pieces, spread between both France and Britain. If Lloyd George hoped to remove infantry formations from Haig's control and ship them to Italy, he would be disappointed.

The Italian general's need for a limited offensive was heavily influenced by geography. The war in Italy had been fought in three distinct areas. To the north, Italians and Austrians faced each other in the Trentino region and the Carnic Alps. This extremely mountainous area included the southernmost Austrian thrust toward the heart of Italy, but the tortuous and limited network of roads afforded the least possible promise for any attacker. Logistical operations in this area were almost impossible. The terrain of these regions also gave a defender innumerable natural barriers with which he could delay, impede, and halt any attack. The Italian First and Fourth armies had successfully defended these regions for some time. To the extreme south, along the coast of the Adriatic, Cadorna had deployed his Third Army. This unit was the pick of the Italian army, for its location was closest to Trieste. Logically, the Third was the attack element in Cadorna's scheme of things. The terrain along the Gulf of Venice was relatively flat, but was inundated with a number of rivers and swamps.

Sandwiched between these two regions, the mountain and coastal theaters of operation, lay the area of responsibility assigned to the Italian Second Army. The city of Caporetto on the Isonzo River formed the center of the Second Army area, but the front itself was east of that town. The terrain here was mountainous as well, but there were some broad valleys, and once an army found itself past the Julian Alps, its maneuverability would be markedly improved. Cadorna's problem was the failure of the Second Army to secure the entire east bank of the Isonzo during the most recent offensive. Thus the enemy-held Tolmino bridge-head area, where the Austrians held ground on the river's western bank, represented a threat to the Italian units that were now east of the river.

Cadorna reasoned that in 1918 the Austrians would deploy units both north and south from the bridgehead, trapping his forces on the east bank. Such a move would at least jeopardize the Second Army, and if that unit was in trouble, the prized Third Army would then become vulnerable to being cut off in the south. It was essential, therefore, that the Second Army seize all of the east bank of the Isonzo prior to the spring of 1918.

The immediate need was for artillery, and the British emissaries were glad enough to get off so lightly. Sending the guns, together with a French and British plan for the immediate reinforcement of Italy in emergency conditions, would be sufficient. The British promised 160 guns and gave the assurance that Cadorna's requirement would be made known to the French. The French agreed to send 40 pieces, and soon the entire 200-gun shipment was en route.

On September 20 Cadorna changed his mind. There would be no Italian offensive in 1917. The general—whose favorite quotation was the Piedmontese maxim "The superior is always right, especially when he is wrong"—began to have second thoughts. It seems that he had gotten wind of a possible early Austrian offensive, and so decided to defend instead. The French and British, while willing to support an attack, had no intention of contributing to a defensive operation. They believed the old fellow had deceived them from the start. So the artillery shipment was turned around. If all that the Italians intended to do was defend, they could do it with what they had.

Italian fortunes, therefore, would rest on the strengths and weaknesses of the Italian army, not on those of the French and British, and in the fall of 1917 this army had many weaknesses. The morale of the forty-three divisions at the front was being undermined by a growing barrage of pacifist messages. Italian Socialist and Communist parties widely advertised the motto: "Next winter, not another man in the trenches." The Italian government, like its French counterpart, failed to maintain effective censorship measures. Antiwar propaganda easily reached the troops through the mails.

The church, usually a psychological bulwark for the regime during war, had already disavowed the conflict, calling it a "senseless slaughter" in the Vatican's 1917 message. In some cases there were also miscalculations in government attempts to support the war effort. When munitions workers in Turin went on strike, the government responded by drafting them into the army. After less than thirty days of training, the laborers were pressed into the defenses of the Second Army. Not only did this foolish measure equate punishment with service to the nation, but it provided the Caporetto front with some dubious defenders.

Alarm signals indicating the deterioration of the Italian army were increasingly noted by foreign observers—but not by the Italian high command. In the spring of 1917 an Italian offensive had resulted in more Italians than Austrians becoming prisoners. In one instance three full regiments had sought refuge in their enemy's care. Given decent leadership and a worthy cause the Italians fought well, but in September 1917 they had callous leaders and little national support for their suffering.

Italy's immediate opponent, Austria, likewise had serious military problems. Composed of a polyglot collection of ethnic minorities, the Austrian army had no central rallying point, no common reason for fighting. A large percentage of Emperor Karl's forces had little at stake in either a German or an Austrian victory. Defections from the Austrian army had become commonplace by 1917. There were constant and well-founded rumors that the emperor and his government were seeking ways out of the war.

The two opponents on the Italian front were roughly an equal match, with the Italians having a slight edge. The Austrians had been giving ground in the second half of 1917, and Karl's generals, like Cadorna, believed the ground they defended was disadvantageous. They too believed that the time had come for outside assistance.

Cadorna's eleventh Isonzo offensive of August and September 1917 threw a scare into the Austrian command, so that with the possibility of a Russian collapse imminent, the leadership in Vienna naturally turned toward reinforcing the Italian front with Austrian units taken from the Eastern Front. Such talk greatly disturbed Ludendorff, who did not want to limit his options for 1918 by having to fill in the gaps left by departing Austrians on the Eastern Front. The German general believed it essential to keep the troops of his allies deployed in the east.

The Austrians, however, went over the heads of the German General Staff. Emperor Karl approached the kaiser directly, with the result that Hindenburg was ordered by his king to find a solution. So Ludendorff had to act swiftly. He narrowed the problem down to its roots. The Austrians believed they were in an untenable position. They were not asking for the war to be won for them; they simply wanted to regain the use of their own troops. Permanent transfer of Austrian troops from the east, however, would constrain the Central Powers during the next year, and the same dismal result would be realized if German troops were permanently transferred to Italy from the west.

Ludendorff summoned his alpine warfare expert, Lieutenant General Krafft von Dellmensingen, briefly outlined the problem, and sent him to Italy. Dellmensingen's hasty reconnaissance of the Italian front was completed in early September. A quick offensive thrust could be made— if the right spot was selected as the point of attack and if the right troops were used. Reluctantly, Ludendorff decided upon an Austrian-supported German main attack, to take place in late October. Not only would the German contingent be light—just seven divisions—but its employment would be brief. Once a successful breakthrough was effected, the bulk of Ludendorff's forces were to be withdrawn for more vital work elsewhere.

The choice of a rapid, brief German attack solved the problem for Berlin. Its ally, Vienna, would be supported in its hour of need; no mass withdrawal of Austrian troops from the east would be required; and no permanent dispersion of Ludendorff's western forces would be necessary. Germany's alpine units would provide the spearhead for the attack, but their numbers were so limited that other, less prepared troops also had to be readied for the offensive. Ludendorff chose General Otto von Below, a proven leader with a sound reputation, to command the main attack force, which included seven Austrian divisions augmenting a similar number of German troops. Following the usual German practice, Dellmensingen, the "brain" of the operation, was named as Below's chief of staff and charged with detailed planning.

By September 10, one day prior to the British visit on the other side of the lines, Dellmensingen had already picked his "right spot" for the attack. His choice was the Tolmino bridgehead. If secrecy was preserved, the German planning team believed they could get their forces into the bridgehead area before the Italians could react. Crossings of the Isonzo were also planned, both above and below Tolmino. The objective of the operation was to plunge so deeply into Italian lines that the entire front would be pushed back to the Tagliamento River, forty miles to the rear. Once that river was reached, German forces could then be withdrawn.

The initial task was to knock the Italians aside, or to bypass them, so that German forces would hold the last significant terrain features of the Julian Alps. That would give the attackers a position overlooking the plains below, including Cadorna's headquarters at Udine, and probably force an Italian withdrawal to the Tagliamento. General von Below's appraisal concluded that a key terrain feature, Mount Matajur, a 4,500-foot peak, would be a prime tactical objective. He promised the coveted German medal, Pour le Mérite, to the officer who took the peak.

Dellmensingen's plan relied on skilled mountain troops such as the Alpine Corps and the Württemberg Mountain Battalion to secure the critical heights, and more conventional troops to achieve the initial penetration of Italian lines. From the outset there were more critical heights than specialized troops, so that regular infantry formations were given a fast-paced course in mountain warfare and a measure of reorganization. The Austrian army, which was more skilled in these matters, assisted their German allies in overcoming the mysteries of pack artillery and mess equipment, using searchlights for signaling and illuminating enemy positions at night, and moving through rugged terrain.

Logistical requirements presented formidable obstacles. The basic problem in mountain warfare is that normal transportation—rail, wagon, and truck—becomes useless when located miles behind troop units. Each of the German divisions had to be supplied with one thousand pack animals. Motorized cable systems were constructed, as well as roads and trails, so that adequate supplies of food and ammunition could be made readily accessible to the attack formations. Even so, the planners had to acknowledge that an average load of seventy-eight pounds per man would have to be borne up the steep terrain by the assault elements. Each German division had a wireless radio assigned to it, but most of the Austrian units had none. The plan called for each lead battalion to lay wire for telephone communications as the attack progressed. Since no vehicles could follow the offensive from the Tolmino bridgehead, the planners were hoping to capture Italian stocks of food and ammunition.

As early as October 6, Italian intelligence officers began collecting the telltale indications that a large-scale offensive was imminent in the Second Army area. Construction activity and reports of German units sighted near Tolmino convinced some of these officers that the enemy-held bridgehead over the Isonzo would be the focal point of the attack. Three days later, an estimate was made forecasting an attack for the last week in October. On the twentieth an Austrian officer defected to the Italians, informing them that the attack was scheduled for the twenty-sixth, that the assault troops were to be primarily German, and that the main thrust was to be made from the Tolmino bridgehead.

The report should have been a disturbing one to the Italian leadership. The Austrian-held bridgehead faced only one Italian division, the Nine-

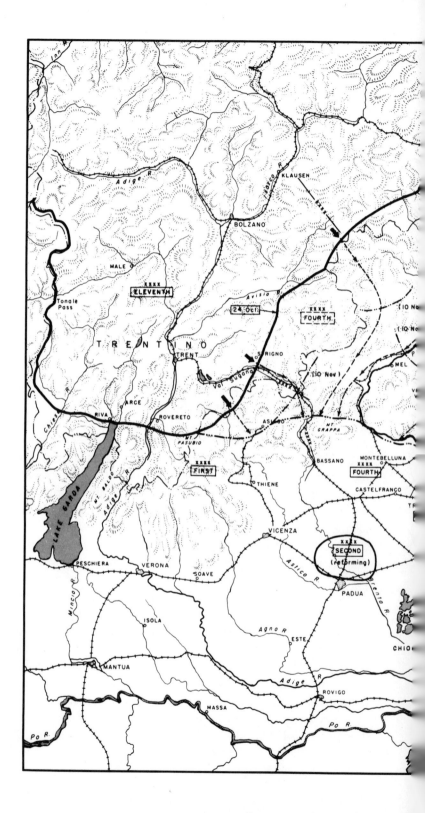

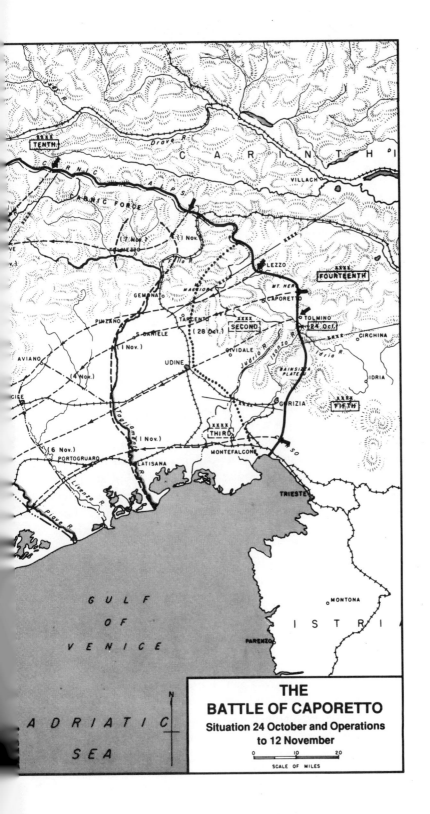

THE
BATTLE OF CAPORETTO
Situation 24 October and Operations
to 12 November

SCALE OF MILES
0   10   20

teenth, under the command of General Villani. His troops were stretched over four and a half miles of front. The general did have five brigades under his command and the backing of a reserve division immediately to his rear. However, the terrain he was defending was so rough that many ravines and potential attack corridors could not be kept under continuous observation.

Twenty-four hours later additional defectors confirmed the story, adding that the artillery preparation would be short and violent: four hours. Then an enterprising Italian intelligence operation, involving the tapping of an important Austrian telephone line, revealed that the artillery preparation was not scheduled for October 26 but was due to begin at 2:00 A.M. on the twenty-fourth.

A few days earlier, on the twentieth, Cadorna became convinced that his intelligence officers were accurately forecasting what was coming, and he moved rapidly to ready his Second Army for the onslaught. General Luigi Attilo Capello, the Second Army commander, was ordered to withdraw his heavy artillery from its position forward of the Isonzo River. Cadorna also directed Capello to pull back some of his infantry from the front positions to save them from an expected heavy preparatory artillery bombardment. Even so, Cadorna's instructions fell short of what a full use of available intelligence information might have produced. He was proceeding on the unfounded premise that his enemy was interested only in regaining some lost positions, not in mounting a full-scale offensive.

What loomed as a moderate threat to Cadorna appeared to be an opportunity to General Capello. Popular with Italian politicians, and considered by some to be the best officer in the Italian army, Capello ignored what he viewed as conservative orders from his commander. The Second Army commander believed his forces could cut off the attacking enemy units by striking them in the flanks as they moved forward. To achieve that, however, his artillery and infantry would have to be well forward, so few of Cadorna's instructions were implemented. The Second Army was also deprived of the full vigor of its commander, for Capello was fighting an apparent case of influenza.

The information derived from the telephone tap was accurate. At precisely 2:00 A.M. on the morning of October 24, most of the 2,430 German and Austrian guns opened up. Capello had 231 of his 353 battalions on the front line. The artillery preparation was carefully targeted on headquarters, road junctions, and Italian artillery positions for the first two and one-half hours. A large number of nonpersistent gas rounds were fired during this phase, primarily against Italian artillery units. The result was that Italian counterpreparation fire was weak and ineffective. Then came a lull in von Below's preparatory fire. Italian searchlight crews, expecting the infantry assault at this time, found that their vision was obscured by falling rain in the lower elevations and snow on the heights. After two hours of relative quiet, all the German and Austrian guns suddenly opened up again. This time the prime target was Italian infantry.

At 7:00 A.M. German and Austrian foot soldiers moved into the attack. The assault ranged over an eighteen-mile front and included almost all of von Below's fourteen divisions, but in the mountainous terrain the attack was not in the form of a linear human wave. Instead, most of the initial objectives were ridge lines. Valleys and ravines were usually avoided unless they were essential to subsequent objectives. Von Below had instructed his commanders that mountain fighting depended on the possession of high points, and that valley floors were death traps. There was to be no pause for flanking units to catch up, he declared; in fact, it was doubtful that the attacking units would even see friendly formations to their left or right. Heavy resistance along the slopes was to be bypassed, and if at all possible, an assault on these hard points would be made from the rear.

At least one of the German assault units, the Württemberg Battalion, needed no instructions in mountain warfare. This organization had been very successful during the Romanian campaign and other Eastern Front actions staged in hilly terrain. Its part of the assault was to take place one hour after an infantry unit had secured an initial penetration of the Italian front positions. The assault was aimed at von Below's designated prize, Mount Matajur, located four miles south and west of Caporetto, nine miles beyond the front lines. The battalion was a large one with eleven companies. The lead four companies were under the command of an experienced young officer of great promise, Captain Erwin Rommel.

Rommel and his men had already marched a long distance to their jump-off position prior to their 8:00 A.M. attack time. Before the beginning of the artillery preparation, they had to dodge enemy searchlights along the narrow mountain trails. Now, just before the assault, Rommel realized the full difficulty of the task ahead. Most of his heavy machine-gun team members were carrying a full ninety pounds, and their attack corridor led up the steep Colovrat Ridge, with Mount Matajur miles ahead at the end of the ridge line. There was no single enemy line. Instead, his men had to confront a series of hilltop positions, some with machine guns, some with artillery, and some with both, each ringed with

heavy strands of barbed wire and placed in checkerboard fashion between his battalion and its objective. He could hear the fire of friendly
troops to the front and occasionally the return fire from Italian machine
guns. At 8:00 A.M. he moved his men forward.

Moving through the friendly infantry battalion to his front, Rommel
and his troops encountered the first group of Italian prisoners being
shoved to the rear. The young captain deployed his men in a rather
narrow skirmish line along the slope of the ridge, and the troops began
weaving their way in and out of trees and scrub brush, already deep in
autumn colors. Passing the last friendly position, the attackers moved
into enemy territory. Within a few minutes, a camouflaged machine-gun
position revealed itself and the men of the Württemberg Battalion dived
for cover. Leaving his point element in contact with the enemy position,
Rommel worked his way around the flank and spotted an opening. Maneuvering a section through it in single file, the captain brought his men
to the rear of the Italian machine-gun position, making the occupants
his prisoners. Sending them to the rear, Rommel continued his attack up
the ridge through the rain and mist.

The bold German use of infiltration tactics was not restricted to the assault corridor of the Württemberg Battalion. General von Below's other
elements were also achieving successful penetrations of Italian defenses.
The artillery preparation had done its grim work. Reinforcement efforts
by the Italian defenders were stymied by the shelling of road networks,
headquarters operations were severely disrupted by the bombardment,
and communication lines were severed. Italian commanders rapidly lost
contact with their units at the front. Although there were numerous instances of Italian soldiers quickly surrendering to the attackers, other
elements in the southern sector of the Second Army stoutly contested
the offensive. Well to the north of Tolmino, however, Italian defenses
dissolved with blinding speed. In much of this area the Isonzo had to be
crossed by the assault elements, but they encountered little difficulty in
doing so.

By midmorning Rommel found himself at the head of a single file of
his German troops more than half a mile long. Bypassing some scattered
resistance, the soldiers soon came upon deserted batteries of Italian artillery, guns and ammunition intact. By noon, Rommel's column was in
the area of his enemy's heavy artillery positions.

In the late afternoon General von Below knew that he had achieved
a fifteen-mile-long breach of the Italian Second Army's defensive positions. He also knew far more than his adversary about what was hap-

pening. Most of his lead battalions had been accompanied by telephone wiremen. Receiving progress reports, divisional headquarters kept the corps and army headquarters apprised of the fast-changing situation and the growing accumulation of prisoners. On the other side, Cadorna knew little but suspected much. The old soldier was at his best in times of crisis, and knew that a major event was in the making. But with his subordinate headquarters displaced and his communications disrupted, information was coming to him very much delayed.

As night fell, Rommel settled in for a fitful few minutes of sleep. During the day he had advanced about a third of the way toward the peak of Mount Matajur and had reported the capture of 17 artillery pieces, 7 officers, and 150 Italian soldiers. Much else had been bypassed, and he knew that his enemy was moving to the rear, attempting to organize a new defense. The attack had not been characterized by hard fighting as much as brutal marching and maneuvering up steep terrain. One man in the Württemberg Battalion had died of exhaustion.

By 7:00 P.M. Cadorna finally knew the scope of his army's situation. He knew that one of his corps, the Twenty-seventh, was rapidly giving ground. That corps had the Tolmino bridgehead in its sector and was the superior command to the Nineteenth Division, which had been stationed at the bridgehead. No one had heard from the Nineteenth Division; its commander, General Villani, had committed suicide. To the north of the bridgehead, another corps, the Fourth, was also withdrawing. Although the rest of the Italian army was holding out, Cadorna realized no local counterattacks could remedy the plight of the Italian front.

Considering his options, the Italian commander knew that even though the First, Third, and Fourth armies had not been damaged, the status of the crumbling Second Army threatened the others. Once behind the Second Army, Cadorna's enemy only had to turn north or south to reach the rear of the Third, Fourth, or First armies. The Italian commander decided the first task was to establish a line of high ground in the rear of the Second Army where that force could rally its retreating elements. By midnight the Italian commander dispatched orders that outlined his concept. One of the high points that Cadorna designated as an essential defense position was Mount Matajur.

Germans and Austrians continued their attack through fog and mist on the second day of the offensive, October 25. Enough progress had been made on the first day to allow the forward displacement of von Below's supporting artillery. The advance of Rommel's unit outpaced the telephone wiremen, but they managed to catch up early in the morning.

As the troops of the Württemberg Battalion moved up the ridge, the foliage began to thin out. Thus far much of their success had depended on the skillful use of cover, but now it seemed that they had only the protection of bad weather to obscure the defenders' visibility.

However, the German and Austrian attack leaders had another factor working in their favor: complete confusion in the ranks of the Italian Second Army. Rommel spent the early hours of the morning surprising isolated, uninformed Italian detachments. The first encounter was little more than a matter of waking up sleeping enemy soldiers, disarming them, and sending them to the rear. A second group of Italians was caught bathing. By noon, when the sun broke through the clouds, Captain Rommel had already collected several hundred prisoners. He then encountered the first real resistance of the day. His men repeated their now-familiar flanking and rear-attack tactics, gathering more Italian captives. Rommel estimated that by then he had sent no less than a thousand enemy soldiers to the rear.

In the early afternoon his easy successes seemed to be over when his flank was suddenly attacked by a battalion-sized unit. However, the Italian commander had not seen the lead elements of Rommel's force. When the German leader wheeled into the flank and rear of the attackers, the unnerved Italians threw down their weapons. In this brief encounter Rommel's take was twelve Italian officers and 500 soldiers.

All during October 25, the second day of von Below's offensive, incidents such as those experienced by the Württemberg Battalion were taking place throughout the defensive zone of Luigi Capello's Second Army. Sick, defeated, and dispirited, the Italian army commander moved his headquarters farther to the rear and turned over the helm to a subordinate, General Montuori. The new leader attempted to rally his units for a stand. The army, however, emulated its former commander, and most of its elements refused to resist the oncoming Germans and Austrians. Those units that did stand and fight quickly became isolated and were captured. The attack became a rout.

By midafternoon Rommel could see that his position overlooked one of the Italian lines of communication, an important road running through a little valley. Taking 150 men with him, he dropped down to the road and established a hasty ambush position. Within a few minutes he was the proud captor of 100 more prisoners and 50 wagonloads of supplies. His soldiers hungrily tore into captured foodstuffs. The feast was rudely interrupted by the approach of a large enemy force coming down the road. Rommel stepped into the roadway and tried to signal to the advancing troops, gesturing that the opportunity to surrender was at hand. The surprised Italian soldiers saw the opportunity in another light, and a brief firefight broke out. When the Italians discovered that Rommel had carefully placed several machine guns to their disadvantage, however, they lost heart. The young German captain quickly handled the familiar surrender procedures, sending the Fourth Bersaglieri Regiment, with its 50 officers and 2,000 men, to the rear. Regaining the ridge and rejoining the rest of his unit, Rommel continued his climb toward Mount Matajur in the gathering darkness.

On October 25 Generals Cadorna, Capello, and Montuori met. Capello urged a general and immediate withdrawal for the whole army behind the Tagliamento River. The other two favored a staged, orderly retreat to the river to protect the Third Army to the south, which was now becoming exposed by the collapse of the Second Army. The latter idea seemed feasible because the two Second Army corps nearest the Third Army were holding well. If these two units could begin a wheeling movement and reorient to the north, they could resist any attempt by the Austrians in that sector to get behind the Third Army during its retreat. Capello's immediate and wholesale flight was dismissed. Cadorna dispatched orders for the staged withdrawal to the Tagliamento River.

Later that night General Cadorna, frustrated by the lack of news from the Fourth Corps north of Caporetto, sent orders for the relief of the corps commander. The latter gentleman did not know that he had been fired and the newly appointed commander had no idea where to find the corps headquarters. An already confused situation on the left flank of the Second Army became even more muddled.

During the night of the twenty-fifth, Captain Rommel found a spot to rest most of his exhausted soldiers while he conducted a brief reconnaissance. Deep in the enemy rear, he knew that his enemy was badly confused and uninformed. Surprise and shock were playing a big role in the German success, because an accurate appraisal of the extent of the penetration was not known by Italian regimental and battalion commanders. Rommel could hear enemy units marching to and fro in the darkness—some attempting to reach critical delay positions, others trying to reinforce areas of the front, and some milling about in aimless fashion.

Early on the twenty-sixth, again commanding the lead element of the Württemberg Battalion, Rommel continued up the steep approaches to Mount Matajur. Reconnaissance the previous night had revealed an occupied enemy trench line, which he took in the rear as the first task of the day. After a short fight the young captain organized the 37 disarmed officers and their 1,600 Italian soldiers into a north-bound march column. Moving on south, he made a chance contact with a large Italian unit forming in a clearing. Approaching them and indicating a surrender opportunity with a white handkerchief, he saw the unit's officers make a few menacing moves. Suddenly the Italian soldiers pushed aside their leaders and rushed toward the German officer. When they reached him, they lifted the surprised Erwin Rommel to their shoulders, shouting "Long live Germany!" The 1,500-man First Regiment of the Salerno Brigade seemed to welcome their new status as captives. A 1,200-man Second Regiment that Rommel encountered a bit later put up a fight, but soon succumbed as well.

Rommel and his men captured Mount Matajur on the afternoon of October 26. For the first three days of the offensive, his losses amounted to six dead and thirty wounded. His detachment of the Württemberg Battalion had taken over 9,000 prisoners and eighty-one artillery pieces in those three days. As so often happens in war, through an error the promised medal for capturing the mountain went to another officer in the battalion. Rommel was presented the Pour le Mérite award later. There was no shortage of opportunities for the daring German officer on the Italian front.

The full extent of the disaster was now known to the world. Cadorna set his Third Army on the coastal road toward the safety of the Tagliamento River. In London, Lloyd George ordered two of Haig's divisions in France to entrain for Italy. Authorities in Paris discussed the dispatch of a French general to Rome; an on-the-scene report would be necessary. There was no lack of interest among the Central Powers as well. General von Below began to consider greater things. Perhaps Italy could be put out of the war. A request to retain German units in Italy might be welcomed in Berlin.

Civilian refugees began to clog the roads south, complicating Cadorna's problems. Yet in the midst of a clear and ringing defeat for the Allies, several positive but somewhat obscure aspects began to emerge. Although attention was largely centered on the increasingly desperate condition of the Second Italian Army, the First, Fourth, and Third armies remained under control and responsive to orders. In spite of the fact that the Third Army along the coast was in danger of being outflanked, its withdrawal had begun without much pressure from the Austrian forces facing it. There was also little pressure on the First and Fourth armies. Then too, as the refugees began streaming down the roads, Italian soldiers started to realize that the war was taking on a different character. In retreating southward to escape German and Austrian control, the people of northern Italy were choosing sides. Clearly they did not want to live under enemy rule. For the Italian soldier the war was no longer a geopolitical scheme to acquire Austrian territory. Almost overnight, it was being transformed into a new conflict—the defense of the homeland.

Coming out of Austria, the Italian army was staging one of the world's strangest retreats. There was shame, despair, determination, discipline, disorder—no single characterization could describe this massive movement. One more general, Rubin, who was in charge of the Thirteenth Division, shot himself. Some units marched steadily southward in good order; others disintegrated into dangerous, pillaging rabble. Some bridges and supply dumps were methodically torched, others abandoned for the use of the Austrians and Germans.

The luckless Second Army had only four bridges over the Tagliamento River to carry it to safety. One of the bridges was washed away in a flood and another was only a footbridge. This caused many units to march laterally toward the river, producing vulnerable flanks and the intermingling of troops at the crowded bridge sites. On the other hand, the withdrawal of the Third Italian Army was just that—an unhurried movement to a better defensive position. The Third Army had seven bridges over the Tagliamento in its sector and the unit was destroying everything of use in its wake.

General Cadorna chose the evening of October 27 to inform the government in Rome of his plans to put his army behind the Tagliamento. It was the first accurate report of the actual situation that the politicians had received from their military leader.

During the next two days, October 28 and 29, Cadorna calmly continued to orchestrate the withdrawal of his forces, while the Allies began to step in to support their retreating ally. There was not much the Italian commander could do about the Second Army. It was shattered, and the primary Italian effort was to retrieve as much of it as possible. The plan was to order the Fourth and Third armies to occupy the defenses of the Tagliamento and to assemble the remains of the Second well behind the river. The withdrawal would greatly shorten the defensive frontage, and there was little difficulty in assigning appropriate sectors for making a stand. Meanwhile, the French picked their general to send to Italy, Ferdinand Foch. Paris also directed four divisions to join the British reinforcements. The earliest date that the French and British soldiers could expect to arrive on the battlefield, however, was November 6. Both

Lloyd George and Painlevé, the French prime minister, decided to visit the threatened front.

The Germans were racing south. Early on the morning of October 29, the relentless 200th Division forded the Torre River and drove toward Udine, the site of both Cadorna's headquarters and that of the Second Army. The lead elements of the 200th Division arrived at the outskirts of the town two or three hours after the Italian staffs had departed. Following his troops closely, General von Berrer, the German corps commander in this sector, motored into the town in his staff car. An alert and brave Italian carabiniere spotted the German commander, raised his rifle, and shot the general dead. The act did not make much of a difference to the German troops. They continued their attack southward. The 200th Division was now between the two fleeing wings of the Second Army. Not only was the Second being pressed hard, it was now divided.

General von Below knew an opportunity when he saw one. Hoping to defeat the Italians and put them out of commission for good, he made plans to extend his thrust over the Tagliamento; on October 29 he telegraphed Ludendorff. The German field commander recommended the new plan and requested the retention of five of the seven German divisions.

However, von Below's forces began to experience some difficulties. For the first time in months, Italian horse cavalry entered the fray. Placing themselves between the Germans and the retreating Italian infantry, several squadrons began attacking exposed lead elements of the attackers. In the fluid situation, the Italian horsemen did well, checking the German advance in several areas and giving their comrades badly needed time. These scattered actions took place on the twenty-eighth and twenty-ninth, but a major encounter involving two cavalry regiments occurred on the thirtieth. The Genova and Novara Lancers caught an advancing German infantry unit on the road and went into the attack. Pressing the foot soldiers back, the cavalrymen gained a small town, dismounted, and set up a hasty defense. A house-to-house battle took place when the Germans resumed the fight. Although the Italians gave up the town, they remounted and made a courageous but unsuccessful charge back into the streets. One of the squadrons was quickly reduced to ten survivors; its officers had all been killed.

Stiffening resistance was not the only problem that von Below's forces encountered. General von Hofacker, who had taken over from the fallen von Berrer, decided to switch the direction of attack. Instead of pressing the Italian Second Army back to the Tagliamento, he shifted toward the southeast, attempting to get behind the Third Army, cut it off, and trap it against the coast. The ill-coordinated effort caused little more than massive confusion in the German ranks. Several German units were very quickly intermingled on the sparse road network and large-scale traffic jams developed. Von Below countermanded the order on October 30, but the damage had been done. Time was being lost and the Italians were escaping.

On October 31, most of the Italian forces were behind the Tagliamento River. The exception was the ill-fated Second Army. Bridges were destroyed before some elements of the Second arrived at the river. Thus much of the Second Army was captured. However, General von Below continued to experience difficulties, since some of his lead units were still tangled up on the roads. Unable to imagine the extent of the Italian collapse at the start of the attack, von Below had failed to assign boundaries for his units so far to the south. October 31 was used by the Germans to reestablish some degree of order on the front.

By November 1 the Italian Third and Fourth armies were behind the Tagliamento, and even some small elements of the Second Army had been saved. The Germans and Austrians were having trouble bringing up artillery, ammunition, and supplies, which had not kept up with the infantry. Lead German and Austrian units were dangerously exposed, without essential logistical and fire support elements.

Despite his logistical problems and lack of artillery, however, General von Below threw caution to the winds and hurled his troops forward in an attempt to break the Italian defenses along the Tagliamento. The German and Austrian infantrymen found the defenses to be much stronger than they had experienced heretofore. Even so, on the night of November 2, the Austrian Fifty-fifth Division forced a crossing over a partially destroyed railroad bridge at Cornino. When the German Twelfth Division seized a footbridge at Pinzano, the Italian defenses started to crumble once again.

Seemingly unperturbed, Cadorna ordered the Tagliamento defenses abandoned. He had already decided that the Italian stand would be made yet farther to the south, on the Piave River, and he had placed his heavy artillery accordingly. The Italian infantrymen continued their retreat for another twenty to twenty-five miles. By then the withdrawal was causing near panic in Rome, but Cadorna's purpose was a single-minded desire to save his army. At this point, ground did not seem to be important.

By November 9 Cadorna and his troops were behind the Piave. It was all too much for the Italian government, and the general was relieved of his command. His last order was for an all-out stand in the new defenses. There was to be no further retreat.

As the Germans and Austrians continued their approach, the Italian high command learned that their troops would have to face the renewed attacks alone. The British and French leadership decided that eight divisions would be the extent of the support they would ship to Italy, and furthermore that no French or British units were to man the front along the Piave.

Most of these decisions revolved around the judgment of the French general, Foch. He believed the Italians had to regain their self-confidence, and that it would do no good for French and British troops to step in temporarily to achieve what in the end the Italians would have to do for themselves. A firm advocate of the supremacy of the Western Front, Foch managed to convince all concerned that it was in the overall Allied interest to have the French and British contingent remain in the rear of the Italians. Paris and London would back up their ally, but they would not do the job for Rome.

The first concerted effort of General von Below to continue his advance beyond the Piave came on November 16. His attempt to get across the river failed. On the twenty-second he tried again. This attack also collapsed in the face of the determined Italian defenders. The next day saw another attack and another failure. Confident now in the Italian ability to defend and convinced that the army had regained its self-respect, Ferdinand Foch left Italy. Soon the winter rains began to destroy the usefulness of the Italian roads. Another front of the Great War sank once more into the mire of stalemate. The Caporetto offensive was over.

The bold and briefly successful German fall 1917 campaign in Italy had been achieved through special circumstances. General von Below's initial gains came largely because of the poor condition of the Italian Second Army, and were not the result of any type of new doctrine, organization, or novel system that could be repeated on other fronts. The infiltration techniques that the Germans and Austrians used were typical of those essential to mountain warfare. Mountain fighting demanded an approach to operational planning similar to a chess player's forethought. Position was all-important, and multiple, narrow-front attacks on selected terrain, as opposed to an advance on a broad front, was the rule. Both the Austrians and the Italians had used such methods for over two years prior to von Below's arrival in Italy.

Capello's Second Army, although reflecting many of the ills of the Italian armed forces as a whole, was particularly vulnerable during the time of the attack in October. It is unlikely that von Below would have been as successful against any other Italian army. To be sure, pacifist propaganda, questionable war aims, public disaffection, and callous leadership were not unique to the Second Army, but that army had already suffered much just before the Central Power's offensive, and also had the misfortune to be under vacillating guidance from a sick commander. There is no indication that in the critical first hours of the attack Capello's immediate subordinates knew whether they were supposed to withdraw or counterattack. Capello's untimely departure from the scene heaped more confusion on an already mystified army. The infusion of unreliable troops just before the assault also worked to the disadvantage of the defenders of the Julian Alps. The Second Italian Army would have failed in any event.

Curiously, the disaster at Caporetto worked to the benefit of the Allies. Despite the loss of 10,000 killed, 30,000 wounded, 293,000 prisoners, and 400,000 deserters, the Italian army was in effect reborn. The shock of the retreat forced the people and their government to stand behind their army for the first time in the war. Just as the people of France had elevated Clemenceau at a moment of crisis, and just as Britain pressed Lloyd George into the leadership role, Italy now found Vittorio Orlando. Like his British and French counterparts, Orlando's sole aim was to win the war. Once a champion of free speech, the Italian leader now began attacking pacifist voices, and Italy joined its political allies in a temporary suspension of democratic procedures. Socialist advocates of a separate peace found themselves facing investigation for undermining the will of soldiers. After Caporetto the Central Powers had no chance to remove Italy from the war through diplomatic means. They had gained an implacable foe, fighting for national survival on its own soil. Although British and French troops stood at the ready behind the Italian army, the stout defense at the Piave was an Italian feat of arms, one that von Below could not overcome.

The campaign in northern Italy may have been viewed by Austrian and Italian leaders as an end in itself, but others saw it as an integral part of a larger event. Ludendorff acquiesced in the use of German troops in Italy only as a necessary and unwelcome prerequisite for continued Austrian cooperation. His aim was to ensure adequate strength for the coming battles on the Western Front and sufficient force structure in the east. The temporary deployment of a small segment of his army was successful in causing the French and British to subtract from their strength in the west, but his move failed to divert the attention of one French general from the true objective.

Ferdinand Foch went back to Paris before the climax of the German attempt to break the Italian defenses on the Piave. Not only did he seem to know that the tide had turned, but he correctly sensed that Ludendorff would not reinforce success in Italy. In failing to advocate more French and British forces for Italy, he probably disappointed Lloyd George. But the French general's thinking was in complete agreement with that of Ludendorff. General Foch returned to the only place where the long war could be brought to an end, the battlefields of France and Belgium.

FIVE

Maneuver by Machine: Cambrai

AS THE COLD AND WET WINTER OF 1917–18 began to settle over the battlefields of Western Europe, there was a general expectation that the weary commanders and their staffs would begin planning for the spring campaign. A winter offensive was not seriously expected by most observers. The movement of supplies, units, and munitions would be too uncertain in severe weather. Much transportation still depended on animal power, and even in mild weather the road networks of France and Belgium were not reliable.

Even though major offensives were not expected, the filthy and disease-ridden trenches had to be manned. So the soldiers of both sides expected to endure a winter's cold and to trade occasional raids, and hoped to survive shellings. To them the future offered a few months' respite until there were better conditions for battle.

However, even before the last British assault was made at Passchendaele and well before the Italians stabilized their defense on the Piave, leaders were calculating the balance of power and how that balance might be tipped by yet another offensive.

Since every attempt had been made to hide true conditions, an adversary's future capabilities could only be roughly estimated. Although Haig held the initiative on the Western Front, his own horizon appeared dark. The lack of infantry replacements, the slow commitment of untrained Americans, and increasing high-level intimations of the transfer of more of his forces to Italy painted a grim future, particularly with the forthcoming reinforcement of Ludendorff's ranks by German units released from the collapsing Eastern Front.

Yet Haig would have been reassured had he known Ludendorff's actual thoughts. The German general also had to consider the Italian front, and had diverted several western-bound units to the south. Then too, Ludendorff was far better aware of the real situation in Russia. Despite the overthrow of the czarist regime, the nature of that front would require the presence of considerable numbers of German troops for an indefinite period. Germany's Austrian ally was not strong, and the chaos in Moscow made it difficult to reach any sort of concrete agreement worthy of past German sacrifices. Never fully aware of the French troubles, Ludendorff was also counting the Americans who were landing in France. The U-boat campaign had failed, and it appeared that President Wilson would place his entire growing army at the disposal of the Allied commanders on the Western Front.

Perceptions differed from facts, but in the process of military planning, perceptions weigh heavily. Haig and Pétain knew they enjoyed an advantage in the short run—the coming four to six months—and Ludendorff saw the situation in the same light. Their perceptions, however, differed for the midterm—six to twelve months out, including the June to December 1918 time frame. In that calculation Haig and Pétain estimated that the Americans would still be unprepared and that hordes of Eastern Front German and Austrian troops would reinforce the west. Ludendorff could hope for that midterm condition, but he was too much the realist. His Western Front troops were badly depleted, he could not count on favorable results in the east, and he had to plan for the combination of Allied industrial superiority and American manpower becoming an early, powerful determinant. On prospects for the long run—the year 1919—Haig, Pétain, and Ludendorff could probably agree. The Allies would win—if their will did not break first. The democracies had the numbers: men and machines.

Perceptions drove logic, and logic dictated the nature of the plans. For the short run Ludendorff had to continue his defense, and he believed Haig would continue the attack at Passchendaele. Germany must therefore bend every effort to end the war in the midterm: spring 1918. That was essential, because Ludendorff knew that if the war lasted into 1919, German failure was inevitable.

Haig and Pétain had reason for some doubt in the long term: it was a political matter, a matter of national resolve. In the midterm they feared a coming imbalance that would give Ludendorff a temporary but dangerous advantage. In the short run they had the advantage and intended to use it. They must continue to attack before the Western Front was in the full grip of winter.

The operations plan for the new offensive did not originate with Haig. It was the combined conception of several British officers. As early as June, Lieutenant Colonel J. F. C. Fuller, the primary planner for the emerging British Tank Corps, had created a scheme for a massive use of tanks in a large-scale raid in the relatively peaceful Cambrai sector. Fuller's agenda had as much to do with demonstrating the power of the new armored formations as it did with furthering the Allied cause in the west. An effective show of massed tanks would perhaps undercut those who continually insisted on using the growing number of tanks as mere infantry-support implements. The tanks had been parceled out to those sectors that had obstacles the tank crews might handle.

Fuller intended no ultimate breakthrough, no final exploitation, and no major offensive. At the same time, innovative artillery officers in the British Ninth Division had become enamored with the idea of unregistered, surprise supporting fire for the attack. It was the same concept that the Germans had already demonstrated on the Eastern Front, and the same technique that Plumer's Second Army used in the Passchendaele offensive. When both schemes were presented to General Julian Byng, the British Third Army commander, he added his own twist. All during the summer and fall of 1917, Byng's army had played a secondary role, supplying infantry and artillery units to Gough and Plumer in the lowlands campaign. Byng had seen one German unit after another peeled off from his front and rushed toward the Belgian coast to defend against Haig's attack. Despite the less-than-impressive gains achieved in the Arras offensive, Byng had great confidence in his army, and now saw an unusual opportunity presented by German weakness. Combining the surprise artillery technique with the idea of massed tanks, Byng planned for a large-scale offensive that would break through the German defenses, enter their rear, and turn north, rolling up the German northern front. With Ludendorff's strength focused on Passchendaele, it could well work.

Haig had been given the outline of the concept in mid-September. Byng's troop list estimate amounted to practically all of the British tanks and nineteen divisions, including the exploitation arm, horse cavalry. The habitually optimistic Haig encouraged Byng to continue his planning, but did not lend his full approval. Certain limitations were imposed. If a breakthrough was not achieved in forty-eight hours, the plan must incorporate a halt and switch to defense. Haig's eye sought out a terrain objective that would signal a successful breakthrough and trigger the exploitation phase. For the lowlands campaign, the objective had been Roulers. For Cambrai, he settled on a wooded high spot west of the city: Bourlon Woods. The commander of the British forces then turned his attention back to the agonizing progress of the lowlands campaign, while Byng and his staff began detailed planning.

When French liaison officers learned that the British were planning for an offensive at Cambrai, Pétain made a bid for participation. If a breakthrough could be achieved by the British, exploitation should not be directed at rolling up the German northern line alone. Pétain insisted on five French divisions driving through the gap and turning south on reaching the German rear. Thus Lieutenant Colonel Fuller's notion of a tank raid had grown into a full-blown offensive, involving twenty-four Allied divisions aimed at a weak German sector containing only two or three enemy divisions. The objective of the revised plan was no less than the destruction of the German army in the west. The key element in the plan was to achieve a breakthrough by the use of machines. The Battle of Cambrai would give birth to a new age of armed conflict: mechanized warfare.

The new kind of warfare was based on three machines that utilized the internal combustion engine: the truck, the airplane, and the tank. Although much of the munitions and supplies were hauled by animal or rail, the British were increasingly using the more efficient and flexible transport means provided by the truck. The truck allowed military planners to shift troops, munitions, and supplies quickly from one area to another. For Cambrai, fourteen of the nineteen designated British divisions had either recently returned from the lowlands offensive or were yet to be transported south from the fighting around Passchendaele. The vehicle could also be used to support the exploitation phase following the capture of Bourlon Woods.

The airplane, which began the war as a means of observation, had quickly been transformed into a counter-reconnaissance implement, or fighter. The next step in its utilization had been as a bomber, targeted on vulnerable points in the enemy rear. The Royal Flying Corps planners for the Cambrai operation projected a need for about three hundred aircraft. Airplanes would have a close support role, assisting the tank crews and infantrymen by strafing and bombing enemy forward positions. Additionally, raids were planned on German airfields at the outset of the initial assault, in the hope of catching enemy aircraft on the ground.

However, the centerpiece of this maneuver by machine was the new tactic planned for the 476 tanks that were now being moved under cover of darkness to the Cambrai front. As with any new branch of an armed force, British armor officers believed the units under their care had been improperly employed by unknowledgeable higher commanders. At Cambrai the tank zealots largely had their way, and were allowed to determine the tactics and conduct brief preparatory training sessions for the accompanying infantrymen. Unfortunately, the roles might more

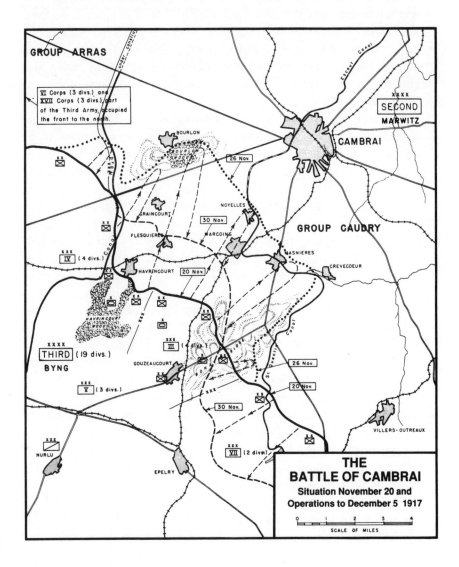

THE
BATTLE OF CAMBRAI
Situation November 20 and
Operations to December 5 1917

properly have been reversed, because the tank had been designed and developed from the ground up as an infantry support device.

The British tank project had begun early in 1915 with the idea of providing the infantry with an armor-plated machine that could cross trenches, crush barbed wire, and destroy machine guns. Winston Churchill, an early advocate, had seriously suggested that the accompanying infantrymen carry bulletproof shields during the passage of enemy forward defenses. The amazing feature of this project was not the initiators' failure to foresee the ultimate destiny of their mechanical prodigy; what was astounding was the accomplishment of British engineers, soldiers, and sailors, who were able to construct a workable prototype in about one year. The weird-looking "landship" actually crossed trenches, crushed barbed wire, and mounted the protected firepower to destroy enemy machine guns. Moreover, it did all of these things with some degree of reliability.

However, the British tank was never designed or developed to operate alone, and certainly not in the enemy's rear. It was not meant to be an exploitation device. It could manage no more than five to six miles of combat before it broke down, ran out of fuel and ammunition, or exhausted its crew in the super-hot interior of the shell. It had sufficient power to achieve an infantryman's pace—and not much more.

In 1916 and 1917 the tank crews had accomplished their assigned missions about 30 to 40 percent of the time, figures that considerably exceeded the success rates of British corps and army commanders. The tanks, and the brave soldiers in them, had proven the worth of the original concept.

Although they would generally condemn him after the war, citing the "premature" employment of the tank in 1916, British armor officers owed much of the growth of their organization to Sir Douglas Haig. Despite the tanks' lackluster performance in the Battle of the Somme, Haig dramatically revised their planned production rate upward. Although a few hundred tanks at the most were envisioned even by the most ardent supporters, Haig's order was for a thousand improved versions. The general took an energetic officer from his own staff, Major Elles, and put him in charge of tank matters for the British Expeditionary Force. He gradually provided him with an organization, and ultimately promoted the young officer to the rank of brigadier general.

The piecemeal employment of the tank from the summer of 1916 until the fall of 1917 would have been a dubious policy had it not been for the fact that few Germans viewed the tank as a serious threat. A handful of Ludendorff's field commanders contemplated the new weapon with alarm, but its initial use in widely separated parts of the battlefield and its mixed performance led the German General Staff to view it as no more than a minor irritant. Haig had greater faith in it and was now ready not only to employ tanks in mass, but to permit Elles to prescribe the tactics for the breakthrough at Cambrai.

Elles turned to his bright assistant, Fuller, for the tactical scheme of the initial assault. The attack would be launched by two British corps. Elles and Fuller assigned 216 tanks to the Third Corps and 108 to the Fourth Corps. The tank crews were organized into nine battalions of 36 tanks each. The assault battalions would keep 6 of their tanks in reserve to replace losses or reinforce as necessary. Fifty-four of the machines and their crews would be assigned as a general reserve. Each of the assault tank battalions had several "grapnel tanks," vehicles that had been fitted with trailing cables and hooks designed to pull away large segments of the barbed wire once the tank had rolled over the entanglements. Additionally, a number of the machines had been designated as supply and communications vehicles. Several of the assault machines had been configured to carry large ten-foot-long rolls of bound wooden poles, which were rigged to be dropped in wide German trenches. These rolls, or "fascines," would allow the tanks to traverse the wider German trenches without crew exposure or external assistance.

Fuller's tactical concept envisioned the infantry closely following each of the assault tanks in two single files. Once the tanks had crossed the German trenches and had swept parallel to them for a distance, firing into the overrun enemy positions, the foot soldiers would enter the trenches and eliminate German resistance. The whole process would then be repeated until all of the enemy trench lines had been penetrated.

The five assault divisions were trained in the new attack procedure and their commanders accepted Fuller's doctrine—all except one. The leader of the Fifty-first Division, Major General G. M. Harper, insisted that his infantrymen put more distance between themselves and the tanks. He also wanted his men to be on line behind the tanks, not in single files. It was this division that was to carry the attack in the center of the offensive corridor.

The flanks of the corridor were bordered by two canals, the St. Quentin and Canal du Nord; the latter ditch had been under construction at the outbreak of the war. An area of tall trees, the Havrincourt Wood, was located just behind the British lines and provided an excellent spot to hide some of the tanks and some of the more than 1,000 artillery pieces being assembled. The Germans were believed to have only about 150 guns in the area. Their defenses in this sector generally consisted of three lines of double trenches, with a distance of about one mile between each of the three lines. The double trench lines were separated by an average gap of 200 yards. The British assault divisions would primarily be pitted against the defending German Twentieth Landwehr and Fifty-fourth Divisions. To the south, a segment of the German Ninth Reserve Division sector was also to be attacked.

What the British did not know was that another German division, the 107th, was en route from the Eastern Front to Cambrai. Yet even with this unknown factor the German soldiers would be overwhelmingly outnumbered in men, guns, tanks, and airplanes.

The British would also have the vital element of surprise in their favor. The front-line German troops had reported hearing tanks as well as abnormal movement behind British lines. On November 18, two days prior to the planned attack, German soldiers captured several British infantrymen. One of the captives, a noncommissioned officer, told his interrogators enough to lead them to forecast a tank attack. However, in this sector, an area of relative peace, such news was received with considerable disbelief. Both subordinate field commanders and Luden-dorff's own staff discounted a major British push at Cambrai. A continuation in the lowlands was believed to be more likely. There was yet another reason to discount the prisoner's story. If a substantial offensive was in the offing, where was the registration of British artillery?

At 6:20 A.M. on November 20, the quiet, dark skies twelve miles southwest of German-held Cambrai were bathed in a brilliant flash as close to one thousand British guns suddenly opened fire. At the same time, three hundred tanks rumbled their way across British lines, attacking northeast. Adding to the deafening roar of the artillery and the nerve-shattering whine of their shells in flight, the massed tanks contributed a new sound to warfare. This attack was different from the others in many ways. British officers in a number of units had taken up rifles, assaulting enemy positions alongside their infantrymen. Brigadier General Elles was in command of the lead tank.

The Battle of Cambrai, seemingly just another effort after three years of efforts, would have a special quality. It would be a story of mechanized warfare, a logical outgrowth of the industrial age; yet it would not prove man's subservience to or replacement by machines. The event seemed to enhance man's willingness to sacrifice. Cambrai was a battle that would forever be marked by courage. Initially, in the morning hours, that courage was almost wholly on the British side. But as the day wore on, a special spirit, an ennobling quality, quickly spread among the badly outnumbered and outgunned German defenders.

At first the German soldiers were immersed in darkness, mist, and clouds of smoke, the latter carefully placed by the British artillery. The British gunners had developed their surprise unregistered fire techniques in apparent ignorance of an almost identical German program. Precise measurement of each gun's firing characteristics, use of meteorological data, and calculations with accurate maps and survey data paid off. The guns were on time and on target.

"Wire-cutting" fire was not necessary this time. The tanks would take care of that. Most of the screaming shells were laid into the creeping barrage sequence, just in front of the rolling tanks. The line of outposts was quickly overrun and most of the occupants were hurriedly killed or captured. Next came the first trench line and its protective wire. British artillery planners had left nothing to chance, so their smoke rounds had largely obscured the defenders' vision. In the combination of smoke and mist, the front-line German soldiers were aware only of the growing roar of hundreds of tanks and thousands of artillery shells. At the first blast of artillery, some of the Germans dived for the "bombproofs" within the trench system. These men would be either killed or captured. For those whose fate was to endure the oncoming and ominous sound of barbed wire and pickets being crushed beneath unseen mechanical monsters, the choice was often to quit the open trenches and run to the rear through the hail of artillery shells. The first trench line was taken in darkness.

By 9:00 A.M. a five-mile breach had been opened in the first German defense system. Many of the tanks did not have to drop their fascines, as the trenches were narrow enough for them simply to roll over the top. In some cases, the British infantry had to struggle to keep up with them. Men were burdened with 170 rounds of ammunition, and many carried picks or shovels for the inevitable defensive phase. In the area of Harper's Fifty-first Division, however, the tanks were considerably out of touch with the infantry, whose deployment in line instead of file brought troops up against numerous areas where the wire had not been breached by the tanks.

By 10:00 A.M. a pale sun was slowly burning through the mist, and the impatient airmen of the Royal Flying Corps ran to their planes. Some of their comrades had already made it to the German airfields through the marginal early morning weather, catching the pilots there as they scrambled for their aircraft. By machine-gunning and bombing, the British had rapidly destroyed the German aviation capability in the Cambrai sector. The men of the Flying Corps methodically went about their tasks, striking headquarters, road junctions, and artillery positions, giving close support to the advancing ground troops, and providing observation reports. The view below appeared to indicate a British triumph—but one that was not clearly understood in Byng's headquarters.

The pilots saw the tanks making steady progress on both flanks of the British attack, the regions near the canals. Rapid progress in the center sector of the offensive, however, was not clearly evident. Harper's Fifty-first Division was not keeping up with the companion units to the right and left. On the ground there was great confusion as to just where the attacking forces were and what they had seized. The confusion was not due to the lack of planned means of communication. One tank had been designated as the "telephone tank." Playing out wire behind it, the crew of this machine relayed up-to-the-minute reports back to headquarters. Kite balloons were sent aloft for the purpose of carrying observers high enough to view and report on the situation below. Messenger pigeons were released by forward units and used for the same purpose. There were many messengers, afoot and on horseback. All of this was for naught, however, because Byng and his corps commanders never got a clear grasp of what the situation really was that day.

The urgent need for accurate and timely information from the battlefield centered around the cavalry. That was the designated exploitation arm, and this offensive had been designed for an exploited breakthrough. It was essential for Byng to know when to release the mounted units, and what path they should take to avoid areas that had yet to be breached. Throughout the day cavalry units moved from one place to another, mostly on false information. The British army and, for that matter, all others in this war were not prepared for breakthrough situations. Byng's headquarters was too far back to either receive or immediately act on information. There were many opportunities on this day, including the opening of roads and paths to the northeast. But Byng was depending on the complete achievement of every facet of a complex plan. Alternate courses, on-the-spot modifications, and sudden shifts were unlikely in an army that had been a slave to set-piece plans for almost three years. Byng's plan depended on a uniform advance in a corridor that was five miles wide. The plan was not being fulfilled, for a knock-down-drag-out fight was developing in the center of the attack corridor around the little village of Flesquières.

The village was in the sector of the German Fifty-fourth Division, an organization that had been in a state of chaos since dawn. By late morning an entire regiment was considered completely lost, its commander and all of its battalion commanders dead. The violent artillery storm, the raiding and unopposed British aircraft, and the marauding tanks had badly disrupted the division's communications. The German Second Army headquarters was receiving only bits and pieces of information from the Fifty-fourth. The division's troops had mistaken the British smoke barrages for a gas attack and donned their masks, which restricted vision and induced fatigue. It was a scene of near panic. But with the arrival of a young regimental commander, order began to be reestablished.

Major Krebs, commander of the German Twenty-seventh Infantry Regiment, marched into Flesquières with some of his men under orders to reinforce the battered Eighty-fourth Infantry Regiment. Krebs began to stop many of the fleeing troops and organized dazed groups of leaderless soldiers into a hasty defense of the village and its surroundings. On his flank, at a small knoll, lay the remnants of one of the division's artillery units. Seeing Krebs's rallying efforts, the German artillerymen responded by practicing what they had recently been taught. It was a quirk of fate that this organization was one of the few German artillery units that had been drilled on using their pieces in a direct-fire mode at moving targets. They had been trained to fight tanks.

As the British attack emerged from the smoke and mist, Major Krebs's supporting artillery began firing with a rather high degree of accuracy. When a number of the tanks were hit, the accompanying infantry faltered. Krebs brought in more troops, placing them on the terrain and paying particular attention to the machine guns. The British resumed their assault, and soon the attack reached the very outskirts of the village.

The commander of the German Eighty-fourth Regiment was badly wounded and Krebs took command of all forces defending Flesquières. Soon he too was hit, but he continued his efforts. In sporadic communications with the artillery and his higher headquarters, Krebs pleaded for reinforcements. He also called for antitank ammunition. The Germans had developed a munition called the "reverse bullet," a blunt-nosed round that had a steel core. On striking the tank, the bullet's core would sometimes penetrate the compartment, but more often the munition would simply distort the shell of the tank and cause a spalling of metal on the other side of the armor plate. These fragments could wound and disable the crew as effectively as a round that penetrated the interior of the tank.

For Cambrai, the tankers were wearing metal chainlink mail visors on their helmets to protect their eyes from these metal fragments. But tanks could be destroyed or disabled in many ways. Brigadier Elles's tank had been "ditched," or turned over on uneven ground. Some of the more courageous German infantrymen had approached those tanks that were too far in front of British infantry and placed grenades under the tracks. In one instance the Germans grabbed onto the guns of a tank to prevent accurate fire. They learned to direct their machine-gun fire at the vision slits on the tanks. Once a tank was disabled, some of the engineer troops that Major Krebs had incorporated into his defense would go forward, subdue the crew, and seize the Lewis machine guns. Taking them out of the tank, the engineers would then add to Krebs's growing firepower. The tanks and their crews needed infantry to protect them. Harper's Fifty-first Division did not fully understand this at the beginning of the attack, and was learning the hard way. By the end of the day, Krebs, a young but brave and intelligent officer, was gaining the upper hand around Flesquières. The British center came to a halt.

However, Major Krebs and his gallant band of defenders were being surrounded. Far to their south and rear, British cavalry had broken through to the last areas of the German defensive system. Near the village of Masnières the horse soldiers galloped into open ground and saw a German artillery unit. In a scene more in keeping with a previous century, the British cavalry quickly formed for the charge and launched their attack. The German artillery unit, low on ammunition, prepared to receive the charge using pistols. The fight was a brief one. When the ill-trained troops of a German recruit depot appeared on the scene, the cavalry withdrew.

It was now 4:30 P.M. and light was rapidly fading from the battlefields. Although the British had achieved surprise in the morning, their advantage had begun to slip by midday. Ludendorff had been informed of the attack at 8:30 A.M., but the reports were so confused that he did not immediately react. By noon, however, the German general was fully aware of the seriousness of the British offensive. The Second Army commander had rushed in the rest of the 107th Division, choosing the region immediately to the rear of Krebs's fight. The Eastern Front division had little ammunition for such a task, but began organizing a defense. Other local units were hurried forward, many of them using confiscated cars and trucks to shuttle their men into the face of the British attack. With Ludendorff fully alerted and the Second Army staff working throughout the afternoon, seven reserve regiments had been stripped from organizations surrounding the sector and pressed into trains, trucks, or any other available transportation bound for Cambrai. By late afternoon Ludendorff had committed seven divisions to stop the British.

The attack had actually stopped itself. The natural inclination for British commanders was to pause when resistance was encountered along the line of attack, and to resume the attack when the resistance was cleared up. It was important for them to be on line, so as to present no opportunity for the enemy to exploit a flank advantage. Harper had now stopped to regroup in the center, and his pause had a paralytic effect on the whole offensive. The German third defensive system had been breached at several points, but there was no one present with both the knowledge and authority to continue the advance. As darkness settled on the fields, a great Allied opportunity began to fade.

Major Krebs took stock of his situation in the early evening hours and decided there was little hope of holding on to the village of Flesquières. For all intents and purposes, he and the men he had gathered and led were surrounded. They would be easy prey for the British in the morning. The only hope lay in a quiet move to the rear under the cover of darkness. The wounded officer collected his charges and began a silent retreat. Unaware of their foe's plight, the British had failed to close the trap. The commander of the Twenty-seventh Infantry even managed to take some of the artillery with him. A light rain covered his withdrawal. Soon he encountered friendly voices, the forward elements of the 107th Division. His regiment had been reduced to battalion-size strength. Krebs brought out 32 officers and 512 men, losing 52 known dead and 705 missing. Unaware of the full extent of his achievements, the young major would later learn that he was leaving behind thirty-nine destroyed or disabled British tanks in what had been the center sector of Byng's attack.

Overall, the attack had been a rather successful one for the British, especially in comparison to other offensives. In some cases an advance of almost six miles had been made. Surprise had been achieved. Despite Harper's troubles, the tanks had proven effective when employed in mass. The surprise unregistered artillery technique worked. The Royal Flying Corps performed with great distinction, accomplishing many varied missions. In addition, some 4,200 German prisoners had been taken, along with a hundred guns.

On the debit side, Haig had determined that more had to be done before his forces would be in a position to exploit the breakthrough. At 5:30 P.M. he had called Pétain and informed him that use of the French exploitation forces would have to be delayed for at least twenty-four hours. The British counted about 4,000 casualties. The order was given to complete the breakthrough the next day.

For the British, November 21 would constitute an attempt to bring their five divisions on line, which meant that the Fifty-first Division would have to catch up with the others. For the Germans, it was another day of frantic troop movements. Before sunrise, Harper's division moved into Flesquières. Finding the village deserted by the Germans, the unit continued to press forward. Harper found his enemies soon enough, however. The division reported that it was being counterattacked. Actually, what the Fifty-first was facing was less a counterattack than a meeting engagement. The Second German Army staff had decided to move reinforcements forward until they ran into resistance.

By midmorning combat was taking on an odd character. There were few trenches, so that encounters were often in the open. Resistance and assaults seemed to center around villages and road junctions. Now there was less barbed wire and prepared ground, and fewer pillboxes. By afternoon serious fighting began to develop around the town of Noyelles. British tanks were increasingly being hit with German artillery and anti-tank ammunition. Then too, German airplanes made their appearance over British troops. The Germans had been in possession of Noyelles at noon, and the British were determined to take the town. Reinforcements were ordered, and some units intended for the exploitation force were thrown into the fight. Against machine guns the British cavalry was helpless, so they attacked dismounted.

The British were also in close proximity to Bourlon Woods. That objective was the key to signal the exploitation phase, and another locus of intense combat developed there. Taking cover in a sunken road, the lead British infantry units reported that the wood was being defended by numerous German machine-gun crews just inside the tree line of the elevated forested area. While artillery support was being coordinated to bring fires on Bourlon Woods, the seesaw battle at Noyelles reached a conclusion. At 4:00 P.M. in the gathering darkness, the British took the town. The British forces had now gained some semblance of a line, but the forty-eight-hour time limit that Haig had set on achieving a breakthrough would now be exceeded. Bourlon Woods was still firmly in German hands.

Douglas Haig was now caught up in Byng's larger view of the Cambrai offensive and began ignoring the restrictions that he had placed on the planners. He decided to use the next day for preparation and try again on the twenty-third. Calling Pétain once again, the British commander advised another postponement. Bourlon Woods was still the prime objective. Unfortunately, Haig was already using elements of his force that were reserved for the breakout. An obvious reason for the now-discarded time limit was that if a breakthrough could not be achieved quickly, German reinforcement of the threatened area would bring about another stalemate. Firmly in possession of the initiative, Douglas Haig did not want to let it slip from his grasp.

By the evening of the twenty-first, Ludendorff had four divisions on line in the threatened sector, and five more nearing the vicinity. He was now stripping units out of Flanders. The general had also begun planning for a counterattack. Considering his rate of buildup at Cambrai, he calculated that a major counterattack could not be undertaken before a week's preparation at the earliest. For the first time since the early morning hours of the twentieth, however, the German General Staff could breathe a sigh of relief. All of the initial confusion had been swept away, and the size of the British effort was now identified. The Germans had identified the attacking British units, so that their order-of-battle specialists could confidently state that new and unidentified elements were not present. In short, the threat was now known. Speed was still essential and there was an undeniable element of danger, because the defensive system in the sector had been destroyed. But the momentum of the British offensive had been arrested.

During the night Haig pondered his options. Orders were already being dispatched for a continuation of the offensive, with the immediate focus on the seizure of Bourlon Woods. But what if the attack failed? His forces were now in a salient, an exposed indentation in the line surrounded on three sides by his enemy. Salients were expensive to defend, requiring more manpower than a line and exposing rear areas to enemy artillery. On the other hand, they could be used for offensive springboards, and the defender would have to employ considerable forces to keep a three-sided region contained. Haig's decision had much to do with the nature of the terrain and his original choices for this campaign. If Bourlon Woods could be seized, the attack would continue. If there was a failure to take this high point, he would order a withdrawal, a retreat back to Flesquières. In other words, he would not attempt to defend a salient with weak ground. It was not an easy choice. Neither politician nor soldier welcomes the surrender of ground recently won in blood.

On the next day, November 22, Haig rode to Flesquières, carefully inspecting the ground. The weary soldiers of the Fifty-first Division continued slugging their way forward to further straighten the lines against stiffening resistance. The communications problem had still not been solved. British artillery fire was being coordinated by mounted messengers—telephone lines were still almost impossible to maintain. Preparations for the attack on the next day were made and Haig rode back. On his return he was greeted with bad news. A message from London informed him that further reinforcements and replacements could not be expected, and there was a stronger indication that more of his units might have to be sent to Italy.

The twenty-third of November brought a cold, wet, and windy day. Byng's plan for taking Bourlon Woods included 100 tanks, the Fortieth Division, 50 aircraft from the Royal Flying Corps, and the support of 432 guns. The attack was scheduled for 10:30 A.M. The battle began with the tanks fighting well, despite a large number of losses. One battalion lost 10 of its 13 vehicles, another lost 6 of 11. Byng had dismounted more of his cavalry to fight as infantry. German aircraft began to contest control of the skies and a hot fight developed overhead. Baron von Richthofen's "Flying Circus" was reported in the area now, and the results of the fight seemed to confirm the report. The British lost 30 percent of their aircraft. There were also 200 German artillery pieces to contend with. The Fortieth Division and the dismounted cavalrymen, however, were not to be deterred. Despite heavy casualties, the British held most of the woods as darkness fell. Snow began falling during the night.

Expecting to use their captured high ground to advantage on the next day, the British attempted to take the rest of the woods and the nearby village. On the right, the exhausted Fifty-first Division was providing a supporting attack. But by now the German Second Army was gaining strength hourly. Gains began to be measured in yards. Hours of fighting yielded little. The Fortieth Division's casualties mounted. Within three days, this unit lost 4,000 men. The progress of the Fifty-first Division was little better. By November 26 the Germans had seven divisions on line, four of them grouped around the British attack. The supporting German artillery now numbered 500 guns. Their counterattacks were becoming increasingly effective, forcing the British to retake ground time and again.

On November 27 the British Cambrai offensive came to a disappointing end, and with it the Allied hopes for decisive results in 1917. Byng had committed the Sixty-second Division and thirty tanks to the attack. His forces were almost immediately hit with a ten-battalion German counterattack. Enough of the high ground had been taken around Bourlon to merit retaining the salient, but the casualties and overall strength problems of the British army pointed to a suspension of any further attacks. Haig passed the word to defend for the winter.

But he and Byng did not realize that their adversary would not be content to defend as well. Although the British leaders could not help but notice the steady buildup of German forces at Cambrai, they never translated Ludendorff's capabilities into an intent to attack.

On that day, the twenty-seventh, Ludendorff was busily providing guidance to his staff and subordinate commanders. For the first time in a year, the German army was going over to the offensive on the Western Front. It would be the first major offensive against the British army since 1915. Ludendorff's plan was to deliver the main attack on the southern side of the British salient. German forces would be advancing toward the north in hopes of cutting off the forward nose of the British position, bagging the concentration of Byng's units around Bourlon Woods. The woods themselves would have to be attacked. Otherwise, British forces there would be free to reinforce their companion units in the south and possibly escape the trap.

Since the British had most of the high ground around Bourlon, the northern German attack would not be easy, for preparations, assembly, and advance could be observed from the wooded knoll. The German high command planned for the employment of twenty divisions and a large number of aircraft. The main attack would be delivered under the control of Group Caudry, with assistance from the German Twenty-third Corps farther to the south. The secondary effort would be launched from the Group Arras sector. It was decided that the main attack would be delivered first, possibly easing the burden of the German soldiers who would have the unenviable task of assaulting Bourlon Woods.

The twenty German divisions that had been assembled in the Cambrai sector had not been sent there with the idea of an offensive operation. They had been selected purely on the basis of immediate availability in the first few desperate hours of the British tank attack. Their mission had been to defend, to contain the British advance. Now they were expected to put together an attack in a hurry, under unfamiliar headquarters staffs and with previously unknown units on their flanks. The offensive would have to be delivered quickly, since the weather could now be expected to close in, limiting air operations and making observation and supply operations difficult at best.

The German attack entailed high risk, but unknown to the planners, the British were providing them with some welcome assistance. Byng was unwittingly helping Ludendorff by releasing a large number of his aircraft and tanks for employment elsewhere on the front. Moreover, the British were going about their winter defense tasks in a somewhat leisurely fashion. Ludendorff set the attack date for November 30.

FOR THE ALLIES, THE FAILURE TO ACHIEVE an exploited breakthrough at Cambrai was a serious blow. It was not simply another failed offensive. With the capture of some of the German soldiers of the 107th Division, French and British intelligence officers now knew that the long-dreaded transfer of enemy troops from the Eastern Front had begun. Coupled with the serious manpower problems of both the French and British, the tide appeared to be turning. Cambrai might well turn out to be the last Allied offensive. Dark thoughts were in the air, because by late November the great hope of the Allied coalition, the Americans, looked none too promising.

The problem was that the Americans were now known to be terribly unprepared and apparently unwilling to fight as well. The initial impression was wholly discouraging. The first blooding of American troops had been nothing short of disastrous. Two battalions of the newcomers had finally been put on line in a quiet French sector. The first unit, under French command, took its assigned position on the twenty-sixth of October. As the second battalion was moving into its place on the front, news of the first American action was relayed. A trench raid by a Bavarian unit had caught the Americans by surprise. After they killed three of them, the Germans carried away eleven American prisoners. All the Americans had to show for the event was two German bodies and one dispirited soul who had stayed behind on purpose, hoping to end his service to the kaiser. It was not much of a beginning for Pershing's troops.

The Americans had practically nothing to fight with. Although four American divisions were in France in November, they were ill-supplied, ill-equipped, and woefully in need of implements of war. The British experience in this war held that about 40 percent of the total troop strength had to be devoted to logistics: supply and transport. The Americans had virtually no logistical troops and no hint of a logistical system. The supplies that had been sent to support their huge 28,000-man divisions were scattered throughout France and England, and no one seemed to know where they were. Even if they had been accurately located, there was little capability to transport them. The U.S. Army had fewer than thirty trucks in France. The staff officers of the American divisions were hard pressed to keep their men fed. As a result, the horses of the first units of the American contingent were actually starving to death. Neighboring Allied officers were reduced to pity and tapped their own resources. In the fall of 1917, eight months after U.S. entry into the conflict, the extended hand of American assistance had its palm up.

Even if the Americans were given the implements of war, there was not much hope that they could use them. Most Allied officers expected that the first American units, the First and Second Infantry Divisions, would be composed of professionals. They were soon disabused of that notion. The army and Marine Corps units that formed these organizations had been drastically understrength at the outset of the war. "Regiments" had only about 700 men, and had to be given as many as 2,000 raw recruits as they embarked for France. Once aboard their transport ships, the staff of the First Division had to introduce themselves to each other. The four American divisions were actually undergoing basic training in the rear areas of a theater of war. Then there was the matter of officers. Some held that the reason for the enormous American divisions was that having fewer of them overall would require fewer senior officers. Since the Americans had a very limited number of experienced professionals, the convenient melding of big divisions and few experienced officers seemed more than a coincidence.

For all of these reasons and more, many Allied officers well understood General Pershing's reluctance to take the field of battle with his recruits. To Haig and Pétain, the American "hope" was proving to be a faint one.

With a growing casualty list, practically no replacements, an increasing enemy, and allies in questionable circumstances, Sir Douglas Haig set about plans for defense in a stormy spring. His first trial would come much sooner. The first clues came from the front-line British commanders in the recently won Cambrai sector. There were noises. The sounds of troop movements across the lines had been reported on the evening of the twenty-eighth of November. There was also the matter of German artillery activity. Some doubted that the firing indicated the registration phase of a forthcoming offensive. The argument was that the Germans were simply settling into their new winter defense positions. Even when the preparation firing began, it appeared to be an odd, unfamiliar sequence. Since the British had not established much wire in front of their positions, protracted "wire-cutting" shelling was not necessary. On the twenty-ninth British units were still evacuating the salient, destined for other parts of the front.

The blow fell in the morning hours of November 30. It came at 7:30 A.M. in the southern part of the salient, and it came like an irresistible flood. The British Seventh Corps was short of the St. Quentin Canal, and its commanders had been concerned about recent German activity. As a precaution, some units had stood to arms at 6:00 A.M., and artillery was briefly fired at German positions. Enemy artillery replied at 7:00 A.M., but did not cease. The bombardment grew in intensity. Suddenly, British observation posts began reporting distress flares from forward positions. In the few instances where communications wire existed, units began to report that they had been attacked from the rear. At the first hint of light, the British were subjected to swarms of low-flying German aircraft, bombing and strafing throughout the sector. Many of the first reports from infantry battalions were identical: the Germans were already attacking command posts.

Throughout the southern part of the salient, small groups of British soldiers began fighting their way to the rear, often intermingled with north-bound German units. British artillery was often silent, not knowing where to fire. Survivors who reached the safety of an island of British control reported that the German infantry was not on line. There were no assault waves in the German attack. Instead, the penetration was reported to have been accomplished by small, heavily armed infantry units with light machine guns and flamethrowers. The retreating British soldiers remarked on the accuracy of the enemy artillery and stated that it appeared to be controlled by German infantrymen with signal lights and colored flares. The Seventh Corps commander asked for reinforcements and was told none were available because the situation in the Third Corps, also facing south, was more serious.

The character of the fighting in the British Third Corps sector was much like that in the Seventh's area, but more German forces appeared to be involved. The attack on the right flank was so swift that one brigade commander's first knowledge of the progress of German infantry came when they almost captured his entire headquarters. The intensity of the air attack drove some retreating British elements into the comparative safety of wooded areas. With near total disruption of organizational alignment, British officers found themselves picking up small groups of retreating men and staging phased withdrawal tactics, defending in place to delay the attackers and then retreating to the next likely spot. By 9:00 A.M. the lead German infantry units were already moving into the town of Gouzeaucourt, an important terrain feature at the base of the British salient. Ludendorff's trap was about to snap shut.

The full impact of the situation dawned on a number of British field officers in midmorning, and frantic cooperative efforts were made to put together a hasty defense line a thousand yards west of Gouzeaucourt. Third Army headquarters finally sensed the danger and ordered cavalry, infantry, and tanks to the town. The first reinforcements to arrive were the Twentieth Hussars, who boldly rode to the rescue, topped a hill that faced the attacking Germans, and promptly dismounted, joining the ad hoc defense. Thirty minutes later the infantry arrived, in the form of two battalions of the Coldstream Guards and one of the Irish Guards. Bayonets were fixed, lines were dressed, and the assault began. An hour later, the Germans had been evicted and the British were establishing a line just east of the town. The tanks did not arrive in time to assist in the successful counterblow.

The German attack on the southern part of the salient had been made with bewildering speed and great effectiveness. Some of the British troops who fought that morning were veterans of the fighting around Passchendaele, and were familiar with German counterattack methods. But this was different. Here the Germans achieved surprise. In Flanders an immediate counterattack could be expected after gaining ground. There the Germans had little time to prepare, because the chosen area of battle had been determined by the location of the British attack. But here in the Cambrai sector, it was the Germans who chose the spot to assault, and they had obviously prepared accordingly. The Germans had the full, traditional advantages of the attacker: surprise, choice of location, preparation time, and, initially, superior numbers at critical points. In short, they had the initiative.

In the eastern part of the salient, in the defense area of the British Fourth Corps and Bourlon Woods, the story was entirely different. Here the attack was not delivered by Group Caudry, but by General Moser's Group Arras. There appeared to be no attempt at surprise; German troops were seen forming for the attack in daylight by British observers. The attackers did not attempt to infiltrate small groups of heavily armed infantrymen into the British rear, but advanced in linear waves. And finally, at Bourlon Woods the Germans relied on sheer manpower. They were destined to fail.

The Germans opened with a distinct artillery preparation at dawn, firing a mixture of high-explosive and gas shells. The bombardment continued until 8:50 A.M. when the firing intensified. The assault was then launched. Raising observation balloons to compensate for the lack of elevation, the Germans adjusted their artillery fire along the high ground with great accuracy, concentrating on British machine-gun and artillery positions. The woods were again witness to a dramatic air battle overhead. Part of the forested area was taken by the attackers, but they were hotly contested. German infantry was exposed for long periods during assaults that went on all day long. Although they did gain some ground, the cost in human life was terribly high. British machine-gunners and artillerymen were quite successful in their grim work.

At noon General Haig reacted with decision. The Twenty-first and Ninth Divisions were stripped from the First Army and dispatched to Byng's support. Their expected arrival date would be on the next day, December 1. The day following, Plumer's Second Army would see to the arrival of the Twenty-fifth Division, plus two artillery brigades. On the third and fourth of December, three additional brigades of artillery and five batteries of heavy artillery could be expected. Haig also called on Pétain for support. The French general sent two divisions and a corps headquarters.

Fighting went on in the reduced salient for a few more days. The British managed to gain a tenuous advantage in the air, but their exposed Bourlon Woods positions were shelled heavily. Nevertheless, this piece of high ground remained in British hands. Examining the ground and the condition of his troops, Haig told General Byng on December 2 to select ground for a winter defense. The decision was made the next day. Bourlon Woods was to be evacuated. The British would withdraw back to Flesquières. They would not attempt to defend poor ground, for they knew the German army on the Western Front would be continually reinforced in the next few months. Haig informed London of his decision, adding that his choice to pull back was based on the lack of available reinforcements. The Battle of Cambrai, a trying two-week ordeal, was over.

On the first day of the German attack, the British had lost much of the ground that they had fought so hard for during the previous ten days. They had also lost 158 artillery pieces, overrun in the swift German attack. Of most importance, 6,000 irreplaceable British officers and men went into captivity. Ludendorff's costs had not been light either. From November 30 through December 6, German losses were estimated at about 14,000 men, a healthy percentage of them incurred in the stand-up fighting at and around Bourlon Woods.

Overall, the campaign that had begun on November 20 had resulted in something of a draw. British losses totaled 44,200, those of the Germans were estimated at 53,000. In terms of ground won or lost, the British could claim that they now held the high ground around Flesquières, an advance of about two miles from their original starting line. But to the south, where Group Caudry had attacked on November 30, the Germans had not only recovered lost ground, but had overrun the original British starting positions for the campaign and were now defending a fresh two-mile advance of their lines. Byng had used fifteen of his nineteen divisions in the offensive and subsequent defense. Ludendorff had apparently used all twenty of the divisions that had been rushed to Cambrai. Considering the relative strengths of German and British divisions at this point in the war, the numbers of men committed to battle by the opposing sides had been roughly even. Thus, overall and viewed from a distance, the campaign could be characterized as an equal contest with equally sanguinary results, one that had effected no change in the stalemate on the Western Front.

Yet on closer examination, there was a difference. A breakthrough of the German defensive system had been achieved at Cambrai. Open ground had been reached on both flanks of the British attack. At Passchendaele during October the German defensive system had been defeated. Plumer's short, jablike attacks had steadily rolled back the German defenders. The German defense system had been designed to recover lost ground through immediate counterattacks. In Flanders that had not worked. The cost had been very high, but in the end the British had defeated Ludendorff's system. The Germans had been placed in the position of continually having to reestablish a new line of defense after the British had overrun most of the old one. The system had failed because a line could not be held, but could only be successively withdrawn. In November the British had not simply pushed the German line back, they had penetrated the defense system by using mechanized attack, a wholly new form of warfare. The problem was that although a penetration had been achieved, the British did not possess the professional skill to enlarge or sustain it.

The British offensive had faltered in the first few hours at Flesquières. Once this obstacle was encountered, the entire offensive began to deteriorate, grinding to an eventual halt. There was no one present with the authority simply to order that Flesquières be bypassed. No attempt was made to shift the main thrust of the attack to either the right or left. In the British military establishment such a decision would have had to be made by the Third Army commander, if not by General Haig himself. The British army was devoted to the set-piece plan in all of its details, and placed little trust or responsibility in the judgment of lower commanders. It was a highly autocratic system and did not possess the professional skill that promoted flexibility. Subordinates were not only told what to do, they were told how to do it.

This characteristic severely limited the British, because there would always be a "Major Krebs," a German officer who would foil at least one of the particulars of any plan. In order to succeed, the British would have to delegate enough authority to amend plans as necessary, or else design their plans broadly enough so that details of execution could be entrusted to the competence of junior commanders. At this stage, the British military system did not allow for that type of operation.

Even if a penetration could be effected and held, the British did not have the means to exploit it. The tool that Haig and Byng had planned to use for exploitation was cavalry, even though time and again cavalry had been shown to be useless in the face of the machine gun. When it was used at all, it was almost always in a dismounted role, essentially as infantry. The logical alternative was the tank. Of the 476 tanks allocated to the Cambrai offensive, less than half, 216, had been used in the initial assault. Overall, 179, or about 37 percent of them, had been lost. The largest cause of loss was mechanical failure; 71 tanks had experienced this problem. Enemy action had accounted for 65 of the losses, and 43 machines had "ditched."

All of this had occurred within an area of about six miles. An exploited breakthrough would probably involve a maneuver of fifty to sixty miles. While losses would decrease in the enemy rear, there was little doubt that a tank formation in 1917 would not be able to sustain a march of ten to twelve miles. That left only infantry to exploit a breakthrough, and there is no indication that the British were prepared to use their foot soldiers in this role. Thus, although the British army had demonstrated that it could achieve a penetration, it was poorly prepared to sustain a breakthrough, and had little hope of taking advantage of it.

The German army exhibited capabilities that were in sharp contrast to its British opponent. Ludendorff had gained almost as much ground on the first day of his attack as the British had in their offensive of November 20, and this despite the fact that the Germans, unlike the British, faced considerable enemy forces in the salient when they launched their assault. Initially Byng had to deal with only two or three divisions in a quiet sector. Ludendorff faced much more. In addition, the Germans had no tanks at Cambrai, and their ability to dominate the skies was marginal. They were also at a distinct disadvantage in artillery, in both guns and ammunition. The German success had been obtained despite a glaring material weakness.

In part, the rapid German advance could be explained by the fact that the British army was quite unaccustomed to a defensive role against the German army. It had been two years since it had to hold against a major German offensive. But by the same token the Germans were equally unaccustomed to attacking the British army on the Western Front. The British had devoted five months of planning for the offensive at Cambrai, while Ludendorff had only a week to piece together an offensive. There had not been adequate time for the Germans to make logistical preparations. Lacking time and material advantages, and facing considerable strength, the German army had done rather well in comparison to the British.

A revealing aspect of the German attack is the vast difference in the degree of success obtained by Group Caudry over that achieved by Group Arras. While the latter attempted to defeat the British on the heights of Bourlon Woods by a linear-wave attack, so typical of previous World War I offensives, the former used infiltration tactics and depended on small groups of infantrymen. For the most part, the German success at Cambrai had been gained by Group Caudry. Many German squads of that organization had advanced two to three miles behind British lines. It was obviously a method of attack that could not be rigidly controlled. Ludendorff and his officers were depending on the leadership, motivation, and initiative of very junior infantry leaders who were alone in enemy territory. In that respect the difference between the British and the Germans was stark. Britain, a democracy, had produced an extremely autocratic army. Germany, an autocracy, appeared to have fielded, at least in part, an army in which individual initiative and lower-level discretion were prized.

The German success, however, was only partial. If Ludendorff's forces were to have any chance of defeating the Allies, they could not afford any more attacks such as the one at Bourlon Woods. The Germans would have to imbue their entire army with the methods of attack that characterized the assault of Group Caudry. Ludendorff would have to revise the methods and tactics of the army in the midst of a war. That work had already begun.

SIX

Maneuver by Skill:
The German Offensive of 1918

IN THE SUMMER OF 1917 GERMAN INDUSTRY launched a major manufacturing effort called "The Amerika Programm." The object was to field a large air force on the Western Front before the expected air armada of the United States could make its weight felt in the war. If the proponents of this program had known the actual American combat aviation capability, they would certainly have renamed their project. The first intimation of the American "air armada" would not come until March of 1918, when two U.S. Army pilots would fly two borrowed French unarmed aircraft over the front. One of the pilots was a race-car driver named Eddie Rickenbacker who had just learned to fly. On landing safely, Rickenbacker was asked by his accompanying instructor if he had seen any enemy aircraft during the flight. Eddie answered no, and was then informed that there had been more than ten German aircraft visible in the sky. The Americans had a lot to learn.

Staying alive in the sky or on the ground required skill. In early 1918 there were two ways to gain skill: by experience or by training. The veterans of the Western Front on both sides preferred to train their new recruits before blooding them in battle, and there were a large number of schools on both sides of the wire.

By far the most effective schooling system was operated by the German army. The "Amerika Programm" was only part of an overall plan that Ludendorff was directing to conclude the war in 1918. The plan included a weapons production program, a manpower utilization scheme, a revision in army doctrine, and a comprehensive training schedule. The effort was keyed to use forces transferred from the Eastern Front early enough in the west to obtain a favorable decision, before America's contribution to the Allies could blunt a German offensive. The training program was being accomplished in an extensive system of schools behind German lines.

The weapons production plan included not only aircraft, but also tanks, transport, munitions, and new weapons. However, German industry was severely crippled. There had been a growing number of strikes by workers, and the blockade imposed by the Royal Navy limited the resources available to manufacturers. Despite these restrictions, large numbers of high-quality aircraft were being produced. The German air arm had a fleet of bombers that was now being used against England. Its fighter aircraft were as good as any in the Allied inventory, and Ludendorff was receiving a substantial number of observation balloons used to direct artillery fire and provide information on Allied movements. Germany was producing tanks too. Their model was vastly inferior to the latest British versions, however, because of the late start in development. Ludendorff also insisted on diverting a substantial number of tracked vehicles into a production line fabricating supply transports that would have off-road mobility on the churned-up soil of the Western Front. The manufacture of antitank rifles was also going at full tilt. The famed Krupp works was producing enormous artillery pieces that could be fired from railroad cars. All told, it was an impressive program, but one that Ludendorff could put little faith in. In almost every category the Allied matching projects were superior in both numbers and quality. Germany could not win through material means.

The German manpower situation was nothing short of desperate. The very young as well as the middle-aged had already been drafted into the army. Some efficiency could be obtained by restructuring the elements that had to be left on the Eastern Front. All soldiers there under the age of thirty-five were transported to the Western Front. If fighting was resumed with the Russians, the Germans would be operating at considerable risk, because their Eastern Front units were composed of the old, the previously wounded, and a growing number of non-German nationals.

Every opportunity was examined to bring in additional manpower. Even the industrial work force was tapped. About 30,000 workers were combed out of that force, with 1 million kept at work so that the munitions program could continue. The young and the fit were assigned to west-bound units, and it was hoped that the war was finally at an end in Russia. Staff calculations pointed to a slight advantage in manpower over the Allies in the west in the early spring. It was expected that by March Ludendorff would be able to employ 136,000 officers and 3.4 million soldiers in France and Belgium. That would give him 194 divisions, with the possibility that 10 more would become available during succeeding months. The increase amounted to a 30 percent growth in German combat forces in the west and provided a 10 percent advantage in combatants over those of the Allies. With the continued arrival of American troops, of course, that edge would disappear. The traditional rule of thumb is that the attacker should have at least a two-to-one advantage over the defender. By that reckoning, the German manpower advantage was so slim as to be inconsequential. Germany could not win by superior manpower.

Without a decided edge in men and machines, the German leaders turned to the intellect. Their only chance to win lay in doctrine, training, and leadership. On January 1, 1918, Ludendorff's headquarters published a pamphlet written by a young captain, Hermann Geyer, entitled *The Attack in Position Warfare*. This description of offensive doctrine was not particularly new since it essentially recapped infantry infiltration tactics, the system of using teams of foot soldiers organized around light machine guns to penetrate behind enemy positions. That system had been in development since 1916 on both the Eastern and Western fronts, but it had never been standardized for the entire German army. Geyer's pamphlet did that and more. His concept detailed the follow-up forces that would support the lead infantry units. They were to be composed of light artillery that could be manhandled through the battlefield, engineers equipped to destroy enemy strongpoints, and heavily equipped infantry to hold the shoulders of a penetration against counterattacks and to reduce bypassed Allied pockets of resistance. Much of Geyer's pamphlet had to do with the role that German aviation was to play in support of the attack. So there was a new and fundamental change in the way that the German army would conduct warfare. The stalemate was to be broken in the west, once and for all.

All during December, January, February, and March, German units were drilled in the new doctrine. Officers were not excused from the training, and had to compose themselves into infantry squads, going through the live-fire courses so that they thoroughly understood what their infantrymen would be doing on the battlefield. The courses were held at several locations behind the lines, and a new system of artillery fire was incorporated into the doctrine. Colonel Georg Bruchmuller, an Eastern Front artillery specialist, taught Western Front artillerymen a technique of fire that involved careful, detailed briefings of the lead infantrymen, and held sessions in which artillery officers were required to answer the questions of private foot soldiers. The result was that artillerymen and infantrymen gained confidence in each other.

The technique also involved the clever use of gas and high-explosive fires designed to neutralize but not destroy an enemy defensive position prior to an attack. Bruchmuller believed in unregistered preparation fire lasting about four to five hours. His system had been proven in the east, and would now be used in France and Belgium. By mid-March of 1918, fifty-six German divisions had been trained in the new doctrine.

Ludendorff knew that doctrine and training would not be enough; the key element that would make the new techniques effective was leadership. Officers long accustomed to using infantry in wave-type attacks must be imbued with a belief in infiltration tactics. Those who had insisted on close adherence to plans had to be transformed into supporters of a new, opportunistic philosophy of determining an enemy's weak point during an attack, so that forces could be shifted into soft corridors. Set-piece plans were out, and infantry, not artillery, would determine the pace and often even the point of attack. Leadership would have to be exercised on the battlefield, not in a rear area headquarters.

Altogether, the new system would be based on professional skill. If Germany was to win the war, it would have to be without any sort of significant advantage in numbers of men or machines. Germany would win with leaders willing to place themselves at risk in enemy territory, leaders who would ignore their flanks and press forward without waiting for artillery support, and leaders who would depend on their wit and ingenuity to outsmart their adversary. Maneuver would return in the west— through skill.

Ludendorff outlined the new system and the forthcoming offensive on November 11, 1917, before the British attack at Cambrai. He knew that conditions in Germany, the failure of the U-boat offensive, and the growing American buildup demanded an all-out German offensive at the earliest possible date in 1918. In the waning weeks of 1917, he pondered several options for securing a quick victory.

One option was to attack the British in Flanders. An attack there offered a short path to a decision, since the coast was relatively close to German lines. A simple move forward would shorten German lines, and even a moderate penetration would seriously threaten Haig's coastal ports, offering a great strategic advantage. A deep penetration could well seize the ports and lead to the possible collapse of the British army. Further, there was some doubt that the French would seriously reinforce

Haig, particularly if some sort of deceptive feint could be aimed at Paris. The negative aspect of an offensive in the lowlands was that normal early spring rains would again turn that well-worn battlefield into a morass, favoring the defense and inhibiting the power of the new offensive methods.

A second option would be to attack between the British and the French, near the Somme battlefield of 1916. This would offer the possibility of physically separating the two allies. Perhaps Haig would curl his lines to the north, falling back on his all-important ports, while the French would be prone to bend back to the south, protecting the approaches to Paris. An attack on the Somme was not likely to have the disadvantage of poor mobility in the early spring. Unlike an offensive in Flanders, one on the Somme could be launched quite early, well before the American commander, Pershing, would be able to field significant strength. The British would likely reinforce their own lines and the French theirs, and a penetration between the two might be relatively easy. On the negative side, there was no doubt that the Allies could and would reinforce swiftly and in sizable numbers.

The third option involved an offensive against the French in the south. The closer to the Swiss border, the rougher the terrain—good defensive territory, a negative factor for the German attack. There was also the fact that they would be taking on the largest of the Allied armies. The southern sector did not have a serious sensitive target, there were no ports, and it would be rather difficult to threaten Paris if the offensive was aimed in that direction. The advantages of a southern attack included some real soft points in the Allied defense, a considerable number of forested areas to hide a buildup of forces, and an offensive against a French army that had shown little disposition for major operations during the past year.

Ludendorff made his decision in late January of 1918. By that time, conditions on the Eastern Front and negotiations with the Russians were at a point that ensured the availability of reinforcements for the west. His choice was for a multiple-phased offensive at several locations. There would not be a single attack or single location. He would not try an all-or-nothing throw of the dice. All of the army group commanders were told to prepare offensive plans. Then, in consultation with them, he decided on the sequence of the multiple attacks. Only one major effort would be made at a time, because Ludendorff's slight numerical advantage would not permit simultaneous offensives. His major objective was to break the British army.

The first attack would be the offensive on the Somme, between the British and French forces. The ground there favored the new tactics in early spring. There should be little mud, and the terrain was relatively flat. Ludendorff calculated that Haig would strip the defenses in Flanders to reinforce the Somme. When that occurred, Ludendorff would then shift his attack forces to Flanders and stage a major drive, if possible, all the way to the coast. By the time of the second attack, the ground in the lowlands would probably support an offensive. The German commander, however, hedged his bet and had the staff plan for an offensive against the French in the Aisne sector, just in case a good opportunity came to hand. In essence, Ludendorff intended to "whipsaw" the British, attacking in the Somme to divert Haig's forces from the prime target: Flanders. Once the British took the bait, the Germans would quickly move north and put on their main drive. The scheme was timed to normal weather patterns and the limited availability of the incoming American forces. The British, licking their wounds from the difficult fighting in 1917, were going to be facing not one but two all-out German attacks in early 1918.

Ludendorff had chosen well. By the first week in January of 1918, Haig had 1,097,906 fighting troops in France and Belgium, about 10 percent less than he had during the first week of 1917. Lloyd George had withheld infantry from his commander, keeping 300,000 men and 600 aircraft in Britain. At the same time, Haig's defensive responsibilities had been increased. Discounting the peripheral and secondary sectors of the Western Front, there were about 275 vital miles of the 440-mile-long front. Haig was now responsible for 125 miles, the French had the other 150. The British commander was holding only eight divisions in reserve. Sensitive to his essential ports, he had overbalanced his defense in the north at the expense of the southern sector where the British and French lines met. In that region, Gough's Fifth Army had only seventeen divisions for 42 miles of front. To Gough's left, toward the north, General Byng's Third Army had seventeen divisions covering 26 miles of front. Thus Ludendorff's plan would strike initially at the thinnest part of the British defense.

Despite extraordinary measures to conceal the buildup of attack forces opposite Gough's British Fifth Army, a few indications of the impending storm began to flow into Haig's headquarters. German officers who were familiar with the plan were required to take a special oath of secrecy, and any officer who visited the planned attack sector had to remove all insignia so that the front-line troops would not be able to identify interest in their area by other elements of the army. However, a gradual concentration of German aircraft in the southern sector was noticed by British aviators. For the first time in the war, they sensed that they were outnumbered. They would have been surprised to learn that the actual figures would come to 730 German aircraft to 579 British machines on the Western Front. Although the German soldiers who manned the trenches across from the Fifth Army knew little, the occasional prisoner or deserter revealed that the German trenches were becoming crowded. By mid-March Gough was anticipating some sort of attack and requested reinforcements.

Haig could not afford to give the Fifth Army commander very much assistance from his own depleted resources, and he appealed to his allies. Pétain promised to position some of his reserves closer to Gough, but would not relieve his British neighbor of any responsibility for defense on the lines. Pershing had only four of his divisions ready for combat, and even those had limitations. The American First, Twenty-sixth, and Forty-second Divisions were outfitted with equipment and were largely trained. The American Second Division was still undergoing the final stages of training, and was widely dispersed. Pershing had one more division, the Thirty-second, arriving in France, but it would have to go through a considerable amount of preparation before being ready for combat. The chief problem with the Americans in mid-March, from the standpoint of their allies, was that the American commander insisted on his own sector and was not amenable to any suggestion that would parcel out U.S. combat units as they were needed.

The United States Army had thirty-five other divisions in various stages of organization within America or in the early phases of deployment to Europe. Not only were these units without equipment, but some of them were experiencing high rates of hospitalization due to a strange malady. Increasing numbers of sick soldiers were experiencing rapid weakness and a growing deterioration, with symptoms of high temperatures and pneumonialike indicators.

It was clear that the British would have to face the German thrust with their own units, and Haig sent three divisions to Gough. Although Ludendorff had scheduled the offensive to begin on March 21, the first action heralding the battle took place three days before the assault. The British had gathered a number of air squadrons in the southern sector to counter the German air concentration and conduct reconnaissance over suspected areas that might be holding Ludendorff's hidden legions. Five British bombers and twenty-four escorting fighters lifted off from Haig's airfields on the morning of March 18. Crossing the lines below, the British suddenly encountered overwhelming opposition. In short order three bombers and seven fighters were transformed into smoldering wreckage. The German fighter squadrons only lost one aircraft. It was apparent to the British airmen that 1918 might well be of a different character than the previous year.

Had the British pilots attained unimpeded access over the German positions, they would have observed one of the greatest concentrations of combat power in the history of warfare. Ludendorff had assembled sixty-seven divisions in the south, each with some role in the forthcoming attack. Not all would be assault units. Some were designated to defend the flanks of the expected penetration into British lines, and others were assigned wholly defensive roles. The most that the British and French could be expected to put into the threatened area in the short term was about thirty-three divisions. By skill, secrecy, and careful planning, the German army had managed to attain the necessary two-to-one advantage at the point of attack.

Starting at the southernmost point of attack, the link-up point between the French and British, General Oskar von Hutier was to drive into the Allied lines and orient his Eighteenth Army to prevent the French from closing the gap. Von Hutier had just come from the Eastern Front and was largely unknown to the Allies. To his north and on his right flank was the German Second Army under General Georg von der Marwitz. Although this unit was largely targeted, along with von Hutier's army, at Gough's Fifth British Army, the extreme right flank of the Second German Army would be attacking into the southern flank of Byng's Third British Army. On von der Marwitz's right flank lay the final German offensive formation, General Otto von Below's Seventeenth Army. His attack would be almost wholly centered on the Third British Army. Ludendorff regarded the planned effort by von Marwitz as the main thrust, but made it clear that the tactical philosophy of reinforcing success would be followed at the operational level. If the Second Army was held up in the assault, either of the other two advancing organizations could receive additional troops to press home the attack.

Shortly before 5:00 A.M. on March 21, 1918, the most concentrated and effective artillery preparation of all time opened up from six thousand German guns along a front of over forty miles. The implementation of Bruchmuller's bombardment plan involved a heavy concentration of trench mortar fire on the forward trenches of the British positions and a simultaneous use of medium artillery firing a mixture of gas and high-explosive shells on Gough's and Byng's "battle zone," the main defensive

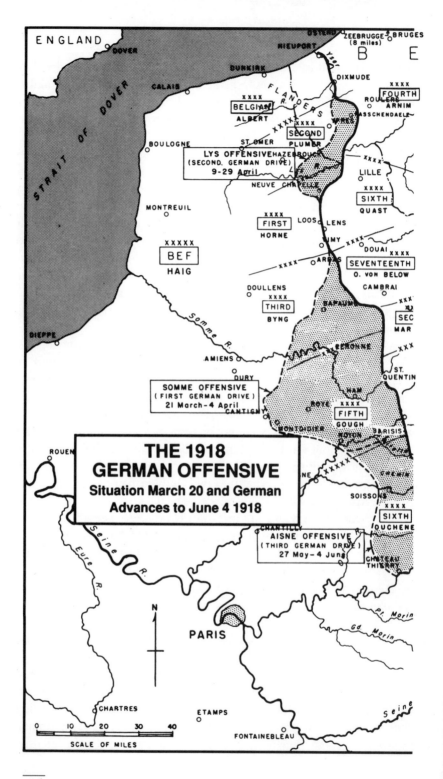

ENGLAND

DOVER

STRAIT OF DOVER

CALAIS

BOULOGNE

MONTREUIL

DIEPPE

ROUEN

OSTEND ZEEBRUGGE BRUGES
(8 miles)
NIEUPORT B E

DIXMUDE

FLANDERS

XXXX
BELGIAN
ALBERT

XXXX
SECOND
PLUMER

LYS OFFENSIVE HAZEBROUCK
(SECOND GERMAN DRIVE)
9-29 April

NEUVE CHAPELLE

XXXX
FIRST
HORNE

XXXXX
BEF
HAIG

DOULLENS

XXXX
THIRD
BYNG

Somme R.

AMIENS

DURY

SOMME OFFENSIVE
(FIRST GERMAN DRIVE)
21 March-4 April

CANTIGNY

**THE 1918
GERMAN OFFENSIVE**
Situation March 20 and German
Advances to June 4 1918

XXXX
FOURTH
ARNIM

ROULERS

PASSCHENDAELE

YPRES

LILLE

XXXX
SIXTH
QUAST

LOOS LENS

VIMY

ARRAS

DOUAI

XXXX
SEVENTEENTH
O. VON BELOW

CAMBRAI

BAPAUME

PÉRONNE

HAM

ROYE

XXXX
FIFTH
GOUGH

MONTDIDIER

NOYON

XXX
XVI
SEC
MAR

ST.
QUENTIN

LA FÈRE

THE

SOISSONS

XXXX
SIXTH
DUCHÊNE

CHANTILLY

AISNE OFFENSIVE
(THIRD GERMAN DRIVE)
27 May-4 June

CHÂTEAU
THIERRY

Seine R.

Eure R.

N

PARIS

Pt. Morin

Gd. Morin

CHARTRES

ÉTAMPS

FONTAINEBLEAU

Seine

0 10 20 30 40
SCALE OF MILES

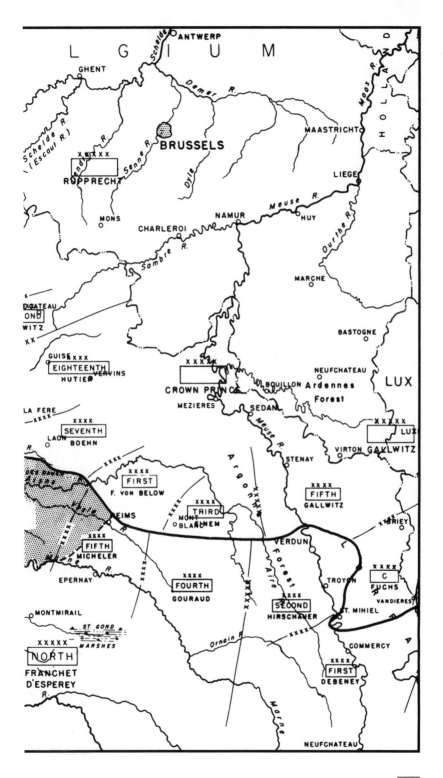

positions one to two miles behind the forwardmost lines. Persistent gas was placed on those areas where German infantry was not expected to attack, with the more temporary gas agents fired into the areas of resistance that the attacking foot soldiers had to breach. Special attention was given by the German gunners to headquarters, artillery positions, and routes of communications within the battle zone. After about fifty minutes the forward lines became the prime targets for the bombardment. There, a withering fire was pounded down on the helpless defenders for over an hour. The next phase involved another sudden shift to the battle zone, hoping to catch exposed movement within the main area of British troop concentration. The succeeding shift was back to what was left of the forward lines. Finally, the familiar rolling barrage and infantry assault commenced.

The bombardment was not meant to destroy the physical barriers of the defenders. That would have taken several weeks of observed and adjusted artillery fire. This attack preparation was designed to neutralize or paralyze the defenders. Enough damage was done that gaps could be found in the British lines, and with the German infiltration tactics that was all that was needed.

At 9:30 A.M. in an eerie fog, the German infantrymen rose to their long-awaited task and began moving forward. Most of them had their rifles slung across their backs. With great courage and daring, they were determined to fight their enemy at close quarters, and they wanted both hands free to use grenades. The small groups of foot soldiers were being entrusted with a considerable degree of faith in their own judgment. The forces that followed these lead elements were depending on them to eliminate what resistance they could, leaving behind only those British elements that the lightly equipped infantrymen could not handle. Additionally, the infantry would pace the attack. As the artillery fire increasingly ranged to the British rear, the German gunners began to stand by for requests for assistance from the front.

Ludendorff's offensive was launched. In many ways, it was now in the hands of his very junior officers, sergeants, and soldiers.

In the southern sector, General von Hutier's advancing infantry achieved amazing results. Throwing themselves forward with little regard for their own lives and no concern about their flanks, the German soldiers managed to completely overwhelm the British defenders responsible for holding the Fifth Army center. In this part of Gough's lines, his Eighteenth Corps had eight battalions in the forward positions. Only about fifty men of these units survived the onslaught. Two of the battalions simply disappeared. The early morning fog had helped. It had been no obstacle to von Hutier's well-briefed and well-rehearsed squads. However, by 11:00 A.M. the sun began to burn off the fog and the exposed German infantry began taking casualties from hastily emplaced British machine-gun crews and some of the pockets of resistance. As the visibility improved, both the attackers and the defenders witnessed a strange phenomenon. In many areas there appeared to be a footrace to the rear, the British outpacing the Germans here and losing the lead there. In short order not only were the forward positions in German hands, but the assault had carried the center of Gough's battle zone as well. Open country had been reached in less than ten hours.

As news of the success filtered back to von Hutier, the German follow-up forces began their move forward. Heavily equipped infantry and engineers began eliminating the remaining positions of British fighters that had been bypassed. In many cases there was little to do but accept a surrender. On the left flank the Germans started their defense preparations against the French forces to the south by digging in along the east-west flowing Oise River and Canal and emplacing heavy machine guns. Light and medium artillery were displaced forward so that the attacking forces could continue to be supported in their rapid advance. The attackers had fabricated wooden treadways to lay over the pockmarked battlefield to help move the artillery, but it was a difficult struggle for the artillerymen, who were reduced to manhandling the heavy pieces in the wake of a fast-paced infantry advance.

The clearing weather allowed the air support element of Ludendorff's offensive to be launched. British airmen responded quickly and fought against the tide. Eight German aircraft were shot out of the sky and seven British planes spun to the ground in flames. Most of the British pilots found that they had to refuel and rearm at different airfields from those they had left in the morning.

So rapid was the German advance that Haig's air arm had ordered withdrawals to fields farther to the rear. Yet the view from the sky revealed a salient fact, one that gave some slight reason for hope among the leaders of the British Western Front command. The German progress, almost unbelievable in the south, was not nearly so advanced against Byng's Third Army toward the north. Byng had failed to comply with Haig's defense instructions. The southern sector of his area—next to Gough's troops—contained the old Cambrai battlefield, and the forwardmost trench lines were loaded with troops, twice as many as in Gough's forward positions. Haig had directed that the front zone be

lightly held and the strength of the defense be centered in the battle zone
to the rear. This explained much of the initial rapid advance in Gough's
Fifth Army area, because the young general had followed instructions.
Byng had not. Von Below's Seventeenth Army assault had a far more
difficult time achieving progress against Byng in the early hours, a fact
noted by the watchful Ludendorff. What Ludendorff did not realize was
that while von Below's progress was slow at the start, he was defeating
most of Byng's troops in the initial part of the offensive. On the other
hand, many of Gough's battle-zone forces to the south had escaped being
killed or captured.

To the north, a large percentage of Byng's army had been exposed
to the devastating artillery preparation and shock attack of German infantry in the extreme forward positions. Byng also had the hard-won
Flesquières position in his defense area. General von der Marwitz determined that this entire position would have to be bypassed, so his
Second German Army situation maps indicated that the high ground
around Flesquières was still in British possession. The main German
effort under von Below and von der Marwitz was not moving with the
speed of the secondary and protective thrust under von Hutier.

As night settled over the battlefield, the sounds of combat quickly
faded. Soon the entire region was cloaked in silence. It was a quiet caused
by sheer fatigue. The young German infantrymen simply slumped over
and fell asleep. Most of the British soldiers did the same. Here and
there British officers led hushed parties forward in hopes of retrieving
abandoned artillery pieces. It was possible to do this because there were
no lines anymore.

While most of the soldiers slept, Haig's and Ludendorff's staffs were
working feverishly to establish accurate situation maps. In the center of
von Hutier's attack sector, the southern part of Gough's defense lines,
the soldiers of the Eighteenth German Army had advanced about eight
miles. On the flanks the advance was not so dramatic; only about three or
four miles had been gained there. In the north von der Marwitz's and von
Below's troops had averaged a one- to two-mile advance against Byng's
Third Army. Altogether, it was unlike anything that the Western Front
had seen. The German offensive was an entirely new form of warfare.
Over much the same ground the British and French had gained 98
square miles in 1916 at a cost of 500,000 casualties. Ludendorff's March
21 attack had taken 140 square miles at a cost of 39,329 casualties. The
Germans had done it in twenty-four hours; by contrast, in 1916 the
Allied Somme offensive had taken 140 days.

British tank going into action.—*National Archives*

American infantry training for combat, somewhere in France.—*U.S. Army Military History Institute*

U.S. Marines ready to march to the front.—*National Archives*

Infantryman of the Thirty-eighth Regiment, U.S. Army, en route to Chateau-Thierry, June 1, 1918.—*National Archives*

Stokes mortars being fired at the enemy at Chaussers, France, by troops of the 165th Infantry Regiment (the "Fighting 69th"), June 1918.—*National Archives*

American troops advance on Cantigny, under protection of French tanks. —*National Archives*

A 155-mm howitzer battery of Fifth Field Artillery, in position near Ploisy, Aisne, France, July 1918.—*National Archives*

A team of reluctant army mules is coaxed forward on the road to the St. Mihiel salient.—*National Archives*

American infantry of the 167th Regiment, dug in at St. Benoit during the St. Mihiel salient operation.—*National Archives*

Captain Eddie Rickenbacker in the cockpit of his S.P.A.D. fighter.—*National Archives*

German prisoners, captured on the first day of the American assault on the St. Mihiel salient, march rearward in the rain.—*National Archives*

Gun crew from Regimental Headquarters Company, Twenty-third Infantry, firing a 37-mm gun on an entrenched German position.—*National Archives*

Major George S. Patton and tank.—*National Archives*

Brigadier General Douglas MacArthur and staff of the Forty-Second Division, awaiting patrol reports, between Bemy and St. Benoit in Woevre, France.—*National Archives*

Sergeant Alvin York.—*National Archives*

Arrival of the Soviet Russian delegation at the Brest-Litovsk Peace Conference, January 1918. The Russian in profile is Leon Trotsky. —*National Archives*

The British were stunned, unable to grasp the magnitude of the loss. A large part of the problem was the lack of reports, in some measure due to the fact that the Germans were herding 21,000 British prisoners to the rear. To the south, Pétain was already making an adjustment despite his inability to get accurate information from his British allies. The French general ordered three divisions to get on the road to the north, with instructions to find Gough's new flank.

The morning of March 22 dawned with fog hugging the ground as in the previous day. Once again the attackers were favored with their infiltration tactics, and the German foot soldiers began fighting their way forward. The fog lifted by 11:00 A.M., and some of the German artillerymen found that they were exposed in the direct sight of British artillery positions. On several parts of the battlefield artillerymen on both sides took aim at each other and fired away in a fashion reminiscent of Napoleonic warfare. With the sun came the battle overhead. On this day the large number of German aircraft made their weight felt. Nineteen British aircraft were gunned out of the sky. The German airmen lost eleven of their planes. As the advance continued, Ludendorff's pilots began to experience difficulty in determining where their lead infantry units were. So too did German artillerymen. The infantry had outpaced their supporting arms. Communications with the front started to deteriorate. However, this lack of contact did not impede progress, because the British army was beginning to lose cohesiveness.

The British had not been trained in techniques of retreat, because it had been decided that such training would be bad for morale. Now Haig's troops were trying to learn the hard way, but so much confusion was being caused by the probing German squads that it was difficult to determine just where the attackers were. It was easy to assume that the enemy was on the flank and that a continued withdrawal was in order. Then, too, many units had lost much of their leadership. Toward the afternoon the retreat became a rout, particularly in the Fifth Army sector. Discipline began to break down, and in some areas officers were gathering groups of fleeing soldiers at pistol point. In the north, the defenses of Flesquières were being pounded with an artillery preparation, and the isolated defenders awaited the inevitable end at the hands of heavily armed German mop-up units. Toward the evening Gough finally received a reinforcement division.

As night fell, von Hutier was able to report that he had completely taken the entire battle zone of the British Fifth Army. The center of his attack had picked up an additional six miles and his flanks advanced another two miles. In the north, von der Marwitz's and von Below's progress was about the same as the day before: one or two miles. However, a gap was just beginning to develop in the center of Byng's position. There von Below's troops had advanced about six miles since the beginning of the offensive. Ludendorff's attention, however, was now clearly focused on the unprecedented advance in the south. Although the overall plan was constructed to strip Haig's defense of Flanders, it was tempting to back von Hutier's play. The Eighteenth Army was not the designated main attack force, but perhaps success deserved reinforcement. The performance of von Hutier's troops caused the German staff to reevaluate the strategy.

On March 23 the dam broke. Up to this time isolated pockets of resistance had given the German attackers some difficulty, particularly in the British Third Army area. Now a decision was made to evacuate Flesquières, and a withdrawal began all along what remained of the British southern front. Haig was moving units to the south, but his prime focus was on Byng and not Gough. The British reinforcements did not counterattack. It was all the fresh units could do to find some semblance of order on which to anchor a defense line. Too often the new units simply joined in the withdrawal. It was a situation of utter chaos.

Strangely, this odd condition presented the attacker, Ludendorff, with a serious problem. He was gaining ground with ease. In some areas his forces were advancing without resistance. But he was not defeating the British army, because the British army was not fighting in place. Simply put, Ludendorff was capturing more French soil than he could defend. He was now creating a giant salient, and he had failed in the attempt to trap Haig's reinforcements south of his planned main penetration site. Instead, the primary penetration had been made next to the French lines, in the south. Thus Haig's forces were increasingly on the extended German right flank. Similarly, Pétain had been rushing units northward, but they too had not attempted either to counterattack or place themselves in front of von Hutier's advancing infantrymen. The French units, now numbering twelve divisions, were gathering on Ludendorff's badly extended left flank. What had been sought by both sides in this war, a battle of maneuver, was now at hand. Ludendorff's decision was whether or not to continue the offensive.

The German general decided to keep on with the attack that was being so successfully prosecuted by his young infantrymen. To stop now would simply mean a resumption of trench warfare once again, a war of attrition —a war that Germany could not win. At some point the British would have to stop and dig in. They would have to defend. And at the present rate of German progress, Haig would not have the time to prepare a stout defense. In open warfare, Ludendorff could place his trust in his soldiers and their officers. Where initiative counted and material superiority was secondary, the German soldier had no equal.

Ludendorff's choice had two prime effects on subsequent German actions. More forces than originally planned were put into the offensive, so that if the second step in his plan for 1918—the attack in Flanders— was to be implemented, it would have to be pushed with fewer troops. And, in the ongoing attack, the relatively slow pace of the northern part of the offensive made it imperative that a shift be made.

General von Hutier's orders were thus changed. The Eighteenth Army was now to press its attack to the west and south. Paris would be threatened. The northern part of the attack was to continue on a west- ward path and proceed farther than originally considered. The overall scheme would resemble a penetration and then a fan, spreading out both north and south in the enemy rear. No longer would it be a penetration followed by a sudden hook to the north.

On March 24 Gough finally received his first reinforcements from Pétain. It was only a rifle regiment, a unit without accompanying artil- lery support. The French soldiers had been hurried to the British with such haste that they only had thirty rounds of ammunition per man. In the face of von Hutier's ever-advancing legions, it was a thin gesture. Gough got more encouragement from his air arm. British pilots were showing courage and aggressiveness. That day a German company com- mander was stopped in his tracks by an intrepid airman who continually harassed the attacking unit. Evidently having run out of ammunition, the British pilot not only knocked down the German officer with his low- flying aircraft, but ran over the humiliated leader with the landing gear. Still Haig's troops continued their move to the rear.

By this time General Pétain was convinced that the British withdrawal was of such magnitude that the entire alliance was in serious jeopardy. His concern centered on the fact that he could not find Gough's con- stantly receding flank. The Allies were becoming separated, and there was little doubt in his mind that the British would swing north to the coast and their ports. He had no choice but to swing south, protecting Paris. So on that Sunday, March 24, Pétain set out to find General Haig.

At 11:00 P.M. the two generals met. Pétain expressed his concern in such grim terms that Haig was left with the notion that he was talking to a defeated man. That was indeed cause for alarm, because the Germans had not yet attacked the French. It was the British army that was in serious trouble. Pétain's statements made it clear that the British could not count on French assistance. Gough's retreat was so disordered, the French general explained, that it was impossible to find a place to make a stand. The result was that the river Somme was established as the new division point between the two allies.

But the real impact of the meeting was that Haig lost faith in Pétain. After the general left, Haig contacted London and requested the immediate intervention of British political authorities.

Haig's alarm over the precarious condition of the British army and Pétain's behavior had already been anticipated by the astute Lloyd George. The British prime minister had dispatched his trusted agent, Lord Milner, and the chief of the imperial general staff, General Wilson, to France. The two emissaries from London had instructions to see Haig immediately, but could not find the general. Then began a bizarre series of missed meetings, separate consultations with the principals, and hurried efforts to get decision-makers in one room. It took forty-eight hours of travel by automobile and train, and incessant use of telephones at various locations.

All the while German infantry moved steadily forward. On the evening of the twenty-fourth, von Hutier's forces were seventeen miles in, while von Below's troops were finally shifting into high gear and had advanced about fifteen miles from their starting point. In the center, von der Marwitz was reporting an overall gain of about twelve miles. On March 25, while British and French politicians and generals were scurrying about in search of each other, von Hutier's Eighteenth Army added another five miles, and von Below's Seventeenth chalked up an additional six. By the time the Allied leaders agreed on a meeting place, there was growing concern that the selected spot, the town of Doullens, might actually be overrun during the projected conference.

With British tanks defending the approaches to the town, the Allied leadership, minus the Americans, assembled for the meeting that would result in a limited form of unified command with a single military leader. Milner, the British war minister, represented Lloyd George. France, at this hour of peril, was represented by both the president, Poincaré, and the premier, Clemenceau. The military figures present included Haig, Pétain, Wilson, and General Ferdinand Foch, who, having returned from the debacle at Caporetto, was by now somewhat accustomed to arriving at scenes of crumbling Allied lines.

As British troops steadily withdrew through the town within earshot of the meeting, the participants quickly reached an agreement. The boundary between the British and the French would be the Somme River, as had been decided earlier. Haig's efforts to reinforce Byng clearly indicated that the British were stretched to the limit and aid would have to come from the relatively quiet French sector. The participants found that Pétain had twenty-four uncommitted divisions that could be used to stem the tide of the German advance. The previous arrangement between Pétain and Haig, cooperation based on mutual agreement, was seen as clearly inadequate. One military authority would have to be appointed to coordinate the Allied defense. All heads turned to Foch.

As the meeting broke up, Clemenceau approached Foch and sarcastically stated, "Well, you got what you wanted." The French general snapped back, "A fine present . . . you give me a lost battle and tell me to win it." The two were not friends. Foch had fallen from grace early in the war for being the advocate of costly, all-out attacks. The French politician had little respect for generals of any stripe. It was not, however, a time for personal preferences, and Foch seemed to have judged the Italian situation correctly a few months before. The grim scene of retreating British troops at the conference no doubt had much to do with the speedy decision and the lack of concern for national prerogatives.

The conferees probably believed that they were turning to the judgment of a prudent general, one who had seriously modified his previous advocacy of bold offensives. If so, they were mistaken. Ferdinand Foch had begun his military career as a private during the Franco-Prussian War. Becoming a student of warfare, Foch rose to be a noted author and lecturer in the pre-1914 French army. At the outset of the war he had distinguished himself as a corps commander and later as an army commander. His reputation was one of a staunch advocate of aggressive, unremitting attack. By the end of 1915 Foch had changed his philosophy. He said that the machine gun, barbed wire, and rapid-firing artillery made defense the king of tactics, and attrition the supreme strategy. Replaced by Nivelle, Foch had gone into eclipse and was only sometimes employed as a consultant. It was therefore reasonable to expect that Foch would shuffle divisions in front of the advancing Germans, establish new trench lines, and resume the grinding, bitter business of war as usual on the Western Front. After all, it was French soil that was steadily being gobbled up by Ludendorff's army. As the conferees returned, they learned that their enemy had gained another three to four miles during the day. Foch had not been given full authority as commander, but his control was destined to grow.

During the next three days Ludendorff's onslaught continued to roll into France. By March 28 the Germans had taken a total of 70,000 prisoners and 1,100 artillery pieces. But now the attackers were reaching serious limits. On that day, a gap in the British lines some nine miles wide was identified. It was a dream come true to any long-frustrated cavalryman of this war, but that branch of the German army had been largely dismounted in order to furnish horses for logistical support of the advancing infantry and artillery. Even so, it had not been enough. Ludendorff's logistical efforts were not keeping up with his advancing forces. And that was not all. German airmen complained of being unable to tell where the front lines were, and of not getting accurate target information from harried staff officers. The artillery was not catching up to the attacking infantry, and ammunition was even slower to arrive where it was needed. Army commanders were also reporting now that the infantrymen were simply exhausted. The German offensive was running out of steam.

Unable to sense the diminishing threat, Haig was still alarmed. By reinforcing his southern sector at various times during late March, he had engaged forty-six of fifty-eight divisions, absorbing serious losses, yet he received little help from Foch. The battle in the Somme sector went on for a few more days, but not at the previous frantic pace, and was judged to be at a lull on the fifth of April. Neither the British nor the French could determine whether the lull was a pause before the offensive was resumed or whether the huge salient, now about twenty-five miles deep, represented the extent of the thrust.

The only glimmer of hope was the Americans. In March 84,889 new troops joined Pershing's command. These numbers did not compensate for Haig's losses, but the British general knew that the Germans had to be absorbing losses as well.

RELUCTANTLY, LUDENDORFF DECIDED TO turn away from the temptation to continue the Somme offensive and return to his original concept for the campaign. Having overcommitted forces to von Hutier, he could not deliver the second blow against the British in the north with the power that had been initially planned. He would be able to concentrate sixty-one divisions there against British, Belgian, and Portuguese forces that totaled thirty-four divisions, but many of the German divisions were not high-quality, well-trained attack units, and even those divisions that had such training were likely to have been badly bloodied in the Somme fighting.

These latter organizations were in the process of being transported northward during the first week in April. To Ludendorff, the saving grace was that Haig was in little better shape. Some of the British troops in the north had seen fighting in the Somme offensive, and if the new offensive were initiated soon enough, he could catch his adversary before recovery and reinforcement.

The goal that Ludendorff set for this second phase of the campaign was to cut off the British Second Army under Plumer, as well as the Belgian army on the coast, from the rest of the Western Front. This could be done, in Ludendorff's estimation, if his forces could seize the town of Hazebrouck, a communications center seventeen and a half miles behind British lines. The town was also an approximate division point between Plumer's Second Army and General Henry Horne's First Army. Horne had sixteen divisions under his command; Plumer had thirteen. Horne would face twenty-eight divisions under General von Quast's German Sixth Army. Plumer would be opposed by the thirty-three divisions of General Sixt von Armin's Fourth Army.

Although the German movement north was well disguised, Haig was concerned enough about his light posture in the north to ask Foch for reinforcements. Foch flatly refused the request and kept seven divisions in the vicinity of Amiens, near the junction of French and British forces to the south. The only interpretation that the frustrated British staff could put on the reaction of Foch was that the new French overlord was focused on Allied offensive plans. He would not look favorably on any deployment of scarce combat power merely to back up a defense. It appeared that Ferdinand Foch was up to his old ways—once again the ultimate advocate of all-out attack. Again, the British would have to take on Ludendorff by themselves.

April 9 was yet another foggy morning, and the violent artillery storm began at 4:15 A.M., shifting to the dreaded rolling barrage four hours later. Close behind the hail of steel came the veteran German infantry. The heart of the attack was directed at two divisions of Horne's First Army, the Portuguese Second Division and the British Fortieth. Within a matter of hours the trenches had been overrun. Progress was particularly rapid in the Portuguese sector, where the first three miles were gained practically without opposition. The German Thirty-fifth and two Bavarian divisions found themselves swamped with 6,000 Portuguese prisoners. British units, rushing into the sector, found 13,000 disordered Portuguese troops in the rear.

Ludendorff had committed 492 aircraft for the offensive. The early morning fog had robbed the attackers of the use of their advantage in the air, but in some measure the infantry made up for it. One British aviation commander, seeing the dissolving front, burned his eighteen aircraft and herded his pilots and mechanics to the rear. Four German aircraft fell during the day. The British launched few of their machines and had far less exposure to ground fire. Only one British plane was shot down. By evening General von Quast's troops were about one-third of the way toward Hazebrouck and Horne's First British Army was in disarray, moving to the rear. To the north Pulmer's Second Army, many of them veterans of Messines and Passchendaele, quietly listened to the ominous rumble of battle on their right flank.

Ludendorff's concept for this offensive was much the same as for the overall campaign plan. Initially, he would hit in the south to draw off the defender's reserves, and then ram home an attack in the north, hoping for a weakened defense. At 2:15 A.M. on the morning of April 10, the northern thrust at Plumer's troops began. At 10:00 A.M. Messines, the scene of Plumer's great success a year earlier, was evacuated by the British. Soon after, Armentières fell. The town had been near the dividing line between Plumer and Horne, and included the river Lys. As the Somme had been the demarcation line between the French and British in the first phase of Ludendorff's campaign, the Lys now played the same approximate role in Horne's and Plumer's withdrawal. The river flowed from the southwest, and the southern thrust of the German forces had already crossed the stream on the first day. Now, on April 10, Ludendorff tipped his hand as his southern arm of the offensive began to head north toward Hazebrouck. However, only a couple of miles were gained.

The next day a rather strident message was delivered to all of the British soldiers. The author was the commander, Haig. It was a dramatic call to arms, and expressed the view that his army was facing the ultimate test of the war. He told his men that their backs were to the wall, that no more ground could be given, and that their enemy would have to be defeated here and now. Haig stated that their cause was just and that a way of life was at stake. It was a short statement, one that British soldiers had not heard before. It was not particularly eloquent, coming as it did from a man often described as inarticulate. It would be scoffed at in later years, when it was fashionable to criticize Haig. But it worked.

At midday a machine-gun battalion of the British Thirty-third Division was marching forward to the front on the main road from Hazebrouck. Its new assignment was to defend the approaches to that important town. Lugging their heavy weapons and ammunition, the soldiers of the fatigued unit had difficulty threading their way through a steady stream of logistical units seeking new positions in the rear. Spotting a convoy of half-empty trucks heading to Hazebrouck, the battalion commander, with Haig's dictum still ringing in his ears, halted the convoy. Using the simple logic that the sooner his men got to the front, the quicker this senseless retreat would stop, the officer demanded the trucks be reversed to transport the battalion to the fighting. The officer in charge of the convoy protested, citing his orders. The battalion commander drew his pistol and renewed the demand. The continued protest of the convoy leader gained him a sharp crack on the skull from the determined battalion commander and the loss of the trucks to the machine-gunners. All along the front, a grim, dogged determination began to grip the British soldiers. Soon, Ludendorff's attack formations were reporting stiff resistance.

Over the next few days, Ludendorff shifted the main thrust of his attack, first to the south, then to the north, always seeking the soft spot. Haig, with no assurance of aid from Foch, threw in division after division to plug the gaps. He ordered his port of Calais to be prepared for destruction, but he had no evacuation plans for his army. Haig's "backs to the wall" message had a meaning that his critics would never really grasp: if necessary the British army would die in place. Outnumbered and absorbing tremendous casualties, the British were fighting on little more than a national characteristic—a well-known streak of stubbornness.

On April 14 Foch loftily declared to a doubting Haig that the German attack was spent. He was right. Some of the same factors that had plagued the Germans during the attack on the Somme were now at work in the Lys offensive. The inability of the artillery and the logistical echelons of Ludendorff's forces to keep up with the superb infantrymen, loss of contact between the air element and the assaulting divisions, and the rapid growth of distance between the foot soldiers and their supporting arms were all much in evidence during this northern attack. For once the ground had been dry in the area, and the initial advance had been speedy. However, there was a factor that had not been present in the initial stages of the Somme attack: fatigue. Many of the attacking formations were still suffering from the losses and effects of protracted, intense combat during March. The weariness was almost wholly centered within the infantry companies and battalions. These foot soldiers had become accustomed to lightninglike attacks that struck deep into the enemy rear and outpaced support. They were now familiar with being grouped in small packets in dangerous territory. Without supplies, they had been forced to live off the land, pillaging the vast supply dumps abandoned by the British. Not only were these soldiers exhibiting an élan and daring rarely seen on the Western Front, they were becoming amazingly self-sufficient. But they were tired.

By April 29 the second phase of Ludendorff's 1918 offensive ground to a halt. Foch had finally released a few units to Haig and the Allies had managed to blunt the drive. Hazebrouck was still firmly in Haig's hands, and his ports were functioning. It had been a bloody month—for both sides. Overall German casualties were estimated at 350,000 since the outset of the campaign in March. The German flying ace Manfred von Richthofen had finally been brought down, evidently by ground fire over the Somme on the twenty-first. Haig had not gotten off lightly; his losses amounted to 305,000 men. But the slight edge that the Germans had enjoyed at the beginning of the campaign was ebbing away. What is more, the Americans had stepped up their deployment of troops. During the month of April, Pershing's ranks grew by 118,642 men. The size of the American army on the Western Front now rivaled that of Haig's.

Ludendorff now had to reassess his strategy. He had been painfully aware that Foch was now, however reluctantly, reinforcing the British. The Allies had not attempted to hold every inch of ground. His attacks had gained territory, but they had not destroyed his enemies. While the French divisions sent to Haig's aid had not immediately been thrown into the lines, they hovered on the flanks of the German thrusts. The deeper the German penetration, the greater the risk that the French and British might attack on each side of his expanding salients. He was also extending the area that he would ultimately have to defend should the offensive be brought to a halt. Then too, the numbers were increasingly important. Although the Americans were not yet ready for major battle, they kept pouring into France. When German casualties and Allied losses were added up, it was clear that Berlin's advantage was slipping. If the Americans continued their increase in combat forces, the Allied advantage would soon be overwhelming. Time was an ally of Paris, London, and Washington. Ludendorff had to win now, or Germany would have to settle into defense.

The German general calculated that his original premise was sound—he must defeat the British army. He could not do that if Foch continued to back Haig with troops. The cure for that was a threat to Paris, an attack in the French sector that was aimed at the French capital. A small, brief thrust would concentrate the French army in the south, laying Haig's battered defenders in Flanders open to a final, all-out drive that could well end with a British surrender on the coast. Ludendorff's decision was to use the new mobility to probe the French quickly, frighten them into a defensive attitude, and end the war in Flanders before the weight of Pershing's army could be brought to bear.

The new operation required transporting a number of attack units one hundred miles to the south and deceiving the Allies as to the exact point of the third penetration. Many of the offensive elements were taken from the Flanders front, with special precautions to mask their withdrawal. Some of the remaining units in the lowlands found themselves marching about in circles, providing British airmen with a scene of activity that belied the actual depletion of the forces facing Haig's sector. The attackers were transported to the south almost wholly at night. As these units off-loaded in the wooded areas opposite the French lines, more precautions were instituted so that even front-line German troops would be deceived. The defenders were told that the newly arrived units had only been sent south to rest. Daily German reconnaissance flights were made over the wooded assembly areas to note any possible troop activity that might be spotted by the British.

Ludendorff chose his attack corridor well. Foch had been gradually building a reserve force by taking units out of quiet sectors and stretching out the defensive responsibilities of those units left on the lines. He had also been adding to the strength of the reserve by refusing to accept recently battered British divisions into it. Instead, those organizations were being given front-line defense roles in the quiet sectors, so that his growing reserve army would be largely composed of fresh French divisions. So it was that a long section of the French front became a weakly held area composed of eleven thinly deployed, understrength, and in some cases recently mauled Allied divisions. It was a defense line that faced north, straddling an approach to Paris. It was known as the Aisne region.

The German forces were not ready to attack until May 27 due to the sheer size of the planned effort. Forty-one divisions were involved in the attack order, only eleven of which were initially located in the vicinity of the target area. The coordination of fire-support planning consumed a tremendous amount of time, since 3,719 guns were scheduled to participate. This aspect—artillery planning—proved to be particularly difficult, for it was critical to the success of the plan that the French not discover the massive movement of German artillery prior to the opening of the attack. Another factor that required careful attention was the need to shift forces rapidly to the north once French reserves had been committed to reinforce the threatened sector. A well-coordinated transportation schedule accommodated the latter concern. Finally, Ludendorff decided to provide his planners with definite limits for the depth of penetration. He established twelve miles as the maximum salient length, so that his subordinates would know when to initiate the switch to Flanders. The German general had calculated that an advance of twelve miles toward Paris would fully alarm the French. Having attained the ability to break through trench lines, the German army was now relearning the art of mobile warfare. The method to break the tactical deadlock had been developed. The problem in May of 1918 was how to exploit the breakthrough to gain a strategic advantage.

Despite the elaborate deception measures, word of the German plans got to the French. It happened in the usual way: prisoners were taken who knew too much. But for the Allies it was too late to do much good. An alert to the defenders forward of the Aisne River went out in the late afternoon of May 26. No units were moved to the threatened sector. An earlier warning issued by the fledgling American intelligence service had been dismissed.

At 1:00 A.M. on the morning of May 27 it all began. For the first ten minutes a cauldron of gas and high-explosive shells was dumped upon the forward trenches of three French and three British divisions. Trench mortars worked over the protective wire. Then came a sudden shift of the light and medium German artillery to the Allied headquarters, artillery positions, and road junctions. This second schedule of targets was blasted for an hour and five minutes. After another brief but tremendous deluge of shells on the front lines, the attack was turned over to the masters of offensive combat: the German infantry. Small groups of foot soldiers rushed forward carrying their light machine guns past the dazed, the dead, and the pathetically weak Allied front trenches. Ludendorff and his young staff officers had masterminded the greatest offensive drive of the war.

On the Allied side there had been gross incompetence. Foch, Pétain, and Haig had all warned their subordinates to man the front trenches lightly, but General Denis Duchene, the French Sixth Army commander, had disregarded his instructions and directed a stout, forward defense. The German artillery preparation had all but destroyed the six Allied divisions, and Duchene had practically no units in the immediate rear to stop the onrushing German infantry. It was a rout.

By midmorning the lead elements of General von Bohn's Seventh

Army had crossed the Aisne River, four to five miles behind the French and British lines. The attack was so swift and so well planned that the Allies had failed to destroy most of the bridges. Refusing to rest, the sergeants and young officers of von Bohn's force pressed on, deeper into the French rear. At 2:00 P.M. General Jean Degoutte's Twenty-First French Corps was hastily shuttled to the battlefield, but at once his troops found themselves outflanked by hundreds of enemy infantry sections. With almost all the French artillery positions overrun, there seemed to be no way to respond to the overwhelming assault. By evening four Allied divisions were reported destroyed and four more were in serious trouble. The breach in the Allied line was now twenty-five miles wide. The depth of the penetration was twelve miles. In less than twenty-four hours, the full objective of the operation had been achieved.

The sudden and brilliant success, far exceeding the achievements of the earlier two offensives, surprised Ludendorff. A prime element in the new tactical doctrine was the dictum that success was to be reinforced. Set-piece plans were to be discarded in favor of seizing the moment; opportunity was not to be lost. Yet the twelve-mile limit, the key to the switch from the southern offensive to the final attack in Flanders, had already been reached. According to the plan, it was now time to begin the movement and assembly of forces against Haig.

Ludendorff reached for his telephone to call his forces in Flanders. Movement would begin. But the movement would be from the north to the south. Units that had been reserved for the lowlands offensive found themselves instead with orders to exploit the breakthrough in front of Paris. The German general had abandoned his strategic goal in favor of exploiting a tactical opportunity.

All during the next day, May 28, the French leaders desperately tried to cobble together some sort of defense that could stem the tide of attacking infantrymen. Degoutte's corps picked up what was left of two shattered French divisions, but the survivors had no machine guns and the artillery could not keep up with the rapidly changing tactical situation. The next reasonable position to make a stand was on the Ourcq River, but by day's end the Germans had punched in another five miles, halfway to that waterway.

Pétain was besieging Foch with pleas for reinforcement. However, Foch treated his countryman in the same fashion that he had handled Haig a month earlier. He would consider the use of the general reserve for offensive operations, but would not hear of committing the Allied trump card for defense. Foch also gave Pétain a dose of the same bitter medicine that Haig had experienced earlier: the supreme Allied leader pronounced the new German drive a mere diversion. Ludendorff was simply throwing in a feint to Paris, Foch claimed; the real German objective was in Flanders. Ferdinand Foch was exhibiting an uncanny talent for intuition. He had divined German plans on two occasions. But this time the plan did not correspond to Ludendorff's actions. Foch had determined what his adversary had planned to do, not what he was actually doing.

Pétain had little choice. Without the forces to plug the ever-widening gap, he proposed placing units of the reserve on the flanks of the penetration, ready for attack. He used his own forces, Degoutte's corps, to delay the spearhead of the German thrust. He also enlisted the aid of Pershing. With the nearby American headquarters preparing to evacuate, the U.S. general put aside his insistence on an American sector under American command and offered up some of his better-trained, readier units to serve temporarily under the French. Pershing agreed that his men could be sent where they were needed, reminding the French only that his forces were still ill-equipped with transportation and would need help getting to the front. The French immediately decided that Degoutte's Twenty-first Corps, the organization facing the almost impossible task of delaying the enemy onslaught, was most in need of reinforcements. An American staff officer was dispatched to find Degoutte to coordinate the U.S. employment, and the French designated one of their colonial truck units to find the American infantry. The U.S. Second Infantry Division was about to get its first real taste of a full-blooded German offensive.

The American staff officer located Degoutte in his hastily assembled headquarters. Showing fatigue and an obvious sense of helplessness, the weary French general tried to define for the American the last reported locations of the speeding German infantry, as well as a rough calculation of his own organization's situation. During the conversation the American noticed that the French officer had difficulty describing what the Germans had actually conquered. Many of the place names, he realized, had an emotional meaning to the general. To the French officer, each of those towns, roads, and streams represented countless thousands of French dead during the hard, grinding fighting of the past three and a half years. Now they were all lost. A decision was made for American employment. As the staff officer departed he looked back to the commander, then quickly hurried out. The French general was crying.

With the exception of the supremely confident Foch, the French leadership appeared to be losing heart. This was in marked contrast to the Americans. The vast majority of Pershing's troops, of course, were well to the rear. But the day before, the U.S. General Headquarters had received good news from the north. A unit of the premier fighting organization of the American army, the First Infantry Division, had distinguished itself in a limited attack just south of the Somme River at Cantigny. Skeptics were quick to point out that the attack had been heavily supported by the French with tanks, flamethrowers, aircraft, and artillery. But in two hours, the Twenty-sixth U.S. Infantry Regiment had gained about 1,600 yards against two understrength German regiments and had thrown off an immediate enemy counterattack. American casualties had not been light. On the other hand, the size of the largely unbloodied American divisions approached the strength levels of German corps-sized organizations, units that were now being diminished through continuous combat. The Americans were optimistic.

To the south the German advance continued as the Americans, under French leadership, received orders for the approach to contact. Racing over the Ourcq River, Ludendorff's lead elements reached the Marne on May 30. Degoutte's corps had not been able to delay them very much prior to the arrival of the Americans. German possession of the Marne valley represented a great threat to the Allies. The river flowed southwest to Paris, and if Ludendorff could achieve firm control of both sides of the river he would have an attack corridor leading straight into the French capital. Bitter memories of the German conquest of Paris and French defeat during the Franco-Prussian War rapidly came to the minds of the Allied leaders.

Pershing committed the U.S. Third Division to the right of the designated American Second Division sector. These two large field units were to blunt the southernmost extension of the German penetration, defend the Marne, and if possible knock back the attackers. The race between the advancing German infantry and the Americans was no longer restricted to the growing deployment of soldiers across the Atlantic; now it also included an oncoming collision across the roads and fields of France.

U.S. Marines of the Second Infantry Division quickly assembled as the French colonial transportation unit arrived, bouncing into the rear-area American camp in mud-splattered, well-worn trucks. Boys from Kansas, California, New York, and Texas tossed their packs into the trucks. Their destination was near a place called Belleau Wood.

As the young Marines climbed into the waiting trucks, they peered into the cabs at the drivers. Orientals. The drivers were from Hue, Danang, Vinh, Hanoi, and Saigon. Little did the Americans know that their grandsons were to meet the grandsons of the drivers—in another war, at another time, and in a distant land. On that now dim and long-ago day, Americans and Vietnamese had a common goal, a common enemy, and a common destination. The convoy pulled out of camp, beginning a bone-jarring journey north.

Reaching the rearward-bound headquarters of Degoutte's Twenty-first Corps, a Marine officer dashed in to effect final coordination. He was shocked by what he was told. It was as if men from separate worlds were meeting for the first time. Dumbfounded and disappointed, the Marine could barely contain himself as he received instructions. The orders outlined a plan for yet another withdrawal. Finally, the American could take no more. He blurted out, "Retreat? . . . Hell! We just got here."

Though it was late afternoon, a new day had dawned on the Western Front.

In the next few days the war hung in the balance. German progress was slowed, due to a lack of ammunition resupply. The Allies took advantage of the brief respite, moving more units into place. Foch began relenting on some of Pétain's requests, in the same way that he had ultimately moved some of his reserves to back up Haig. On the evening of May 31 the Germans had advanced forty miles in all, had taken 50,000 prisoners, and were the new owners of 800 Allied artillery pieces. They were now maintaining a front of over ten miles along the banks of the Marne, and their new long-range artillery was within range of Paris. It was clear, however, that their advance could not continue without resupply, rest, and a movement of more supporting arms to the front. On June 2 the front became relatively quiet, and four days later a formal halt was ordered by the German high command.

On that day the U.S. Marines began a counterattack at Belleau Wood. The Marines were not the only Allied attacking force. Overall, twenty-five French and two U.S. divisions began to hammer at the now-stationary enemy forces. The Marines attacked in waves of four ranks, little different from an American Civil War assault. To the German defenders it was like a flashback to 1916, when they had mowed down British infantry on the Somme. The remainder of the Second U.S. Division exhibited offensive tactics that were little better. In twenty days of slugfest, primitive fighting, the Marines lost half their strength, gaining about one mile for 5,200 casualties. The Third Brigade of the Second Division lost 3,200 men. German officers expressed pity for the young American riflemen, praising their bravery but condemning their careless confidence and the lack of tactical proficiency on the part of their officers.

On June 9 the French Sixth Army commander, Duchene, was relieved of command. He had lost too many men on the opening day of the German attack by loading the forward positions despite orders to the contrary. The Twenty-first Corps commander, Degoutte, took command.

While the battle raged on the Marne, Ludendorff had made a decision to enhance his thrust by gaining ground a few miles to the north. Such an attack would render his only rail supply route into the Marne salient safe from Allied artillery. Besides, a quick shift to the northern part of the sector would have the effect of whipsawing the Allied reserves once more, opening the opportunity for a further expansion of the Marne position. Ludendorff's staff and his well-traveled artillery were unable to keep up, however. The attack was finally launched on June 9, forty-eight hours after the planned jump-off date.

Hastily prepared, Ludendorff's fourth drive allocated fifteen divisions to von Hutier's assault, with an additional seven to be used as follow-up forces. The Allies easily discerned the buildup and Foch moved reserves into the region and further supplemented their strength with tanks and aircraft. Learning the German attack hour, the French lambasted the German assembly areas ten minutes prior to the scheduled preparation bombardment by the attackers. Even so, General von Hutier's attack destroyed three French divisions, gained six miles, and seized 8,000 French prisoners. The attack was continued into the night of June 10, when the Germans discovered that five French divisions and 144 tanks were poised on their flank. Ordering five of his divisions to assault the French, von Hutier soon found himself trying to protect his own forces. The opposing forces slammed into each other in open fields at dawn the next morning. It was a stand-up, toe-to-toe battle, with the Germans finally yielding under heavy French tank and air attack. Under their aggressive commander, General Charles Mangin, the French lost 35,000 men and 70 of their tanks, but they took as much as they had given. Ludendorff had to cancel von Hutier's drive the next day. The massive brawl had been watched by a young American officer, Major George S. Patton.

By the end of June the outcome of the race between the German offensive and the American deployment began to take shape. Through a concerted and almost frantic surge in the rate of embarkation, Pershing's demand for more troops at the earliest possible time had resulted in the dispatch of 246,000 more American soldiers in May. Another 279,000 departed for France in June. Of even more importance, entire American divisions were now coming on line as complete units. By the last day in June, three such organizations were fighting and seven more were entering the trenches.

The German offensive had provoked President Wilson into a decision to create an American army of eighty divisions, a huge fighting force of 3.3 million men. The Americans would soon surpass British numbers on the Western Front, and it was even conceivable that Pershing's army might outnumber the French. This rapid fielding of a combat force had been made possible by an efficient induction and embarkation in the United States, a massive use of British shipping, a machinelike training program in France, and the equipping of the Americans by the enormous capacity of the French armaments industry. It had taken over a year to get the complex system going, and it was not without problems. The biggest holdup now was the marginal French transportation system. Pershing's staff was trading infantry for railway troops in the human pipeline, but obstacles were being overcome each day.

Seeing his thin advantage disappearing, Ludendorff once again pondered his choices. There was little doubt that his third attack had placed Paris in jeopardy. Allied units were still being pulled out of the north. His plan for a final attack in Flanders was behind schedule. But if he switched to the north now, he would leave his new Marne salient without the ability to defend itself, since its forwardmost protrusion was difficult to supply and narrow at the tip, inviting an Allied attack on the flanks. Still, a concerted effort just might break through the Allied defenders on the Marne. Paris might be taken. Yet now that his enemies were gathering on the Marne, what better time to strike at Haig and drive to the coast? If he lost the race with the Americans, trench warfare would be resumed, and the war might head toward a negotiated settlement. In that case, the more French soil Germany occupied, the more favorable terms Berlin was apt to get at the bargaining table.

The choice was complicated by other factors, one of which constituted a new consideration on the Western Front. Many of Ludendorff's soldiers were dying not by the hand of his enemies but by the effects of that same strange malady that had struck American ranks. His only hope was that all of the Allies were suffering as well, and there was an indication that the disease was one of global dimensions. Spain, a neutral nation without wartime censorship, reported that eight million of its citizens were affected. Known as the Spanish Influenza, the epidemic was deadly and was claiming more and more victims on the Western Front. In Britain, the June figures for the military alone amounted to 31,000 cases. The German army had discovered its first cases in April. The Royal Navy had been 10 percent debilitated in May. In that same month, the French Fifth and Sixth armies were evacuating 1,500 to 2,000 cases per day. By June there was no way for military planners to determine which side would be more damaged by the epidemic.

Ludendorff's decision was for a maximum effort on the Marne. If he succeeded, Paris might fall. If that failed, at least the Marne salient might be expanded enough to be held, serving as a prime piece of territory for negotiations. Failure to end the war in the south would not necessarily eliminate the possibility of returning to the original concept and shifting the attack to Flanders. The defeat of Haig's army in the late summer would still remain a possibility. Ludendorff chose the course that kept all options open.

The fifth German drive, essentially a resumption of the third one on the Marne, could not begin until mid-July because of its size and complexity, and the Allies knew it was coming. The German staff made few attempts to conceal their preparations, and perhaps at this stage of Allied alertness, and considering the nature of the terrain, any attempt at deception would have been futile. Prisoners, air reconnaissance, and radio intercepts all told the Allied leadership of the date, location, and size of the forthcoming German attack. Foch knew that one quarter of the German army in the west, or about 50 divisions, would be in some way involved. The attack would be met by about 34 defending Allied divisions, with another 12 or 13 units held out initially for a counterattack as well as even more divisions alerted to reinforce the Allied response. Over 3,000 aircraft would be involved on both sides. There were now 207 German divisions available in the west, but the Allied total had climbed to 203. Not only had Ludendorff's 10 percent advantage dropped to less than 2 percent in terms of divisions, but the real manpower figures would have shown a German inferiority because of the great casualties incurred during the period from March to June. The attacking German infantry would be taking on greater strength, both in manpower and material, and they would have to advance without surprise.

The fifth drive began on July 15, against thoroughly prepared defenders. The attackers often carried portable footbridges to cross the Marne, and in many cases they got across the river. This time, Foch's dictum on lightly manned front trenches was largely observed. The Italians, Americans, and French weathered what was probably the greatest artillery preparation of the war to date fairly well. Allied artillery took a heavy toll even before the Germans started their attack. Despite yielding the forwardmost positions, the right of the Allied defense—General Gouraud's Fourth French Army—held its main defense line throughout the day. On the left, General Degoutte's Sixth Army fought the attackers to a standstill in the morning hours. In the center the easternmost flank of the French Fifth Army held fast, but the left part of its line began to yield early on, putting Degoutte's right flank in jeopardy. In that sector lay the U.S. Third Infantry Division and its Thirty-eighth Infantry Regiment. Even when units on the right of the Thirty-eighth withdrew, the determined American unit held fast for fourteen hours. Captain Jesse Wooldridge's G Company found itself counterattacking throughout the day, led by its courageous commander. When orders were finally received to withdraw, the captain found that he had fourteen bullet holes in his clothing. The Thirty-eighth Infantry had fought off two German divisions, captured prisoners from six different enemy regiments, and demolished the 1,700-man Sixth Grenadiers so badly that the German leadership could only find 150 survivors at day's end.

At tremendous cost, the German attack had gained only about four miles in some sectors, none at all in others. Prisoner interrogations and battle reports clearly indicated the Allied preparation and readiness. Without surprise or any other significant advantage, a continuation of the offensive would be foolish. The next day Ludendorff called the whole scheme off. A few days later, when he was in train for his final blow in Flanders, he had to make the decision to drop that plan as well, for the Allies were now counterattacking in great strength in the Marne region. His staff now resumed the endeavors of a year earlier: defense. The great German offensive of 1918 was over. Foch's insistence upon maintaining a reserve for a future offensive was about to pay dividends.

By professional skill and little else the German army had broken through the trench lines, barriers that had proven to be largely impenetrable for three and a half years. Unlike the one-time British operation at Cambrai, German infantry had demonstrated their new technique time and again. Their skill, daring, and resolute performance had placed their leaders in a position to return warfare to the art of maneuver. In four months Ludendorff's forces had taken ten times the ground that the Allies had gained during all of 1917, a solid year of Allied offensives in the west. Their swift attacks had netted 225,000 Allied prisoners and 2,500 enemy guns. All told, the Germans had inflicted some 447,921 casualties on the British and 490,000 on the French. The late-arriving Americans had sustained only 9,685 dead and wounded during the 120-day period. Tactically, the German army no longer regarded an enemy trench as an impenetrable obstacle. Yet in a larger sense, the newfound German capability was inconsequential. For Germany could no longer attack.

From the end of July 1918 onward, Ludendorff was forced on the defensive because of his losses and the growing Allied strength, and because his breakthrough tactics were not accompanied by an ability to sustain an attack once it reached maneuver ground. His four-month triumph had cost no less than 963,300 casualties. The German army, in particular its cutting edge, the infantry, was badly damaged. Time was needed to rebuild the entire formation, but no time was available. Foch was using his advantage in strength to counterattack.

During the month of July, Pershing's army had grown once again. Some 306,350 American troops had embarked for France that month, and the American headquarters was projecting an ability to employ nineteen of its large divisions in August. The American response to the German offensive had been to deploy over one million soldiers from March to July. The United States had more than replaced the Allied losses. There was no way the Germans could replace theirs. For Berlin to attack now would be to risk the destruction of its exhausted army. Ludendorff had lost the race.

Even if the strength margin had remained in Germany's favor, it is doubtful that a continuation of Ludendorff's offensive campaign would have resulted in any sort of quick victory or the conquest of Paris. The most successful of the drives, the first and third attacks, were characterized by a lack of logistical, engineering, and artillery support for the lead infantry units once they had reached open ground. Additionally, foot-soldier fatigue became a factor at this point, and perhaps the influenza epidemic acted against the fortunes of the attacking Germans more than it did against the more stationary Allied defenders, particularly during the third and fifth drives. The controlling staffs of the attack units lost touch with their spearheads rather quickly and the lifeblood flow of information dried up. Ludendorff's troops clearly demonstrated an ability to break through, but they did not have the material support, the control, or perhaps the physical energy to exploit the breakthrough.

The luxury of hindsight permits one to criticize Ludendorff for continuing the offensive in the Marne sector at the cost of delaying the achievement of his strategic aim to destroy Haig's army with a major attack in Flanders. He appears to have become a slave to tactics, abandoning his overall goal for the sake of pressing a battlefield advantage. Perhaps he knew that his battered but game soldiers were incapable of actually taking Paris or destroying the ever-persistent British army. It is a fact that his prime campaign objectives were aimed at the conquest of territory in front of Paris and the coastal regions opposite the British Isles. In German hands, these two areas would bring a high price at the bargaining table if the war reached a negotiated end. And Ludendorff had already seen the results of a successful negotiation in the east. This German officer may have parroted his predecessors of a hundred years by claiming that the only legitimate goal of war is the destruction of the enemy army, but in his innermost thoughts he might well have harbored a desire for limits.

Whatever his beliefs, Ludendorff now had to hold what he and his men had gained. The German army faced an adversary with growing strength in both men and matériel. Once again, the Germans were to orchestrate the use of trenches, counterattacks, defensive artillery schemes, and the use of reserves to block and parry an attacker. The Allies had demonstrated an ability to defend, but they were now deep in their own territory. The Germans had shown them, no less than five times, a new and successful method of attack. It remained to be seen whether the British, French, and now the Americans could equal or better that example.

SEVEN

Maneuver by Riflemen:
The American Campaign

GERMAN OFFICERS HAD CRITICIZED THE LACK of tactical proficiency among the American Marines' leadership at Belleau Wood, and a similar comment about U.S. Army leadership was made by British soldiers. The observation was made by the officers of the veteran British Fifteenth (Scottish) Division upon relieving the U.S. First Division a little to the north of the American Marines. The First Division had been in the thick of an eighteen-division counterattack that caused Ludendorff to call off his final offensive in Flanders and resulted in a fighting German withdrawal from the Marne salient to a position not far from where their third drive had begun. The British noted the American dead lying in rows on the battlefield, indicating costly human-wave attacks. It appeared to be a terrible waste of good men.

In visiting American units, Haig had privately remarked that, although the young U.S. officers and their soldiers were "active and keen to learn," some of the senior American officers were "ignorant of their duties." The British were particularly astute observers of the U.S. Army. They conversed easily with the American rank and file, and they could reflect back to two years earlier when they had quickly raised their own "New Army." Haig muffled his criticism. More than all the others, he knew the real meaning of fresh Allied units on the Western Front. And despite its shortcomings, the U.S. Army had an unabashed enthusiasm and drive that could be contagious. In the coming months, the Allies would need all the esprit, energy, and élan they could muster.

Now, pushed back deep in their own territory, the Allied leadership began to formulate an overall strategy. For the time being, the effort would clearly be to reduce the threatening salients that had been produced by Ludendorff's spring offensive. The midsummer of 1918 would therefore be spent in counterattacks aimed at regaining lost territory. There was little discussion or controversy about this immediate task. The enemy intrusions were vulnerable, inviting attack. The Germans must not be given the time to construct formidable defenses in their newly won positions. The Allied generals were as alert as ever to the possibilities of a negotiated end to the war. The less French and Belgian soil occupied by the Germans, the more favorable would be the Allied bargaining position. The summer would be devoted to recovering lost ground.

The step beyond that, the Allied strategy for the fall, was now the special province of the senior Allied military authority, Foch. Several factors shaped his thinking. The foremost consideration centered on achieving the best political position for the Allied cause. That led the French general to insist on a continuous military offensive—all summer and through

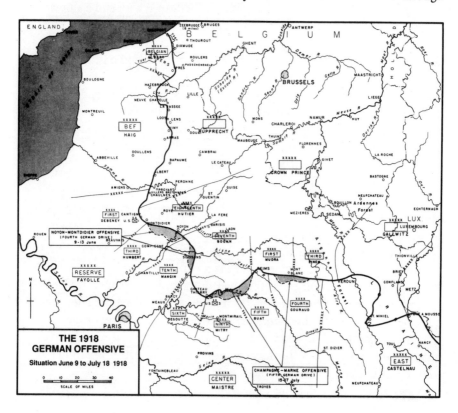

THE 1918
GERMAN OFFENSIVE

Situation June 9 to July 18 1918

the fall. Once the Germans began to give up their gains, Foch believed, they must not be allowed to pause, to reorganize, to reconstitute and strengthen themselves.

The idea of a continuous offensive was, in 1918, somewhat novel. Military thinking was accustomed to planned battles that were limited by time and geography. Foch, however, became so wedded to the idea of a continuous offensive that he began to speculate that the war might be won in 1918. Coming from any other general, such a projection would be put down merely as an understandable but ill-founded encouragement to subordinates. Foch, however, was beginning to acquire a reputation for unfailing intuition.

A more objective analysis could not sustain such optimism. The Allies might have demonstrated an ability to slow and finally stop a German offensive, but there was little evidence to suggest that they could develop and maintain an offensive of their own. Even if the Germans were pushed back, it would be into the awesome defenses of the Hindenburg Line. Breaking that barrier would require the use of vast Allied resources. Then there were intelligence reports indicating that Ludendorff was bringing several more divisions from Russia to the Western Front, as well as all seven German divisions that had been employed heretofore in Italy. There was also a growing Allied industrial problem. Shortages of coal and iron had not only diminished the shipment of U.S. troops, but had placed the production rate of artillery ammunition behind the rate of spring and summer consumption. The Allies were becoming so desperate for iron that Foch had to advise the dismantling of British and American railroads; French industry could no longer supply the new rails needed for increasing lines of communication in France and Belgium. Finally, there was the ominous matter of manpower. The influenza epidemic had begun to wane, but the Allied counterattacks had been costly. American battle casualties per unit had been high in July, but Pershing still had few divisional-sized organizations in the fighting; the prime concern was over British and French casualties. The French were losing men at the rate of 112,000 per month, and the British loss rate was at about 70,000 per month. The British were now drafting men up to fifty years of age. Pessimists within Allied ranks had plenty of fuel for their arguments.

Foch, however, did not depend on mere hope and intuition. He countered the German Western Front reinforcement from Italy with the withdrawal of four of the six French divisions there and two of the five British divisions, adding to his force for the fall campaign. He even persuaded the reluctant Italians to send two of their own divisions. The sum of the Italian front redeployment had Foch one division up on Ludendorff.

He then attempted to check the flow of German troops westward from Russia. To pin down as many of his enemy's troops there as possible, he enthusiastically encouraged a doubting President Wilson to send American forces into the revolution-plagued land. His plea to the U.S. chief of state was wrapped in a piece of logic that he labeled "a decisive military argument." It worked. (The Russian scheme was destined to be of doubtful utility, an action that Americans prefer not to remember but one that Russians seldom forget.)

To cap it all off, Foch persuaded a willing Pershing to request a larger goal for the ultimate size of the American army in France, one hundred divisions in 1919 instead of the existing eighty-division plan. He then gathered the Allied leadership together on July 24 for a general planning session, a meeting that he used to imbue the French, British, and American senior commanders with a vision of final victory.

The enthusiastic French general began the conference with a relatively optimistic assessment. Foch claimed that they were now facing two armies, the well-trained but lightly equipped shock army that Ludendorff had prepared for his recently failed offensive, and another army, designed for defense. The leader of the Allied armies claimed that the shock army was spent, and the other force was being used up in the ongoing Allied counterattacks. Although not quite equal to their enemy in the number of divisions employed, the Allies were actually reaching a superiority in the numbers of combat battalions and reserve forces. The time was at hand, Foch declared, to consider an all-out offensive, one that would position the Allies for ultimate victory in 1919. They should help themselves in the severe iron and coal situation by aiming their offensive at German-occupied French and Belgian industrial districts, adding to Allied might while subtracting from the German industrial capacity. He concluded his appraisal with his firm belief that the reduction of the German salients must be extended to a campaign in which the enemy faced a succession of attacks that would prevent him from withdrawing barrier material, ammunition, and supplies.

The general's performance was wholly dedicated to inspiring a spirit of offense. It was vintage Foch. The supreme commander then asked the Allied leaders for a response. The reply was not encouraging. Haig, whose forces had been battling since late March, said his units were now disorganized. Pétain's appraisal was darker yet. The French leader described his army as "anemic," "worn out," and "bled white." The only glimmer of hope came from Pershing. The American claimed his elements were capable of fighting, although he warned that they were still in the process of being formed.

Despite the general air of caution, however, Haig, Pétain, and Pershing agreed with Foch that the only reasonable course of action was the continuation of the Allied counterattacks at the enemy salients and a transition into a general offensive. To lose the initiative once again to Ludendorff would have too many disadvantages. So, even though still without anything approaching superior numbers, with a critical industrial shortfall, and with no demonstrated ability to sustain an offensive, the Allied leaders set about mounting an attack.

Foch established the overall parameters for the offensive. The immediate actions were to be aimed at reducing the salients. Planning would be directed at final victory in 1919, when Allied numbers might weigh heavily. The fall 1918 offensive would feature a general advance in the center by Pétain's French forces, along with two aggressive and powerful thrusts, one in the north under Haig and another in the south by the Americans. A single bold thrust was never seriously considered, since that would be met by a similar concentration of Ludendorff's defense forces. The northern and southern arms of the offensive were to be aimed at securing industrial and transportation advantages. The British and American drives were therefore targeted on rail centers, coalfields, and iron deposits deep in the German rear. Although the outcome of the July 24 conference was perhaps predictable, there was at least one novel feature: there would be an American campaign.

Up to now, American troops had been fighting under British or French command, executing plans and using tactics that were compatible with those of the European units on the flanks. Pershing was in the process of creating the First Army headquarters, an organization designed to formulate and supervise American plans—plans intended to facilitate American doctrine, use American organizations, and take advantage of American training. Submitting to the coaching of French and British officers, Pershing's officers had patiently waited their turn. In private they had often criticized their European tutors, declaring that their allies were obsessed with the safety of trenches and cowed by enemy machine guns, and that they had become fatigued by Western Front conditions that produced an inordinate degree of reliance on artillery. The American style of fighting would break the tactical deadlock and force the enemy out of the trenches and into open warfare; it would be a brand of combat that would see maneuver, rifle marksmanship, and rapid advance. To the Americans, it was going to be a different kind of war.

Some observers believed it already *was* a different war. Shortly after General Foch held his conference, a young British staff officer, Cyril Falls, a man destined to become one of the historians of the conflict, noted in his diary that if the Allies' forthcoming offensive failed after Ludendorff and his German infantrymen had shown how an attack was to be mounted, the British, French, and Americans might as well give up. For this young captain, the German spring offensive had clearly demonstrated a new and proven offensive method. Never before in this dreary, entrenched conflict had so much ground been covered so rapidly. In the end Ludendorff had been unable to sustain his drives, but the new German doctrine had pointed to methods that were worthy of emulation.

The Americans thought otherwise. American doctrine was based on the 1917 Field Service Regulations, which were hardly revised from the prewar 1911 version. The manual specified that the attack should be conducted under the conditions of fire superiority, with advance achieved by infantry rushes. Fire superiority was to be gained by accurate rifle fire. For the Americans, the bane of Western Front attackers—the machine gun—was viewed as a "weapon of emergency." Although the light machine gun had become the heart of German offensive doctrine, the American system gave it little notice. Machine guns were to be treated as obstacles, weapons to be destroyed by concentrated rifle fire. To be sure, artillery would assist the infantry, but the soul of an American assault was the rifleman.

The major readjustment that the U.S. Army had made in order to deal with the conditions of the Great War was in its huge divisional structure. Pershing had observed that European forces had often been forced to relieve their smaller divisions in the midst of an attack, thereby losing momentum and allowing the enemy to reinforce the threatened area. He insisted on a much bigger American organization, one that could sustain losses and press home an attack to reach open ground. Once there, Pershing believed the "independent character" of the American soldier would prevail over any adversary. To express the special American way of war, Pershing and his officers constantly used the catchphrase "open warfare." In sum, U.S. theory had three components: American independent character, superior riflemen, and a divisional organization especially created to absorb punishment in overcoming trench defense systems.

Not surprisingly, the American theory dominated the leadership of the newly created First American Army, despite an occasional flicker of doubt. One consistently raised concern was Pershing's dissatisfaction with the actual quality of the rifle marksmanship he found among his troops. This produced a flurry of messages back to the United States demanding better training. Unfortunately such messages were usually accompanied by others demanding accelerated troop deployment. Then, too, there was the matter of American performance in raids and patrols. General Robert Lee Bullard, commander of the most experienced U.S. unit, the First Division, had noted in the early spring of 1918 that although the U.S. "tradition of Indian and partisan warfare" should have made raiding and patrolling an "American speciality," actual practice indicated otherwise. Patrol and raid leaders had to be selected carefully, and their troops had to be rehearsed and practiced prior to engaging in these kinds of operations.

These two cautionary indicators—poor marksmanship and the need for careful selection and training of patrol and raiding parties—should have rung some alarm bells in an army that was basing its tactics on superior riflemen and "independence of character," but there was no indication of serious doubt at the higher levels of the U.S. command.

There was also the U.S. notion of "open warfare." One of the American combat leaders, General Hunter Liggett, observed in April 1918 that he could find no definitive U.S. instructions on open warfare. There was little doubt that all the U.S. officers talked about it, but when one attempted to find precise doctrine for its execution, the existing literature was a bit thin. Liggett made his concern known to Pershing's headquarters, and action was eventually taken. New doctrine was published—after the war was over.

In August the staff of the American First Army had little time to revise doctrine. Formally activated on the thirteenth of that month, the new headquarters supervised a massive consolidation of U.S. divisions on the right flank of the active portion of the Western Front, 120 miles east of Paris. The movement of the Americans was a complex matter. During the German spring offensive, U.S. divisions had been plugged in where they were momentarily needed. As a result, fourteen of twenty-nine American divisions were in the French zone, five were in the British sector, and the remainder were in various stages of preparation. Nine of these American units had been involved in the fighting to reduce enemy penetrations, and had already sustained 50,000 casualties. Although Pershing would have preferred to consolidate all of his forces within the newly designated American sector, he yielded to Haig's argument that two U.S. divisions should stay in the north for the biggest of the planned Allied offensives. Two more joined the general reserve. The critical American shortage of transport greatly inhibited Pershing's planners.

The initial American-directed offensive was aimed at the surprise reduction of the St. Mihiel salient, a German-held protrusion that had existed since the early days of the war, and that interrupted direct French rail traffic from eastern industrial areas into Paris. It was in a quiet sector, usually defended by seven German divisions on line, with two additional divisions in reserve. The American staff calculated that the Germans could reinforce the salient with two more divisions in forty-eight hours and another two in seventy-two hours. Since the enemy held high ground overlooking the Meuse River valley on the northwestern face of the salient, the southern face became the selected area for the main American attack. The target date for the assault was September 10.

Pershing's First Army took over the St. Mihiel sector from the French on August 28, but the American commander still needed help from his allies. In addition to his own units, Pershing commanded four French divisions, a welcome role reversal for the Americans, many of whom had long been under French command. General Pétain also assisted Pershing by providing about half the tank crews for the 267 French light tanks, and 900 aircraft and pilots for the armada of approximately 1,500 airplanes scheduled to support the attack. The French also supplied a healthy percentage of the 3,000-piece artillery force that was being quietly assembled in the sector. All told, Pershing would have about 550,000 Americans and 110,000 Frenchmen involved in the operation. The great majority of the manpower was going to be American, but the material of war was almost wholly the product of the prodigious French armaments industry. There would be no U.S.-made aircraft, artillery pieces, or tanks on the battlefield.

The American design for the operation was simple and straightforward. While the French staged a holding action at the nose, the Americans would attack the two flanks of the salient. The assault on the northwestern shoulder of the enemy position would avoid the German-held high ground at the nose of the salient. This attack was the secondary effort under the American Fifth Corps, commanded by General George Cameron, who would have the U.S. Twenty-sixth and Fourth divisions as well as one French division. The main effort was to be on the southern flank of the salient, and would be conducted by two U.S. corps. The First Corps, under the command of General Liggett, had four U.S. divisions: the Eighty-second, Ninetieth, Fifth, and Second. On Liggett's left stood the U.S. Fourth Corps under General Joseph Dickman. This element had the First, Forty-second, and Eighty-ninth U.S. divisions. Additionally, there were six divisions in reserve.

Pershing's First Army staff, a large one of about 500 officers, had learned the vital nature of logistical preparation for a major offensive, and they planned well for the St. Mihiel operation. The attacking forces not only required support in their assembly and initial assault, but would need prepositioned resources to be used during the conduct of the offensive. This entailed 100,000 tons of crushed rock to lay or repair roadbeds, 295 miles of railroad line stock, the designation (and in some cases the construction) of facilities for 21,000 possible hospital patients, 40,000 tons of ammunition, and myriad other important considerations. Despite a host of complications, preparations appeared to be falling into place—until two major and disappointing events occurred.

The first setback had to do with resources; the second involved the entire strategic concept. Colonel George C. Marshall, an operations staff officer on whom Pershing increasingly relied, learned on August 24 that the British would not provide heavy tanks for the American assault. Only French light tanks would be available. The heavy tank was not only a powerful antidote for the machine gun, but a recognized device for coping with barbed-wire obstacles. The Americans would have to improvise.

The second blow came six days later and was directed at General Pershing himself. Arriving on August 30, Foch closeted himself with the American commander and began a carefully reasoned argument for a complete change in the American offensive. The concept involved a shift in the offensive from St. Mihiel to an area sixty road miles north and west, between the Meuse River and the Argonne Forest. The idea would require division of the American forces that were just now being brought together, and a diminished role for the new American command.

"Black Jack" Pershing listened as long as he could, then angrily replied to Foch. There would be no further division of U.S. forces. The United States recognized Foch as the senior Allied military authority, and would go to any area so ordered—but as a complete American force, commanded by an American officer, and to a U.S.-controlled sector. Foch pressed his case, saying, "I must insist." Pershing stood his ground, barking back, "You may insist all you please," but not yielding. Foch departed in a huff, leaving behind an unresolved, contentious issue and a steaming American general.

The essence of Foch's reasoning was that the American drive should start much farther to the north, closer to the vital parts of the German rear. Why not, for instance, let the Germans continue the defense of the St. Mihiel salient? It absorbed enemy troops, troops that could not be used to defend a more important sector. Besides, if the Americans started their drive well to the south, as presently contemplated, it would be some time before they could fight their way north. To the French general, all of this seemed reason enough to revise the plan.

Command and control issues aside, Pershing's reasoning conflicted sharply with that of Foch. It would take a considerable amount of time to pull units out of the gathering concentration at St. Mihiel. If Foch was concerned about continuous pressure on the Germans, he should consider lost time to be an intolerable enemy. However, that was not all. There was a sound operational factor to consider. The St. Mihiel salient lay on the right flank and rear of the proposed offensive in the Meuse-Argonne sector. What if the Germans allowed the new scheme to begin, and then used the St. Mihiel sector as a base to cut in behind the American offensive to the north? To the American commander, elimination of the St. Mihiel salient was an essential preliminary to the Meuse-Argonne operation.

The two generals did not allow the impasse to last. Both men gave ground. Although Pershing's plan for St. Mihiel was not allowed to stand unchanged, he did retain the authority for a consolidated U.S. command operating in a U.S. sector. But he would also have to conduct the Meuse-Argonne operation. The compromise involved limiting the time and depth of the St. Mihiel operation. The Americans were only to pinch off the salient, not continue the drive beyond it. After the reduction they would rapidly shift forces to the Meuse-Argonne and begin an attack there. All of this was to be done in the same month, September.

The immediate result was that Pershing's headquarters, still absorbed in the details of its first major operation, would have to begin concurrent planning for another large task. Because they used many of the same resources, the two undertakings had to be carefully coordinated. For any of the Allied armies the compromise solution would have involved a considerable military feat. For the Americans, with an inexperienced staff, it would be a tall order indeed.

Soon a third problem arose. An element of the planned French support, heavy artillery, could not be moved into place on schedule. For those American staff sections dealing with the new Meuse-Argonne plan, the delay seemed a disaster—there would be two days less to transfer units and supplies from St. Mihiel to the Meuse-Argonne. For those sections dealing only with St. Mihiel, however, it was a blessing, providing forty-eight more hours of planning time, much of which was devoted to the vexing problem of breaching enemy wire obstacles. Operating without the support of British heavy tanks, the Americans did not want to turn to the favored Allied alternative, a week-long "wire-cutting" artillery preparation. American tactical philosophy inclined to the sudden and violent surprise attack. George Marshall and his crew of young operations officers worked eighteen hours a day to find solutions.

Days before the massive September 12 American infantry assault, the scheme for the St. Mihiel operation began unfolding in accordance with a planned sequence of events. The first actions were centered on the French town of Belfort, one hundred miles to the southeast of the German-held salient, a city not far from the German border and the Black Forest. There an American officer took a hotel room in the town and set up a typewriter. Typing out two copies of a piece of correspondence suggesting a forthcoming American troop concentration near Belfort, the officer tucked away the completed letter in his tunic, deposited the carbon paper in the wastepaper basket, and went downstairs for a leisurely stroll. On his return to the room, he noted with satisfaction that the carbon paper had been removed from the basket.

Simultaneously, several U.S. radio detachments arrived near Belfort and began a series of coded messages back to the American headquarters. At the same time, a small element of American tank crews unloaded their light French tanks at a rail siding near the town and began driving the machines along the open edges of wooded areas, ensuring that the tracks would be clearly visible from the air. The bait was taken. Three German divisions began entraining for Mulhouse, twenty-five miles east of Belfort.

At 1:00 A.M. on September 12, 1918, the relative tranquility of the St. Mihiel salient, which had lasted for three years, was shattered by an enormous eruption of flames and shells. Three thousand artillery pieces began a four-hour pounding of German positions. At 5:00 A.M. thousands of American riflemen surged forward. Seventeen months after declaring war, the United States was at last launching its own offensive.

The enemy wire obstacles were overcome with bewildering speed. Each attacking unit seemed to have its own particular method to effect

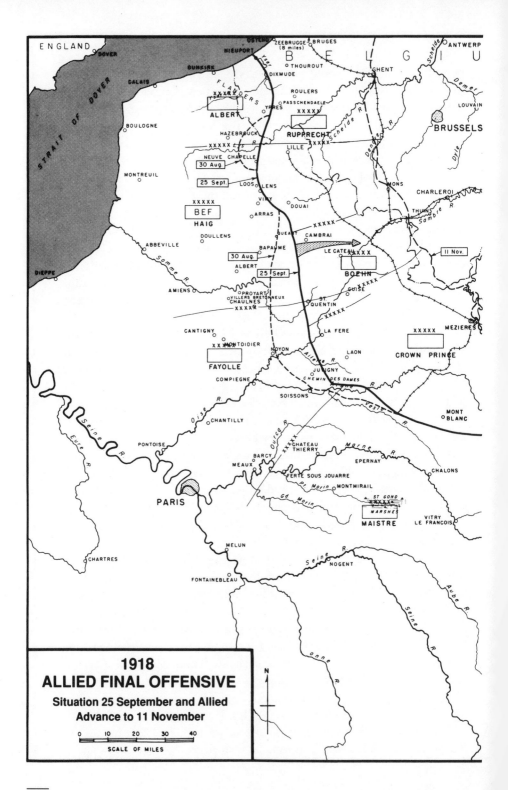

ENGLAND

STRAIT OF DOVER

DOVER

CALAIS

BOULOGNE

MONTREUIL

ABBEVILLE

DIEPPE

AMIENS

DOULLENS

CANTIGNY

COMPIEGNE

CHANTILLY

PONTOISE

MEAUX

PARIS

MELUN

CHARTRES

FONTAINEBLEAU

ZEEBRUGGE (8 miles)

BRUGES

ANTWERP

OSTEND

NIEUPORT

THOUROUT

GHENT

BELGIUM

ROULERS

PASSCHENDAELE

LOUVAIN

BRUSSELS

DIXMUDE

YPRES

XXXXX

RUPPRECHT

FLANDERS

ALBERT

XXXXX

HAZEBROUCK

XXXXXX

LILLE

MONS

CHARLEROI

NEUVE CHAPELLE

30 Aug.

LOOS

25 Sept.

LENS

THUIN

Sambre R.

VIMY

DOUAI

XXXXX

BEF

HAIG

ARRAS

QUEANT

CAMBRAI

XXXXX

11 Nov.

30 Aug.

BAPAUME

LE CATEAU

XXX

25 Sept.

ALBERT

BOEHN

PROYART

VILLERS BRETONNEUX

CHAULNES

XXXXX

GUISE

XXXXX

ST. QUENTIN

LA FERE

MEZIERES

XXXXX

MONTDIDIER

NOYON

LAON

CROWN PRINCE

FAYOLLE

JUVIGNY

CHEMIN DES DAMES

SOISSONS

MONT BLANC

Oise R.

Aisne R.

Vesle R.

Ourcq R.

CHATEAU THIERRY

BARCY

Marne R.

EPERNAY

CHALONS

FERTE SOUS JOUARRE

MONTMIRAIL

Pt. Morin

Gd. Morin

ST GOND MARSHES

MAISTRE

VITRY LE FRANCOIS

Seine R.

NOGENT

Aube R.

Seine R.

Eure R.

Somme R.

Scheldt R.

Dender R.

Dyle R.

Demer R.

Onne R.

**1918
ALLIED FINAL OFFENSIVE**

Situation 25 September and Allied
Advance to 11 November

N

| 0 | 10 | 20 | 30 | 40 |

SCALE OF MILES

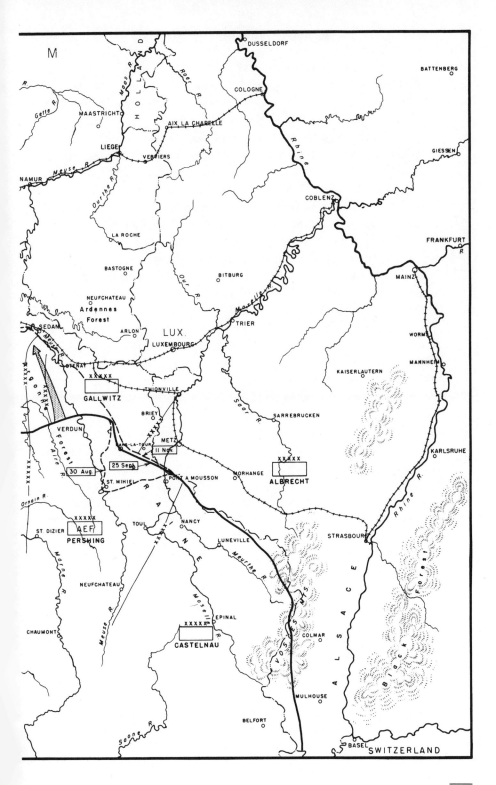

M

DUSSELDORF

BATTENBERG

COLOGNE

MAASTRICHT

AIX LA CHAPELLE

GIESSEN

LIEGE

VERVIERS

Rhine

NAMUR

Meuse R.

Ourthe R.

COBLENZ

LA ROCHE

FRANKFURT
R.

BASTOGNE

BITBURG

MAINZ

NEUFCHATEAU

Ardennes
Forest

Our R.

Moselle R.

WORMS

ARLON

TRIER

LUX.

MANNHEIM

SEDAN

LUXEMBOURG

Saar R.

KAISERLAUTERN

Meuse R.

ETENAY

XXXXX

GALLWITZ

THIONVILLE

BRIEY

SARREBRUCKEN

KARLSRUHE

VERDUN

Aire R.

MARS-LA-TOUR

METZ
11 Nov.

XXXXX

ALBRECHT

Argonne Forest

XXXXX

30 Aug

25 Sept

Rhine R.

Ornain R.

ST. MIHIEL

POINT A MOUSSON

MORHANGE

XXXXX

AEF

ST. DIZIER

PERSHING

TOUL

NANCY

STRASBOURG

Moselle R.

NEUFCHATEAU

LUNEVILLE

Meurthe R.

ALSACE

Black Forest

CHAUMONT

Marne R.

Moselle R.

EPINAL

XXXXX

COLMAR

CASTELNAU

VOSGES MTS.

MULHOUSE

Saone R.

BELFORT

BASEL

SWITZERLAND

175

a breach, and every conceivable way was used to go through or over the wire. The novel techniques seemed to work—one and all. One method was not used: prolonged wire-cutting artillery fire. In some spots the bangalore torpedo, a long pipe filled with explosives, was rammed under a mass of wire, with the following explosion clearing a path. In other areas the American infantrymen carried folded mats of chicken wire to the obstacle, threw the mats on top of the German barbed wire, and simply walked across. There were even instances where the Americans physically tromped down the wire and passed beyond. Some units paused to use vintage wire cutters from the Spanish-American War. In other areas the attackers threaded their way through occasional gaps in the barriers. The lack of heavy tanks was soon forgotten.

Once past the wire, the U.S. infantrymen in the main (or southern) attack found the forward German positions lightly manned, or else discovered that the devastating artillery storm had done its grisly work. When the main defense works were reached, American casualties began to mount—but not for long. It was now daylight, and one amazed German soldier watching the U.S. attack described it as being conducted with "praiseworthy indifference" to danger. The Americans kept coming —and coming in astounding numbers.

In some areas of the main attack, the Americans had pounced on the defenders with such speed that they found their enemy still in bunkers, awaiting the final shells of the American and French artillery. That was the case with Sergeant Harry Adams of the Eighty-ninth Division. Spotting a German soldier darting into a bunker, the game Adams followed him, but the door slammed in his face. The eager American had almost exhausted all of his ammunition in the attack. He was down to his pistol —and had only two bullets left at that. Without hesitation (or perhaps forethought), Adams fired both rounds into the door. Essentially unarmed at this point, the determined sergeant shouted out an authoritative demand for surrender to his prey. The door cracked open. A timid German soldier appeared, hands held high. Adams waved his captive out of the doorway, the empty pistol thrust menacingly forward. Another German followed the first out of the bunker—then another, and yet still more. After Sergeant Adams had gathered his three hundred prisoners together under the rather impotent threat of his useless pistol, he became somewhat apprehensive about his own security. Nevertheless, without losing his stern and soldierly bearing, he herded his charges to the rear. At one point the horde of Germans with their obscure captor was mistaken for a massed German counterattack, but Adams and his small percentage of the kaiser's legions finally reached safety.

The main attack had gone well. The second day's objectives were almost all taken on the afternoon of the first day. To the north, however, the secondary attack had not matched the success of the main attack. The Germans fought harder there, since the attack was aimed nearer to the base of the salient and close to a vital supply corridor for the defenders. Only one unit of the U.S. Twenty-sixth Division gained its first day's objective by afternoon, and that only after the division's reserve was thrown into the fighting. The other elements of the secondary attack had ground to a halt far short of the planned advance. When Pershing learned that enemy troops were beginning to evacuate the salient, he quickly realized that a nighttime pause in the offensive might result in his enemy's escape. Grabbing the telephone, he ordered a night attack, with the goal of effecting a linkup with the main attack forces by dawn. The American commander was now demanding that the entire salient be pinched off in twenty-four hours.

The veteran Twenty-sixth Division sent its weary 102nd Infantry Regiment into the gathering darkness, on toward a front that had thus far successfully resisted the Allied assault. The hastily arranged plan was the soul of simplicity: an attack up a road in a narrow column. To the surprise of defender and attacker alike, the roadway was not blocked. The flanks of the road were defended but not the road itself. The American infantrymen marched forward, reaching the designated linkup point at a little past 2:00 A.M. on the morning of September 13. Along the way they captured an entire German ammunition train. A little before dawn, elements of the First Division arrived, closing off the route of escape for any enemy unit south of the juncture. Pershing's decisive intervention had paid off.

The American air arm had to contend with bad weather during the ground offensive, but its work was not wholly contingent on events below. The American race-car driver Eddie Rickenbacker had by now improved his ability to spot enemy aircraft. Flying a single-seater French fighter, the young captain was on patrol over the northeast part of the salient when he saw four German fighters closing in on a flight of American-piloted bombers returning from a raid over Metz. Climbing into the sun, Rickenbacker turned and dove his craft to the rear of the pursuing enemy, noting the well-known markings of Richtofen's old organization on the German planes. Catching the trailing fighter unaware, the American brought down the plane in a hail of machine-gun fire. Rickenbacker managed to elude the German pilot's three revenge-seeking comrades and save the bombers from probable destruction at the same time. It was his sixth "kill." There would be twenty others before the captain returned to the United States.

German observation balloons were a constant concern of the American attackers. The U.S. air service was hard pressed to destroy the balloons, since they were invariably well protected by antiaircraft defenses. If the balloons were allowed to float uncontested, enemy observers would have been amply warned about the forthcoming American attack. Moreover, elimination of the balloons was just as important after the attack, when the American and French troops established a defense. The better the German observation reports, the more casualties via German artillery. Fortunately, American, French, Italian, and Portuguese pilots in Colonel Billy Mitchell's air element for the St. Mihiel operation were becoming skilled in making rapid and deadly passes at the balloons. One of the best pilots at this dangerous game was Lieutenant Frank Luke. Luke got one balloon on the first day of the assault, two more on September 14, and another pair on the sixteenth. The lieutenant's big day was on September 18: two more balloons and three German fighters to boot. Luke would not return home.

On the ground the American offensive had ended less than forty hours after it had begun. The base of the salient had been reached, and that was the agreed-upon point at which the switch to the Meuse-Argonne deployment would begin. Some of the American officers believed the overall plan was flawed and that the original American concept should have been followed. With the Germans on the run, why not keep the momentum and continue the attack? One such officer, Douglas MacArthur, a brigade commander in the Forty-second Division, had slipped forward on the night of September 13 to a position well within what the Germans should have been defending. Seeing the fortress of Metz, MacArthur claimed his brigade could have pressed on for many miles.

On the surface, a continuation of the St. Mihiel operation appeared to be a sound idea, following the military dictum of reinforcing success. And there seemed to be a wealth of success to reinforce. The bag of prisoners was large. The short American attack had netted over 16,000 German and Austro-Hungarian captives. The haul of enemy weapons was also impressive: 443 artillery pieces and 752 machine guns. Two hundred square miles of French territory were liberated, and the rail line from Paris to northeastern France was no longer imperiled. The Ameri-

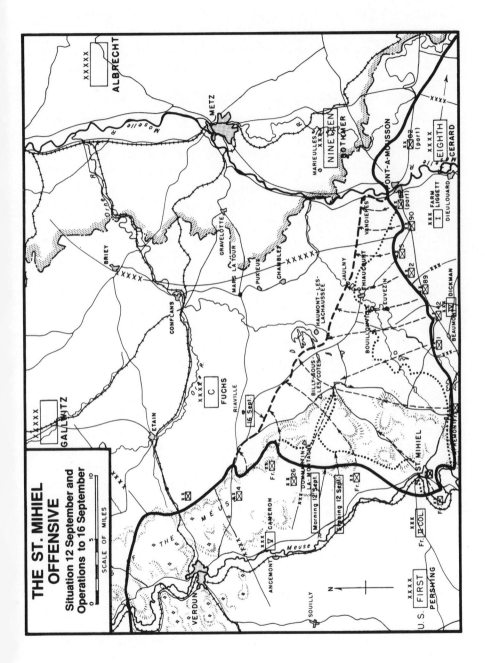

THE ST. MIHIEL OFFENSIVE

Situation 12 September and Operations to 16 September

SCALE OF MILES
0   5   10

179

can doctrine seemed to be sound. The big divisions emerged from the fighting showing little need for relief. The American staff, no doubt with the British and French in mind, crowed that casualties had been light, only about 7,000 men. Congratulations poured in to the commander, Pershing.

On the evening of September 13, when he was certain all of the operational objectives had been achieved, Black Jack Pershing took a few moments to relax and enjoy the accolades. Reflecting on the success, he confided to his intelligence officer, Brigadier General Dennis Nolan, that the reason for the American triumph lay in the superior nature of the American character. Americans were the product, he said, of immigrants who had possessed the initiative and courage to leave the Old World. They were the descendents of those who had the drive, intellect, and daring to make a mighty nation out of a wilderness. Americans had the willpower and spirit that Europeans lacked. With military training equal to that given a European, the American soldier was superior to his Old World counterpart.

Even as the two American officers were speaking, however, evidence began to trickle in to headquarters that should have taken much of the euphoria out of Pershing's attitude—if the evidence were considered objectively. Through prisoner interrogations and captured documents, it was learned that the American attack had been staged against forces that were already in the process of withdrawal. The retreat had begun on September 10, big guns first, and the Germans had no heavy artillery within range of the attack. Although the defenders had forecast an offensive against the salient, their higher headquarters had not thought the area important enough to reinforce. Reserves had been positioned far to the rear, incapable of executing the standard German defense doctrine of immediate counterattack. Total withdrawal had been ordered as early as noon on the day of the attack. The barbed-wire obstacles had not been maintained for some time, a prime reason they were so easy to overcome. Some of the stakes held up little more than fragile belts of rust. Many of the prisoners taken came from the same unit, an Austro-Hungarian division that had little intention of carrying on the war. Numerous members of this unit simply slung their rifles over their shoulders and marched forward, looking for someone to accept their surrender.

An objective analysis would also have considered battle information derived from the Americans themselves. The American boast of light casualties was right—but only if the consideration was restricted to the amount of ground taken. Pershing's pronouncement of about 7,000 casualties did not take into account the French under his command, and was obviously meant to include only the two days of major offensive action. Even then, the casualty rate of 3,500 per day exceeded Haig's accurate prediction of his expected losses for a major offensive prior to the bloody Passchendaele push of 1917. In the next two days, during the consolidation phase, the Americans took over 3,000 more casualties.

An unbiased appraisal of losses would also have considered the intensity of the resistance. In the case of St. Mihiel, the enemy's retreat had as much to do with his desire to withdraw as it did with American pressure to do so. The optimistic conclusions drawn by the U.S. military leadership could be put down to inexperience—but there were Americans who had experience now. Some of the "old-timers" in the U.S. First Division did not regard the St. Mihiel affair as much of a battle. It was an American victory, but along with the elation it should have provoked concern.

Despite the pressing need to set the wheels in motion toward the Meuse-Argonne operation, First Army headquarters did conduct a brief, shallow analysis of the St. Mihiel operation. The results produced several important conclusions: first, there had been severe traffic congestion and confusion on the primitive road net supporting the offensive and second, there had been poor coordination between the American units. The traffic problem was a serious one. An inability to sort out the priorities between infantry reinforcement, ammunition supply, artillery displacement, and casualty evacuation could cripple future offensive actions. The liaison and coordination problem was just as serious. Combat efficiency depended on the ability of one unit either to support or else get out of the way of another unit. Pershing concluded that better training for the traffic control element was essential to rectify the first deficiency, and that more detailed instructions in operations orders were needed to enhance coordination between his forces. The basic American tactical doctrine, however, was not questioned.

TRAVELING AT NIGHT IN ORDER TO AVOID enemy air reconnaissance, American units and logistical convoys made their way northward behind French lines to join in the Allies' great fall offensive. Pershing's army would be on the right flank of the French Fourth Army, and together their thirty-seven divisions would form the southern thrust that complemented Haig's massive assault in the north. The ultimate southern objective, the city of Mezieres, was located in the French-designated sector, about forty miles behind the thirty-six German divisions that were facing Pershing and his ally. Allied possession of this town would sever the vital German lateral rail line that serviced the great majority of Ludendorff's Western Front forces. Success in the southern advance would give the Allies important industrial facilities and deprive the Germans of a considerable amount of resources. There could be little doubt about the importance of the forthcoming offensive. It was not likely that the enemy would voluntarily withdraw this time, as they had from the St. Mihiel salient.

The Americans were taking over twenty-four miles of the front from the French, and the overall plan dictated an eventual U.S. occupation of about one-third of the entire Western Front, or about ninety-four miles. The idea was to feed in the incoming U.S. forces on the right of the French Fourth Army as they became available. Plans were already being drawn up to create another American army headquarters, the U.S. Second Army. Pershing would then become an army group commander and another officer would take over his duties with the First Army. The Meuse-Argonne offensive would therefore carve out the left flank of what was to be a large American sector in France.

The Meuse River formed the initial right extremity of the U.S. attack sector, and the Argonne Forest lay within the left extremity. The main American thrust would be made between the two, in the watershed of the Meuse and Aire rivers. The rolling terrain there was badly churned up and pockmarked from previous fighting around Verdun. During most of the action the Argonne Forest would overlook the main attack corridor, so that the eastern wood line would have to be occupied and dominated by U.S. units. The veteran Twenty-eighth Division was picked to handle this important task.

Possibly the most notable feature of the entire area was a missing element: adequate transportation arteries. There were only three roads in the region that ran parallel with the American direction of attack. Nine U.S. divisions would be using those roads—and that was counting only the front-line infantry formations that were to lead the assault.

Only four of the attacking divisions had any appreciable combat experience; the other five had not even completed their training. Three of these latter divisions had yet to receive their artillery units, and had to be provided with hastily arranged fire-support formations. Fifty percent of the untried Seventy-ninth Division was composed of enlisted men who had been in uniform for only four months. The Fourth, Twenty-eighth, and Seventy-seventh were veteran divisions, but the Seventy-seventh had to be fleshed out with infantry and was destined to receive four thousand riflemen who had been drafted in the United States in July. These new men would arrive only two days before the assault. Clearly Pershing was not putting his best foot forward for the grand offensive. How had it happened?

When Pershing was directed to plan for the Meuse-Argonne operation, he was already committed to St. Mihiel. There he had placed his experienced units in the lead, using his untried divisions for the reserve. Because the reserve force for St. Mihiel had not been used, it therefore remained untested. Three of those units could be shifted rapidly to the Meuse-Argonne sector, and they were. Several U.S. divisions were in the final stages of training during the St. Mihiel operation. Although they would not complete their training in time for the Meuse-Argonne operation, they were at least uncommitted, and therefore were used.

In essence, the First Army staff, having just received the order for the Meuse-Argonne operation on September 7, threw in what appeared to be the most available units. Since the attack was to be made on September 26, the staff had to work quickly. It was a matter of expediency.

The Meuse-Argonne operation was going to be bigger than the one at St. Mihiel, yet in some ways the support for the operation would be less than that used for the first U.S. effort. The perception of ally and enemy alike was that Black Jack Pershing was in command of a rapidly growing, strong army. In reality some facets of that force were showing increasing weakness with each passing day. In addition, there was less planning time than at St. Mihiel: only nineteen days. At St. Mihiel there had been about 1,500 aircraft under Billy Mitchell's direction. For the new operation, only 820 aircraft, 600 of them flown by Americans, would participate on the Allied side. This time there would be only 189 tanks, 25 percent of them with French crews. There was more artillery—some 3,980 guns —but it could not all be brought to bear for the initial assault. More American troops were to be involved; about 600,000 would move into the sector. But these numbers were rapidly being eroded by the mystifying influenza. Beginning in early September, the epidemic returned with a vengeance. American hospital admissions climbed to almost 40,000 for that month. And this wave was deadly. About 2,500 of Pershing's soldiers died from the incurable malady in September. Both figures—hospital admissions and the death toll—far exceeded the wounded and killed for St. Mihiel.

The American intelligence estimate projected that five German line divisions were facing the nine U.S. assault divisions on the first day. Fixed defenses consisted of three well-maintained, well-constructed defense lines about one or two miles apart. Villages interspersed throughout the area had been heavily fortified. Carefully camouflaged machine-gun positions were often present in the basements of houses. While the number of German divisions on the line facing the Americans would be less than at St. Mihiel, the enemy reinforcement capability in the Meuse-Argonne was far greater. General Nolan's intelligence officers predicted the five enemy line divisions would be reinforced with four more in twenty-four hours, two more the second day, and there could well be a surge on the third day of nine additional divisions. If the intelligence estimate was correct, within ninety-six hours of the start of the offensive Pershing's men could be facing twenty German divisions.

To better the chances of success, Pershing and his First Army staff, now grown to 600 officers and 2,000 enlisted men, relied heavily on speed and stealth. The "Belfort ruse" had served well for St. Mihiel, but once fooled, Ludendorff might not be fooled a second time. The American general's intuition proved sound. The Germans actually expected to confront what Pershing *wanted* to do, not what he was *ordered* to do. The enemy staff was looking for the Americans to continue the St. Mihiel offensive. The night movement, front-line reconnaissance done in French uniforms, and other precautions designed to mask the replacement of 200,000 French troops with 600,000 Americans, largely worked, so that Ludendorff was not fully aware of what was about to take place in the Aire Valley. In order to beat those nine third-day German reinforcement divisions to the draw, Pershing directed his planners and commanders to gain about ten miles on the first day. That would put the lead divisions through the successive defense works and into the open ground. Once there, the American infantry was expected to be in its own element.

The First Army plan was once again a simple one. The artillery preparation, one hour shorter in duration than at St. Mihiel, was scheduled to begin at 2:30 A.M. on September 26. There would be less firepower —2,700 guns, used for less time—but the American strong card was thought to be its infantry, and less delay between the start of the artillery preparation and the beginning of the assault would enhance the chances of surprise and minimize the effect of early enemy reinforcement. In order to ensure that the Twenty-eighth Division would secure the wood line overlooking the valley to the east, Lieutenant Colonel George S. Patton's tank brigade was assigned to the First U.S. Corps, which had the attack corridor including both the Argonne Forest and the Aire River. The Seventy-seventh Division formed General Liggett's First Corps's left flank, joining the rightmost element of the French Fourth Army.

Patton's 140 tanks would be advancing with the Twenty-eighth Division on one side of the Aire, as well as supporting the right flank element of the corps, the Thirty-fifth Division, on the other side of that river. General Bullard's Third U.S. Corps would form Pershing's right flank, attacking with three divisions. The rightmost division of this corps, and thus Pershing's easternmost unit, was the Thirty-third Division, which would be attacking up the west bank of the Meuse River. On the left of the Thirty-third Division was the Eightieth Division, and on its left was Bullard's last assault unit, the experienced Fourth Division.

General Cameron's Fifth U.S. Corps would make the main attack and was emplaced in the center, between Liggett's and Bullard's corps. The three divisions of the Fifth Corps, from left to right, were the Ninety-first, Thirty-seventh, and Seventy-ninth. Cameron had no rivers or major streams in his attack corridor or on its flanks, but there were a number of wooded areas, villages, and a few hills. The most prominent hill that the Fifth Corps had to contend with initially was a spot called Montfaucon (mount of the falcon), about five miles behind the German front line. Montfaucon was in the Seventy-ninth Division's sector, Cameron's right flank unit.

On September 26 at 2:30 A.M. the United States Army began its greatest battle to date. At 5:30 A.M. infantry and tanks moved forward in a dense mist made all the more murky by smoke and gas shells. In the main, surprise had been achieved and the forward German positions were lightly held. Through the first two or three hours there were few reports from the front. On the left, however, the Twenty-eighth Division was encountering great difficulty in the Argonne Forest. Trees had been knocked down by the artillery fire, forming obstacles for the attackers and welcome barriers for the defenders. Patton could hear the Twenty-eighth Division's fighting, and the sounds of his tanks with that unit on his left. Across the river, in the Thirty-fifth Division sector, he waited impatiently, but no reports from his tank crews came in. Gathering his party together, he picked up his long walking stick (a device used to gain the attention of his men inside their noisy machines) and marched forward toward the sound of battle. It was 6:30 A.M.

Soon the American tank brigade commander met a disorganized group of Thirty-fifth Division infantrymen walking to the rear. Stopping them, he learned that they had lost contact with their units in the mist and smoke. Adding them to his party, the determined lieutenant colonel continued his advance. Soon the mist began to lift and the group found themselves within range of a number of German machine guns. During the next three hours Patton would release a carrier pigeon with a report to his superior, organize digging parties to get tanks past ditches, direct his vehicles against enemy machine-gun positions, and lead a somewhat foolish two-man attack against one of these positions. While he was busily involved in the Thirty-fifth Division sector, his elements across the river with the Twenty-eighth Division were experiencing considerable problems in their first encounter with German pillboxes in the wood line. Patton was wounded in the leg and turned over his command to his most aggressive battalion commander, Major Brett. While being helped from the battlefield, he concluded that the Thirty-fifth Division was not doing well at all.

Although the left flank of the attack was falling far behind the scheduled advance, at least one unit with the right flank corps was pressing ahead. The Fourth Division had held together in the mist, and when the weather cleared it found itself about a mile and a half beyond, but to the east of, the key terrain feature, Montfaucon. The division's leadership could see that the prized position was still in German hands, but it was in the designated sector of the Seventy-ninth Division, and the detailed instructions cautioned them to stay in contact with flank units. So the Fourth Division settled in, awaiting the advance of the Seventy-ninth.

By late afternoon the offensive was far behind expectations on the left flank and about on schedule on the right. But what of the main attack and Cameron's Fifth Corps? The experienced U.S. units had a saying about the rolling barrage supporting an assault: "Keep your nose in it." In other words, follow it closely, so that you will be on the enemy machine guns before the German crews can react. The Seventy-ninth, an untried and partially untrained unit, had not learned that the prime support in the attack was not concentrated rifle fire but artillery. The new unit had lost the rolling barrage in its advance, and it paid the price. By 9:00 A.M. the lead regiments of the division were pinned down and without artillery support. A French tank unit was sent to assist the stalled division, but the renewed attack ground to a halt on the edge of Montfaucon at dusk. At the same time, Major Brett began counting his losses. Between enemy action and mechanical failure, he had lost 43 of his 140 tanks. With the darkness, the lead elements of the first German reinforcement division began arriving on the battlefield. Pershing's optimistic goal for the first day's gain faded with the sun.

The next day the offensive was resumed against a now fully alarmed and reinforced German defense. Luck was with the defenders; it began to rain. Brett threw in eleven tanks to assist the Twenty-eighth Division, but found that the enemy had begun a concentration of artillery batteries on the edge of the Argonne Forest, hitting the tanks and shelling the exposed American infantry in the open area to the east. The Seventy-ninth Division managed to take Montfaucon at midday, but could not manage a further advance. By holding on to the high spot, Ludendorff's defenders had gained thirty hours. To compound Pershing's difficulties, the fragile routes of resupply and reinforcement began breaking down. Some of the light artillery got forward, but ammunition supply became a severe problem. One traffic jam was seven miles long. Not much was gained on September 27. Brett was now down to eighty-three operating tanks, and the Germans, having built their strength to ten divisions, began counterattacking.

By September 28 the defenders had massed thirteen batteries of artillery in the Argonne wood line. The Thirty-fifth Division, a prime target of the German gunners, began to give ground and to disintegrate as a cohesive fighting unit. The game Seventy-seventh and Twenty-eighth divisions kept hammering away in the forest, but they were not getting much help from the French Fourth Army in the open ground to their left. The rain continued; the roads became nearly impossible to traverse; enemy counterattacks increased; casualties mounted; Brett lost another thirty tanks. The American offensive was slowing to a halt.

It had gone wrong. Even in the best of conditions it was doubtful whether nine divisions could be supported over such a poor network of roads. The Americans were tied to a simple but inflexible plan that called for attacking on line, anchoring flanks with the advance of neighboring units, and keeping within the confines of divisional boundaries, a system that the Germans had learned to abandon long before. Montfaucon should have been taken on the first day, regardless of assigned boundaries. The weather precluded much support from the air, and the initial delay allowed the defenders to bring in reinforcements, six additional divisions by October 3. Most of all, the attack clearly demonstrated that a good percentage of Pershing's army, and particularly its leadership, was not yet ready for effective offensive combat.

The American commander acted. Ordering only local attacks, Pershing began a complex replacement operation over the tenuous lines of communication. The Eightieth Division was pulled out of the line. The inexperienced Seventy-ninth Division was pulled out of action, replaced by the veteran Third Division, the organization that had put up such a stout defense on the Marne River during the summer. The battle-wise ranks of the "Big Red One," the First Division, pulled into the line, replacing the badly mauled Thirty-fifth Division. The Thirty-seventh Division was relieved by the Thirty-second Division, a unit that had been fighting since late July.

Not satisfied with replacing units, Pershing also replaced leaders. The axe began to fall on generals. Several division commanders were replaced. Cameron, the Fifth Corps commander, would be reduced to division, not corps command. For the first time, the American command faced a problem their allies had long known: finding suitable officer replacements. Pershing had lost 521 of his officers, killed in battle during September.

There was little time to make adjustments. Full-scale resumption of the offensive was scheduled for October 4. Prior to the second effort, Pershing was beset with several problems. The fighting in the Argonne Forest was developing into a confused, knock-down-drag-out affair. One group of about 550 Americans from the Seventy-seventh Division had been cut off from American lines and was fighting a desperate battle for survival. The transportation problem had become so acute that the American commander ordered his line-of-communications trucks to the front to serve as troop and ammunition transports. And then there was an unwelcome visit in the form of a French general officer, carrying a proposal from Foch. The idea put forth was that the tactical situation in the Argonne Forest could be solved by moving in the French Second Army headquarters with some French troops and placing the American units fighting there under French command. Pershing dismissed the proposal and concentrated on the forthcoming battle.

It began at 5:00 A.M. on October 4. This time the order permitted division and corps commanders to act independently within their sectors, discarding the notion that each organization had to maintain alignment with its flanking units. Slow, grinding, and painful progress was made, especially by the veteran divisions, but the cost was high. One battalion of the First Division, the Third Battalion of the Sixteenth Infantry, lost 18 of its 20 officers and 560 of its 800 soldiers.

The enemy was not the only cause of losses. During the first week of October 16,000 new influenza cases were recorded. The medical crisis caused Pershing to cut into his requested troop deployments from the United States in order to transport 1,500 additional nurses to the crowded American hospitals in France. All of these losses, whether stemming from the endless heavy combat or a surging epidemic, were cutting into the American army's combat effectiveness.

The isolated unit in the Argonne was finally reached. There were only 195 unwounded survivors from the initial contingent of 550. There had now been 75,000 combat casualties since the offensive began on September 26, almost all in the infantry. Reluctantly, Pershing ordered two of his least-ready divisions to be dismantled, with their members to be used as replacements.

Along with the word of losses came reports of great bravery and skill. The most highly publicized report dealt with an acting corporal of the Eighty-second Division, Alvin York. Leading a seventeen-man element against several German machine-gun positions, York captured a German battalion commander and his party, only to come under attack by the enemy. After losing about half of his men, York set out by himself to reduce the odds. One by one, the skilled marksman dispatched 28 of his adversaries and returned to pick up his prize catch. Leading the defeated German officer around, York persuaded him with his pistol to encourage his men to surrender. In all, the corporal netted 132 prisoners. For those seeking good news from the American sector, it was a banner day.

October 8 also marked the day when the American sector started to expand. The Thirty-third Division secured a crossing over the Meuse River and American units began to form an entirely new attack corridor. By October 12 the American front stretched for ninety miles, and the Second U.S. Army was established. At last a trickle of American-made munitions started to arrive in France: 75-mm artillery shells. The United States was playing a much larger role in the war.

Losses continued to mount. The First Division had taken 9,000 casualties in the first eleven days of October. Such numbers could not be replaced with any sort of speed. Despite the rising number of wounded and killed, the American soldiers continued attacking in the Meuse-Argonne sector, in some cases with astounding results.

Less publicized than the York feat of arms was the case of a professional soldier, acting Captain Sam Woodfill. A veteran of the Philippine Insurrection and the 1916–17 adventure against Pancho Villa in Mexico, the former sergeant found himself on October 12 leading a company of Fifth Division riflemen against several German machine-gun positions near the right flank of the First Army offensive. Pinned down by fire in the middle of an open field, the captain took matters into his own hands. Moving forward, he jumped in a shell hole and determined that the most serious threat was an enemy automatic weapon in a church tower about 200 yards away. Raising up, he quickly fired five rounds from his rifle. The fire from the church tower ceased.

The next threat appeared to be coming from a stable. Locating the gun position, Woodfill repeated his technique—firing five quick rounds with great accuracy. Success once more. Next came the grazing machine-gun fire across the open field. The weapon was concealed in a bushy area, and Woodfill realized he could not use his previous procedure. The deadly machine gun was directly in front of him. He dashed to another shell hole and then began crawling toward a patch of woods on the flank of the enemy position, barely escaping death from artillery and small-arms fire. Reaching a ditch, he worked his way within ten yards of the German gun. Spotting the partially hidden gunner, Woodfill shot him. One soldier after another took the gunner's place, and the captain kept firing until four replacements had been killed. A fifth soldier showed himself and paid the price. Seeing one more, Woodfill brought him down with a pistol shot.

Moving farther into the woods, the veteran soldier bumped into a German officer, who made the fatal error of trying to grab the American's rifle and was shot then and there. Locating another machine gun and crew, the captain eliminated the crew with his now-proven method of picking off the gunner and his four replacements. Surprising two enemy soldiers, he sent them packing to the rear, hands up. Finding yet another machine-gun position, he repeated his technique—five more enemy soldiers died. Bringing his company forward, and still well in the lead, Woodfill was caught in a flurry of artillery shells. Diving into a nearby trench, he landed on top of two enemy soldiers. The ensuing tussle resulted in both Germans being killed—this time by their own pickax. With the enemy position now firmly held by his unit, the captain sent a messenger for reinforcements. His recommendation was disapproved. The company was "too far out front." So Woodfill withdrew from the hard-won ground and abandoned the penetration—the penetration of the Hindenburg Line.

Two days later the First American Army, under the command of General Liggett, began the next phase of the offensive. It was now facing thirteen enemy divisions in the Meuse-Argonne sector. The eight U.S. divisions were ordered to break the Hindenburg Line. Opposition stiffened even more. After forty-eight hours, on October 16, the Americans finally secured the objectives that Pershing had designated for the first day of the attack on September 26. Most of the original attacking divisions had been sent to the rear. The notion that the large U.S. unit could sustain its losses and continue an offensive had not proved out; in actual practice, the average length of stay at the front proved to be about two weeks. As both the Allies and the Germans had learned, divisions must be rotated out of the front in order to reconstitute, feed in replacements, and rest.

At this point, Pershing's problem was that there were not enough replacements to send to Bullard's Second and Liggett's First armies. Two steps were taken to provide an immediate solution. The American commander ordered a reorganization of the large American rifle company, reducing the authorized strength from 250 to 175 men. On the surface this appeared to be merely a paper solution, but in reality the order permitted units that had not been badly reduced by combat to transfer riflemen to divisions that were now seriously understrength at the company level. The reorganization also included measures to dismantle more divisions; the total number of divisions salvaged for replacements now stood at seven. Pershing also ordered an armywide crackdown on stragglers. There were thought to be about 100,000 men milling around the rear areas, either lost, confused, or shirking combat duty. Casualty replacement and filling in for the influenza victims became a major concern. By October 19 the Third, Fifth, and Eighty-second divisions were down to little more than 5,000 combat-effective infantrymen apiece.

The situation in the American sector did not escape the notice of the French political leader Clemenceau. The wily politician knew that Foch, in his position as the overall Allied military authority, had been in direct correspondence with President Wilson. Using his own political position, Clemenceau asked his countryman to take action seeking the replacement of General Pershing. The politician cited the heavy casualties being incurred by the Americans, and their lack of progress in comparison to the British attack in the north being commanded by Haig.

Clemenceau's motive may have been aimed more at diplomatic rather than military objectives. Serious negotiations were now under way with Berlin to end the war, and the basis for the exchange of notes revolved around President Wilson's earlier proposals for peace. Undercutting Pershing and his independent army on the Western Front would diminish the American influence at the bargaining table. Clemenceau had little trust in the American president, and believed that the terms of peace must, above all, suit the needs of France.

It was now October 21. Foch could not ignore Clemenceau's request. The French general had seen much of the American army and its leadership in the past eighteen months. Prior to 1917, American combat experience had largely been limited to minor, punitive campaigns—operations against Indians, Philippine insurrectionists, and various armed Mexican contingents. Some U.S. generals had exhibited an ability to learn their duties in the wholly different arena of Western Front combat, but others had not. None of them had ever commanded the vast number of soldiers they were now attempting to lead. Despite the fact that America had been in the war for a year and a half, their army had been raised quickly—and showed it.

To Foch and his fellow officers, the deployment of the U.S. Army to France had seemed slow indeed. It was clear that the United States had been unprepared to wage modern warfare. The most prominent indication was the lack of American matériel; almost everything had to be given to them—artillery, tanks, airplanes, and machine guns. Once these were in their hands, the Americans had to be taught how to use them. All of this had taken time.

Then there was the matter of American tactical doctrine. There was no question that the individual American soldier fought, and fought well. But the types of attacks they were conducting were extremely costly. Their leaders appeared to have no concern for losses. The American assault was little more than a human wave into the face of German machine guns, a weapon that the Americans treated with contempt. Their doctrine favored the rifle, yet except for a few highly skilled marksmen their use of that weapon appeared to be little different than that of their European counterparts. They insisted on huge divisions, perhaps because they knew they did not have the officers to direct a larger number of more reasonably sized units. However, they were now in the process of reducing the size of these organizations. Pershing was also eliminating some of his more inept generals. And, most important, they were attacking. Losses or not, the Americans kept coming on.

Foch knew the matter had to be handled carefully. The relief of General Pershing might cause a serious and unfavorable reaction in the United States, where the American general was regarded as a hero. The American attack might be slow, but the U.S. offensive was absorbing a growing number of German divisions and, while the American casualties were high, Ludendorff's losses could not be light either. Another 257,000 American troops had arrived in September, and 180,000 were due to reach France during October. No one could replace the casualties being sustained on the Western Front at this juncture—except the Americans.

EIGHT

Attrition

AS FERDINAND FOCH CONSIDERED THE CHOICES for solving the problem of Pershing's slow progress, a number of events occurring in rapid succession elsewhere were influencing the conduct of the war. Most of these developments were adverse to the Central Powers—Germany, Bulgaria, Austro-Hungary, and Turkey. Even so, in late October Ludendorff's forces were still occupying part of France and a healthy slice of Belgium. On the Western Front the war was far from over. Nevertheless, Germany and her allies found themselves on the wrong side of the attrition ledger.

Each belligerent had sought every means to bring the conflict to a quick end by using its mighty armed forces to destroy the opposition or cripple enemy forces so that capitulation would logically follow. Every attempt at maneuver had utterly failed. Battles had been won, but the losers survived. Of the major participants, only Russia had dropped out of the conflict—and even that was not due to the destruction of the Russian army; it still existed. Seven months after the German peace treaty with Bolshevik Russia there were still many German, Austrian, Bulgarian, and Turkish divisions facing Russian troops. Four years after the beginning of the war, large armed forces were still confronting each other.

The Central Powers found it necessary to retain sizable forces in the east—not because of combat, for there was little of that in the east now, but because of the potential for combat. There were still many armed Russians. The confrontation in the east absorbed the combat power of the Central Powers just as if a peace treaty had never been signed.

In a war of attrition, it is the potential that carries the greatest weight. What has been destroyed, and how many men have been killed, are only components in the final calculation. In the end, it is what remains available after the battle that counts. That is the nature of a war of attrition and, above all else, the Great War was just that.

THERE WAS ONE VITAL FACTOR IN THIS war that Foch could now discard from his considerations: the campaign in the North Atlantic. Perhaps it was the most important of all the campaigns. By October of 1918 it had been fought and won by the British, Canadian, and American navies.

Eighteen months earlier the Atlantic campaign had been considered all but lost by two important Allied naval officers. In April of 1917, shortly after the American declaration of belligerency, the American naval representative, Admiral William Sims, had met with his longtime professional acquaintance, Britain's First Sea Lord, Admiral Sir John Jellicoe. The meeting, whose subject was how the United States could actively participate in the conflict, was of vital importance. U-boat sinkings of Allied shipping had risen to alarming levels since the Germans began unrestricted submarine warfare, and U.S. intentions were of little merit if America could not get its men, guns, foodstuffs, and industrial resources across the Atlantic. Even though Sims had been following the war closely, he did not know the actual balance sheet of losses, ships remaining, and ships under construction; few people did. The British had carefully concealed the actual numbers, so that only a handful of top-level officials were privy to the facts. When Jellicoe showed Sims the figures, the American officer was shocked.

"It is impossible for us to go on with the war if losses like this continue," Jellicoe commented.

"It looks as though Germany is winning the war," Sims grimly remarked.

Jellicoe looked at his American ally and said: "They will, unless we can stop these losses, and stop them soon."

"Is there no solution?" Sims asked.

The British admiral did not hesitate to respond: "Absolutely none that we can see now."

Jellicoe was correct in the sense that there was no single solution to the problem. The Allies won the Atlantic campaign by using multidirectional programs. There was little that was not tried. The naval authorities persuaded their governments that new ship construction had to be given the highest of national priorities. Every effort was made to browbeat, cajole, and lure neutral nations into contributing to the dangerous Atlantic crossings. Elaborate schemes were laid out for heavily mining the accessible waters near German U-boat ports. Additional resources were poured into radio intercept facilities that located German submarines. More spotter aircraft were assigned to patrol duties, their crews instructed to look for the telltale wake of a periscope or an unwary surfaced submarine. Japan, the Allied power in Asia with the largest navy, contributed fourteen destroyers to patrol the Mediterranean, releasing a number of British destroyers there for North Atlantic duty. And the United States Navy immediately pressed nineteen of its destroyers into antisubmarine service. America also initiated a crash program of destroyer construction.

Of all the programs, schemes, and actions that Britain and the United States began in that dark spring of 1917, however, none bore more fruit, or was harder to accomplish, than the joint plan of instituting the convoy system for transatlantic shipping. The difficulty was due in part to the fact that acceptance of the convoy method required a complete change in British Admiralty thinking about protecting merchant ships from enemy submarines. Before Germany began its indiscriminate attack on transatlantic traffic, the standard procedure for safeguarding cargo and passenger vessels was to create a secure, submarine-free corridor for transit. This required the allocation of appropriate warships in linked areas of the ocean and the maintenance of submarine hunters in each designated region. The general areas of U-boat operations were established by reported sinkings, sightings, radio intercepts, and simple logic. A relatively new apparatus being used to pinpoint the submerged submarine was the hydrophone, a crude underwater listening device. However, the undersea raider was limited by its need to come to the surface for extended periods, and many were visually spotted. The first line of weaponry against the German submarine was the depth charge, a device created by the Royal Navy during the course of the war. This was a 300-pound drum of TNT with a variable-water-pressure fuse. The weapon was usually rolled from the deck of a destroyer over a suspected U-boat position.

As intelligence data accumulated, the various antisubmarine forces in the corridor's security zones were augmented as necessary. However, the corridor security system was proving to be inadequate to cope with the intensified attacks in the Atlantic that had begun in February of 1917. In the first three months of the unrestricted submarine warfare campaign, only ten of an estimated ninety operating German U-boats had been sunk. During the same period, the undersea force had put some 844 Allied ships on the bottom. The new German submarine construction program was believed to be running ahead of U-boat losses. It was a battle of attrition, the grim statistics of current losses versus future potential, and in the spring of 1917 the Allies were clearly losing the battle.

The proposed convoy system rejected the concept of a transatlantic security corridor in favor of a moving security region, an area that did not extend beyond the physical limits of the convoy. Such a system would permit a higher density of antisubmarine resources in the critical protection zone, the convoy itself. Those who favored convoys argued that their proposal would ensure that no merchant vessel would ever be out of the sight of an antisubmarine escort, and that this in itself would likely deter U-boat captains from attacking. It was in essence a recommendation to guard the cargo and passenger ships themselves, as opposed to the idea of clearing a path for them all the way across the ocean. Simple, but a major change.

There was nothing new about convoying; since the age of sail convoys had been established for guarding merchant ships against raiders. Those who argued against the convoy system now, and there were many, cited a number of reasonable assertions. First, the convoy was only as fast as its slowest ship. The more modern and speedier ships were difficult targets for the slow-moving submarines, but in a convoy the fast ships would trade off their advantage. Second, chaos would result at the debarkation ports, since all of the surviving ships of the convoy would arrive at the same time, overtaxing limited unloading facilities and resources. Conversely, in between the arrivals of convoys there would be no work on the docks. After all, the anticonvoy voices argued, the whole purpose of the transatlantic effort was to deliver people and things to support the war in Europe, and convoys would handle both inefficiently. Ships desperately needed for transportation would now spend days simply awaiting debarkation, the inevitable result of group versus individual ship arrival. Then too, a convoy offered a big, slow-moving target to the U-boat captains, one lucrative enough for the raiders to form packs of submarines, await an opportune time, and launch mass attacks. And, how could merchant captains, members of possibly the most legally independent of all professions, be expected to accept the discipline essential for the conduct of a convoy? All of these arguments and more were made—to no avail.

The convoy system was hurriedly implemented. The problem of varying ship speed was partially solved by grouping fast ships in "fast convoys," and slower vessels with those of comparable speed. In all there were three categories of convoys: fast, medium, and slow. Since no single person or authority could direct shipowners, merchant ship captains, and naval escort groups—all representing various nationalities—to comply with a single plan, convoy grouping was done by committee. Predictably, the committees produced compromise solutions. The same was true of the debarkation problem. The onshore-surge effect caused by the arrival of a convoy was largely solved by allocating prearranged berthing space for the surviving vessels at multiple ports, round-the-clock unloading, organized marshaling of longshoremen, orchestration of port authorities, designated availability of dock space, and careful coordination of subsequent rail traffic.

In the complex debarkation process, committees, arguments, and compromise reigned supreme. The same process was applied so that the traditional and legally supported independence of the sea captain was downgraded. Naval authorities persuaded government contracting officials, the latter persuaded shipowners, and soon the captains of merchant vessels were being informed of the advantages to be gained from surrendering their navigational responsibilities to a convoy leader. The ancient law of the sea, holding each ship master responsible for the safety of his own craft, was not overruled; it was temporarily and partially suspended.

The system worked. The first transatlantic convoy put to sea on May 10, about one month after Sims and Jellicoe had their meeting. Sinkings decreased from over 200 in July 1917 to 148 in August, and were down to 107 in December. Most of the other antisubmarine measures bore fruit as well. U.S. Navy construction contributed seventy-nine destroyers to the cause in short order. Merchant vessel construction and persuasion of neutrals to join the Atlantic convoys went into high gear. By May 1918 the available shipping finally began to exceed the losses to submarines. U-boat losses mounted, and the German submarine construction program was driven into a replacement race. That program did keep up with the losses, but it did not exceed them enough to increase the operational U-boat fleet. When the steadily decreasing number of sinkings was measured against the rapid growth of seagoing tonnage available to the Allies, the implications were clear. The Royal Navy's surface fleet had the German High Seas Fleet bottled up with an effective blockade, and there was little that Berlin could do to alter the downward spiral. By the summer of 1918 the Battle of the Atlantic, a campaign of attrition, had been won by the Allies.

THE VICTORY IN THE ATLANTIC PROVIDED Foch with the assurance that the heavy casualties sustained by the Allies in the fall of 1918 would be replaced. Not only were new troops for the Western Front coming from America, but veteran divisions were arriving by rail from the Italian front. This welcome addition was in part due to the wise decisions that Foch himself had made in Italy during the previous year, 1917.

Italy had put her army back together, and by the early summer of 1918 was again largely holding her own. The Austrians, now without much support from Germany, had attempted another offensive in June, but only gained about five miles at best. The Allies had taken 24,000 dispirited Austrian prisoners, an odd event since the attacker is normally on the receiving end of surrenders.

By October of 1918 Foch had recovered most of the British and French divisions that had been sent to Italy the year before, and had also taken control of two Italian divisions for use in the west. The French general learned that desertions were rapidly depleting Austrian ranks, and he knew that the Italians were preparing for a massive drive north with sixty divisions. Such "massive offensives" had been forecast in the past, however, without much in the way of results. Meanwhile, the Austro-Hungarian Empire had been dissolved on October 16, a federal state had been created, and near-autonomy was being granted to a number of dissident nationalities. The Austrians still held a considerable portion of northern Italy, but their capability to retain what they had gained was now questionable. In truth, both armies, Austrian and Italian, were in difficult straits. Foch expected no miracles on the Italian front.

THE LACK OF ALLIED PROGRESS IN ITALY was balanced in part by success against the Bulgarians to the east, on the Balkan front. Unfortunately for the Allies, that success could not be translated into a strategic advantage in the fall of 1918. If the Italians could actually drive the Austrians back, however, the Allies could threaten southern Germany, causing Ludendorff to deflect resources from the Western Front. The Balkan front offered no such advantages. Bulgaria was simply too far to the east and south to have an immediate effect on the Germans. The victory on the Balkan front, however, had jeopardized the lines of communication between Germany and her ally, Turkey. If Turkey could be taken out of the war, a large number of Allied divisions could eventually be transferred from Palestine and Mesopotamia to the Western Front. Events in Bulgaria constituted an indirect hope for Foch's plans for 1919.

Beginning in 1914, the Allies had accumulated four British, six Greek, eight French, six Serbian, one Italian, and three Czech divisions in northern Greece and southern Bulgaria, a half-million troops in all. Many of the Allied military leaders had protested such a concentration; imagined postwar political advantages had outweighed wartime strategic facts. There was little to do but attempt to achieve some military gain out of this large, polyglot force. It had been argued that with Russia leaving the Allied cause, the Balkans should be reinforced so as to prevent German forces from being transferred from east to west. That rationale, however, appeared to be rather weak, for in the face of the Allied counterattacks on the Western Front in 1918, the Germans had largely abandoned the Bulgarian army, leaving them only three battalions and thirty-two artillery batteries. In the late summer the balance of forces stood at about 574,000 Allied troops versus 400,000 Bulgarian and German soldiers. In mid-September the Allies launched an offensive.

The abrupt failure of the Bulgarian army came as a surprise. By the end of the month, Serbian units had advanced eighty miles, the Bulgarian border had been crossed, and various Bulgarian authorities and parliamentarians had signed armistice agreements: all of this from a front that had been stagnant since the fall of 1916. By late October the Allies were in the process of occupying the Balkans and advancing on Turkey from the northwest. Foch knew that the collapse of Bulgaria could have a profound effect on both Austria and Turkey and an indirect, adverse effect on Berlin. There were those, however, who claimed with some justification that Bulgaria's withdrawal from the war was only partial compensation for Russia's departure from the Allied side.

PERHAPS THE GREATEST SOURCE OF FRUSTRATION for the Allied military leadership on the Western Front was the immense resources that had been devoted by the British to the war against Turkey. In 1918 there were two main fronts aimed at the Turkish Empire, based on Palestine and Mesopotamia. During most of 1917 and 1918 the British had 340,000 troops involved either in the Palestine operation or in the rear of that front in Egypt. To the north and east, on the Mesopotamian front —modern-day Iraq—there were about 400,000 British Empire troops. Fundamentally, London's purpose was little more than an effort to enlarge the British Empire at the expense of the fading Ottoman Empire. Britain had gained Egypt as a protectorate, and by 1917 was attempting to enroll Palestine in the same category. On the Mesopotamian front, the British had placed troops at the head of the Persian Gulf early in the war, so as to secure an oil pipeline. Then they had expanded their horizons, worked their way up the Tigris River, and conquered Baghdad in March of 1918.

Just as Plumer had been sent from the Western Front to Italy in 1917, Allenby had been dispatched to Palestine. With reinforcements Allenby had conquered Jerusalem in December of that year and began a drive north in September 1918. Damascus had fallen to Allenby on October 2. The German commitment to these Middle Eastern campaigns had been small. Ludendorff's overall desire was to tie down as many Allied troops as possible—as far away from the Western Front as possible. The resistance to the Allies was almost wholly supplied by Turkey. During late 1917 that resistance began to disappear.

By 1918 the Turkish army was crumbling. The Turks had fought off a Russian offensive in the Caucasus region with their Third and Fourth Armies. The Sixth Turkish Army was pitted against the British offensive on the Mesopotamian front as well as another Russian drive from Persia—modern-day Iran. The Turkish Sixth Army was in a desperate situation—caused not so much by the British as by a terrific death toll from malaria. Russia's departure from the war had given some respite to the Turks, but they had to send every spare soldier to Palestine. There Allenby's drive from Jerusalem was joined by an Arab revolt against Turkish rule, the latter movement ably assisted by a British colonel, T. E. Lawrence. With the collapse of Bulgaria, Turkey lost its overland link to Germany and the source of a large percentage of its arms and supplies. On October 20 Foch learned that Turkey was asking for terms.

WHILE FOCH HAD MUCH TO BE OPTIMISTIC about, considering the Battle of the Atlantic, the collapse of Bulgaria, and the possibility of Turkish capitulation, Russia presented a continuing problem. In the spring of 1917 the Russians had been fighting no less than ninety-nine German, forty Austrian, twenty Turkish, and perhaps six Bulgarian divisions. All told, roughly 35 to 40 percent of the war against the Central Powers had been carried by the czar's troops. However, Russia was now out of the war. The implications for the Allied leadership in the west were grave indeed.

The reasons for czarist Russia's collapse were many and varied. Certainly one of the more important causes was the enormous losses suffered by the Russian army from 1914 to 1917. During the first sixteen months of the war alone, the Russians suffered an estimated two million casualties. By the end of 1916 Russian leaders were reporting about one million desertions. The huge initial losses and the subsequent inability of Russia to maintain its forces on the battlefield quickly undercut the presumed Russian population advantage. In addition, Russia had neither the industrial capacity nor the capital to equip and finance her large army. Her allies tried to help with the shipment of weapons and munitions, but the corrupt and inefficient czarist bureaucracy was able to place only a portion of these resources at the disposal of front-line commanders. Vast quantities of war matériel had been accumulated at several sites along the trans-Siberian railroad. There it rotted, rusted, or was stolen. This situation, together with the enormous losses of equipment suffered by the Russians during the first few months of the war, produced an increasingly ill-equipped army, one whose troop strength was steadily declining.

The provisional government that swept away the Romanov regime in the spring of 1917 was committed to the continuation of the war. However, the military leadership of the army was little improved, and the government was hardly more efficient than before. The empire, composed of a large number of nationalities, showed a tendency to weaken when the czar fell from power. A minority element of the emerging political organizations, the Bolsheviks, produced an effective propaganda program calling for the end of the war and the disbanding of the army. Thus the Russian Revolution accelerated the disintegration of the Russian army.

The Germans and Austrians had also suffered on the Eastern Front, but their losses and desertions were in no way comparable to the huge casualties, defections, and absences from the ranks of the Russian army. The Central Powers had been able to maintain and equip their forces in the east all the way through November of 1917, when Lenin and Trotsky finally took control of the government in Petrograd. Through a complex process involving losses, declining willpower, industrial and financial weakness, and political change, Russia lost a war of attrition.

Yet Germany found itself unable to exploit its victory in the east to better its fortunes in the west. A considerable portion of the former Russian empire sought independence from the new Marxist regime, and the German leadership saw a distinct advantage in gaining dependent buffer states between their nation and Russia. Finland, Estonia, Poland, Latvia, Lithuania, and the Ukrainian Republic emerged in early 1918, and all looked to the Germans to ensure their security. Ludendorff fully endorsed these new political entities because their existence would solve an old Prussian General Staff problem: German vulnerability to surprise attack from the east. However, some German troops had to remain in the east to safeguard this new measure of security.

While the Bolsheviks publicly called for the end of all empires, their foreign affairs functionary, Trotsky, was shocked at the German demands for the independence of much of the western portion of the old Russian Empire. It was a preview of the now-classic Soviet dilemma: an inability to separate Marxism and Russia. Trotsky's decision was for inaction. He delayed a final agreement with the Germans until Lenin was forced to step in and take charge of the negotiations. The delay had led Ludendorff to authorize another offensive in order to bring the Bolsheviks to terms, an operation that extended the war in the east into March of 1918. The result was that eastern reinforcements to Ludendorff's spring offensive in the west arrived very late. The combination of the German desire to protect the newly independent states and Soviet hostility toward the agreement they were forced to sign caused Ludendorff to leave forty divisions in the east.

RAPID CHANGES IN THE COURSE OF THE war during late October of 1918 were not restricted to the ground and naval aspects. Change was also occurring in the air war. Over the Western Front the Allies were finally gaining the upper hand. German technology had maintained a general technological superiority over the Allies in fighter and ground-support aircraft, but the Allies had an edge in doctrine and a fast-growing dominance in sheer numbers. The kaiser's airmen could not consistently capitalize on their technological advantage because the German manu-facturing practices were geared to the production of a small number of the best aircraft, while the Allied practice produced large numbers of good aircraft. No matter how well the high-quality German machines performed, accidents, weather, and multiple engagements took sufficient tolls to smother any technological edge.

German air doctrine also contributed to the growing Allied air superi-ority. A persistent German tenet had been to defeat enemy fighters over friendly territory, where a front-line ground-warning network and anti-aircraft guns could assist in the air battle. Weather on the Western Front and the increasing speed of successive aircraft models often negated early warning and friendly ground fire, and the Germans found themselves in a defensive battle. This defensive posture skewed the development process as German aircraft builders were driven to compromise their designs in order to create fast-climbing interceptor models. The attri-tion balance in the air was tipping heavily in favor of the Allies. By late 1918 Germany was not producing enough pilots or machines to keep up with the burgeoning Allied air armadas, particularly the Royal Air Force. The American contribution was still frustratingly small, but U.S. plans for 1919 were aimed at a very large air arm. In the realm of fighters, ground support, and reconnaissance aircraft, the Allied potential was clearly greater than German prospects.

Foch could rely on a superb performance from the Allied air forces, yet he was troubled by one aspect of the air war. Cities had been bombed by both sides early in the war, but the damage and actual results had been negligible. Now, however, the practice was becoming a science, and on the Allied side it was an endeavor that Pershing, Haig, Pétain, and even Foch could not influence. Later it would go by the somewhat clinical term "strategic bombing," but in 1918 it was a new, unnamed, and ominous activity, one that raised serious moral concerns.

The aims of strategic bombing varied among the advocates. Some cited the advantages to be gained by spreading terror among the enemy's people, thereby undercutting their will to prosecute the war. Others pressed for targeting the opposition's industrial and transportation bases. Then there were those who appeared to be motivated by a spirit of pure vengeance. In sum, it appeared to be a war against the population: women, children, the old—everyone. That was the unsettling thing. To many of the early twentieth-century soldiers, strategic bombing was a beastly business.

It was not as if it had not been done before. Cannonading besieged cities was a practice of warfare that was at least five centuries old. However, strategic bombing was different. A siege had been at least partially or even wholly decisive; it could signal the end to a war. But strategic bombing appeared to bear no such fruit because it was in the nature of a raid. Soldiers knew that raids were rarely decisive, often extraneous, and normally contributed little to war termination. Besides, military leaders of the Great War were well versed in the recent international agreements to limit the horrors of armed conflict. From the 1890s on, the various Hague conventions had outlawed military operations that jeopardized the lives of innocent civilians. Strategic bombing therefore appeared to be futile, illegal, and morally corrupt.

However, in October of 1918, Allied plans for strategic bombing were absorbing increasing resources. The prime stimulus had been several German raids on London during 1917. On June 13 of that year, a squadron of Gothas hit the city, killing about 600 civilians. Another raid in July was all that the British prime minister, Lloyd George, could tolerate. The Welshman set in motion a train of events that led to the separation of the Royal Flying Corps from the British army, creating a new arm— the Royal Air Force—initiating a major production program for British bombers, and providing guidance for a planned attack on German cities, industrial centers, and transportation facilities. Most of this was done over the objections of British military leaders.

Haig strenuously opposed the efforts of Lloyd George to bring about a large British strategic bombing capability, and he was initially joined by Foch and Major General Hugh Trenchard, Britain's ranking airman. Trenchard stated that the project was not only impractical, it was immoral to boot. However, Trenchard was chosen to carry out the will of the politicians and begin the program. By the time the RAF was formally organized in April of 1918, the rapid advance of air technology gave the advocates reason to expect unprecedented effectiveness for bombing raids. By then, large, multiengine aircraft were carrying 2,000-pound bombs, and incendiary munitions had already been dropped on cities. Trenchard began the operational phase earlier, in October of 1917, with raids on steel manufacturing facilities in southwest Germany. By the end of December both Mannheim and Ludwigshafen had been hit. Trier was subjected to "round-the-clock" bombing with both day and night strikes in February 1918. In March, Cologne, Mainz, Coblenz, and Fribourg were bombed. As growing numbers of British bombers began to reach farther into the heart of Germany, British political leaders sought every device to enhance the status and effectiveness of their new arm.

London began an orchestrated campaign to entice the Italians and French into the rapidly expanding bombing enterprise, announced an ambitious program to field forty squadrons of bombers, and in June created a new air command, the Independent Force of the RAF. The organization was to take its orders from the British capital, bypassing both Haig and Foch. This scheme was too much for one French general, who sarcastically commented, "Independent of whom . . . God?" The protests of ground soldiers and the Allied high commanders in France went for nought. Strategic bombing became firmly embedded in the fabric of war.

By October 1918 the energetic airmen pieced together a concept to give Lloyd George and the British people a bit of revenge: a plan to bomb Berlin. Technology had not yet provided a machine capable of flying to Berlin, dropping a significant bomb load, and returning to the launch base, but the RAF planning staff found a way. In the next world war it would be dubbed "shuttle bombing." The idea was to fly east, bomb Berlin, and continue on to a friendly airfield. The aircraft would then be refueled and rearmed, and the whole process repeated in a westerly direction. RAF calculations proved that fuel loads would permit the operation if the initial launch point were Norfolk and if Prague was used as the first recovery site. The westward route involved a takeoff from Prague,

Generals John J. Pershing and Hunter Liggett.—*National Archives*

U.S. Marines in battle, Meuse-Argonne.—*National Archives*

A Signal Corps sergeant removes a message from the leg of a pigeon, Cornieville, France.—*National Archives*

Corpsmen of the Fourth Ambulance Company treat U.S. First Division wounded at a makeshift aid station in the ruins of an old church near Neuilly.—*National Archives*

An artillery battery of the U.S. Twenty-eighth Division alongside the Aire River, firing a salvo at retreating German columns.—*National Archives*

American infantry moving forward through barbed wire.—*U.S. Army Military History Institute*

U.S. field artillery battery firing on German lines, Le Cotes de Forimont, during the Argonne offensive.—*National Archives*

Scene showing immense traffic congestion behind the American lines in the Argonne, amid the ruins of the village of Esnes.—*National Archives*

Eightieth Division vehicular traffic at Imecourt, in the Ardennes.—*National Archives*

Troops of the 316th Infantry slog through Buzancy on a rainy day in early November, in the Ardennes.—*National Archives*

Black American infantrymen advance toward the front in the Argonne along a screened highway.—*National Archives*

From this position atop a hill, one kilometer north of Grandpre, dug-in German machine guns commanded the valley below, holding up the American advance through the Ardennes until finally captured after three unsuccessful attempts.—*National Archives*

Raiding party of the 168th Regiment making its way to a captured trench near Badonville.—*U.S. Army Military History Institute*

After four years of German occupation, this old French couple in the town of Brieulles sur Bar in the Ardennes are delighted at the arrival of the Americans. The two U.S. soldiers are Philip Tangor (left), of the Seventy-seventh Division, and Allen Floyd, of the Forty-second Division.—*National Archives*

Marshal Ferdinand Foch, generalissimo of the Allied armies on the Western Front, entering the conference hall at Versailles, November 1918.—*National Archives*

the bombing of Essen, and the final landing in England. By using the new Handley Page bombers, the shuttle bombing plan was to be ready for execution in November or December.

The RAF bombing operation was costly. By late October the air campaign against Germany was a year old and had suffered about 140 lost aircraft and 280 crewmen dead or missing. In order to keep losses down, the British airmen increasingly scheduled their raids during hours of darkness, a time when target identification was difficult but avoidance of German interceptors easier. In the final analysis the RAF was not doing much damage in Germany, but civil officials there demanded that the General Staff provide protection against the raids. In response the hard-pressed German military leadership began deployment of antiaircraft artillery in and around German cities and industrial centers. While the British bombing campaign was an expensive way of doing minor damage to German industry, it was at least causing Ludendorff to look to the security of the homeland.

The German armed forces had been involved in strategic bombing from the very beginning of the war. Perhaps too much energy had been expended too soon. The prime vehicle for bombing in the early phases was the zeppelin, but these huge lighter-than-air ships had proved vulnerable both to extreme weather conditions and to interceptor aircraft. The German priority then shifted to large, multiengine aircraft. However, the same factors that contributed to the decline of the German tactical air capability heavily influenced the steady erosion of the German strategic bombing capability.

The problem—as it was with fighters, interceptors, and reconnaissance aircraft—was that the number of bombers being produced was insufficient to keep pace with accident and combat losses. As with the other German airplanes, the bombers were well designed and very airworthy. There were simply not enough of them. At one point in the spring of 1918, Ludendorff's entire inventory of bombers was down to less than fifty working machines. That was at a time when RAF bombers numbered well over one hundred and British production had not even reached its stride. Again, it was a matter of potential. The Allied future looked bright, while German prospects were dim.

IF THE AIR ARM WAS NOT THE GERMAN strong suit, big guns were. In the case of Paris, Ludendorff had tried to achieve the objectives of strategic bombing by using artillery. As early as 1916, he had encouraged the naval artillery division of the Krupp works to design and build a mammoth railroad gun with a sixty-two-mile range. In 1917 Ludendorff revised his requirements—he specified seventy-four miles. The engineers, artisans, and workers labored day and night to build the unprecedented weapons. They named their creations "William's Guns"; the Allies would call them "Big Berthas." When the project came to its successful conclusion, there were two versions: the 8.26-inch gun and the 9.13-inch gun. Both were designed to bring the war to Paris and to destroy the morale of Parisians.

Nothing quite like it had ever been done before. To launch the 250- to 300-pound projectiles as much as 550 pounds of explosives had to be used. That meant that the long steel barrels would be subjected to such heat and pressure that they would be progressively distorted by each firing. The careful design therefore envisioned a varying size to the projectiles and a maximum number of sixty-five rounds before the barrel would become useless. The smaller design launched a 229- to 262-pound shell, the larger gun a 273- to 307-pound projectile. This melding of explosive, ballistic, and metallurgical technology was scheduled to be available for Ludendorff's spring 1918 offensive.

The German army's 1918 attack on the Western Front was supported by the shelling and bombing of the French capital. The bombing started in January, and the German bombers struck Paris seventeen times between the first of the year and September. The numbers of planes varied from a large-scale raid of seventy aircraft to a single bomber. Eleven planes were lost in 267 sorties. With their 615 bombs, the German bombers managed to kill 303 Parisians and wound 539. The specially designed guns had not been as effective. Opening up on March 23, the huge artillery pieces fired 367 rounds, killing 256 citizens of Paris and wounding 620. It all came to an end when the Allied counterattacks pressed the German line beyond the range of the big guns in August, and the kaiser's bombers had been worn down to an insignificant force. By late October Foch could consider strategic bombing and terror shellings an Allied, not an enemy, advantage.

ONE OF THE LAST CONSIDERATIONS FOR Foch was the fleeting and ambiguous peace negotiations among the belligerents. He suspected that the course of the negotiations was the actual reason for Clemenceau's protests over Pershing. President Wilson's fourteen-point proposal of January 1918 had become the operative basis for a possible negotiated end to the war, and Wilson's goals were not necessarily those of the

French political leader. While some of Wilson's proposals, such as a postwar association of nations, freedom of the seas and trade, and a reduction of armaments were vague enough to be harmless, others could drastically affect French fortunes. Included among these was a proposal advocating adjustment of colonial claims, and another calling for a general redrawing of East European political boundaries. Downgrading the American contribution to the Allied effort was a way of undercutting the prestige of Wilson. Nothing could bring this about quite as well as a recommendation for the relief of the American military commander in France.

Foch himself had attempted to influence the course of the negotiations. On October 6, when the Germans had declared their willingness to negotiate on the basis of Wilson's points, they had directed their offer to Washington, not to Paris or London. The European Allies had quickly surmised that Ludendorff was attempting to gain time in the face of the Allied advance on the Western Front. If the German army could obtain some sort of cease-fire, it could consolidate its forces, prepare a new defense, and rebuild during the winter. Few of the Allied leaders believed the German offer to talk was sincere.

Foch quickly drew up his notions for the conditions that should prevail prior to serious negotiations. He informed Clemenceau on October 8 that there should be no cease-fire until Germany had evacuated all occupied territory, allowed the Allies to seize two or three bridgeheads on the Rhine, and forfeited a considerable amount of war matériel. In short, Foch specified that the momentum of the Allied attack must not be stopped unless Germany yielded its wartime military gains and the Allies were assured of overwhelming superiority if the proposed talks were broken off.

By October 21, however, the Allied momentum existed only in the north. Haig had begun his major drive on September 29, with the British Third and Fourth and French First armies battering into the Hindenburg Line. By September 30 a wide gap had been opened through Ludendorff's main defensive position. Haig's primary thrust had been staged by thirty British and two American divisions against thirty-nine German divisions. They had captured 36,000 prisoners and 380 guns.

To the north of this attack, in the lowlands, a force under the king of Belgium consisting of Belgian, French, and British troops had also launched a major offensive. Starting on September 28, this attack quickly gained all of the ground that had been so bitterly contested in the 1917

Passchendaele offensive. By mid-October both northern attacks were steadily moving forward and the German defenders began giving way. As soon as Roulers was cut off, the Germans evacuated the entire coast of Belgium, an action that Haig had predicted a year earlier. The British military leader and his Belgian ally kept up the pressure. Ludendorff could find no respite in the north, and Foch was determined to keep his adversary reeling.

Between October 21 and 23, Foch laid out the immediate instructions for the continuation of the Allied offensive, and in another communication, he composed a carefully worded reply to Clemenceau concerning General Pershing's situation. He told his French and American military subordinates that they were facing an enemy "whose exhaustion increases every day." Important results could be achieved only by a rapid and deep advance. Foch directed the American and French offensive to match Haig's progress to the north. He expected the advance to be made without delay and without concern for the lack of progress of flanking elements. He believed the German army could be destroyed by an acceleration of the rate of German attrition. The war could be won in 1918.

The "American command problem" was handled in a less direct manner. In his letter to the French political leader, Foch suggested that Clemenceau lacked an understanding of both the American contribution and the difficulties that any American commander would be contending with. He pointed out that Pershing had only twenty of the thirty American fighting divisions under his direct command, the other ten being assigned to French and British armies. Pershing's sector contained difficult, wooded terrain, Foch stated, and despite the harsh nature of the fighting, the Americans had demonstrated great skill in being able to shift quickly from the St. Mihiel to the Argonne offensive. The American army was an "improvised army," he stated, and was suffering from the inefficiencies inherent in all such forces. He then outlined a scheme that avoided a confrontation over Pershing's leadership, but gave Clemenceau an answer that was difficult to refuse. If the need arose, Foch said, he could shift more American divisions from Pershing's control, placing them under British or French command. Clemenceau had phrased his challenge in military terms, although probably for political reasons. Foch had replied in military terms and with a military solution, one that kept Pershing in command and offered no political advantage to Clemenceau. The two Frenchmen had never been fond of each other, and on this encounter the soldier got the best of the politician.

Black Jack Pershing was unaware of the Foch-Clemenceau exchange, and even if he had known, it is unlikely that the American leader could have found the time to defend himself. He had only seven days to prepare for another massive American thrust. The date of the attack was scheduled for November 1.

NINE

Continuity and Change

AS THE FINAL DAYS OF OCTOBER PASSED, a growing sense of war's end swept over most of the Allied military leaders. However, the generals were neither certain of it nor in complete agreement on what should be done. Haig believed the Germans were far from beaten, while Pershing and Foch were convinced that victory might be near. Their beliefs influenced their differing recommendations on the terms of an armistice, should that long-awaited moment arrive. Haig favored a bit more leniency toward the enemy than either Foch or Pershing. The British general saw the need for some respite for his hard-driving troops, while Foch and Pershing believed that pressure should be kept on the enemy at all costs. These officers mainly saw what was in front of them—the tasks for the next few days, the ground on the immediate horizon. They could not see, and could not have been expected to see, that a long-enduring political era was collapsing and a new era of militarism and warfare had already been born.

The fighting from September 26 on had been difficult for Pershing and his soldiers. The American general had to relieve four brigade commanders, three division commanders, and one corps commander. His troops had begun the drive facing twenty enemy divisions. Now, in late October, they were up against thirty-one German divisions. The U.S. Army had gained about thirteen miles in its assault and had claimed to have taken 18,600 prisoners, 370 artillery pieces, and 1,000 machine guns. All of this had cost about 100,000 American battle casualties. Although fresh troops were pouring into France and the American army was growing, Pershing's front-line strength was actually decreasing. Between the resurgent influenza epidemic and combat losses, Pershing needed 90,000 replacements, mostly infantry, by November 1, but could count on getting only 45,000. The Americans would also have to launch their new offensive once again with just a handful of tanks. Their hope was that the Germans would be in even worse shape.

On the positive side, Pershing had some newfound strengths. By now, the American First Army was no longer so dependent on Allied support. Most of the French logistical support—ammunition-supply facilities and personnel, rear area communications units, and transportation organizations—had been replaced by similar U.S. units. The strength of the American Expeditionary Force had grown to 1.8 million, and was scheduled soon to overtake the 2.7 million British and Dominion totals. The American army now had experienced staffs and unit commanders. Its fighting elements had pushed the Germans past the Argonne Forest. The terrain ahead was not as closed-in as before, and it would not be as easy for the Germans to defend.

A crude scheme to solve the vexing problem of controlling assault elements had been worked out. Colonel George C. Marshall, operations officer of the First Army, had charged a number of staff officers to accompany the lead units with a contingent of carrier pigeons and their handlers. The young officers were given six birds each and instructions to report progress three times on the first day of the attack and three times the second day. Since reports through channels had consistently failed to provide timely information all during the previous month, the Marshall "pigeon plan" had promise. The hope was that the First Army headquarters would be in possession of accurate information from the front in time to influence the course of battle. All told, the previous air of innocent overconfidence at American headquarters had been replaced with a more realistic atmosphere of disciplined, battle-wise determination.

For one soldier, however, the American changes did not go far enough. When the U.S. plan for the renewed offensive reached the eyes of Ferdinand Foch, the Frenchman was disappointed. The plan contained the phase lines of a general attack—precisely what Foch wanted to avoid. A phase line, or in this case, a daily objective line, could be used to justify a pause in a situation that could otherwise provide the opportunity for a breakthrough. A successful unit could halt at a phase line while waiting for a slower unit on the flank to catch up. The attainment of an objective line could be interpreted as the accomplishment of the mission. What Foch wanted was for his forces to ignore the flanks, just as the Germans had done in the spring, and to set no specified terrain goals.

The Allied leader was also informed that Pershing's original concept had scheduled the attack for October 28, but since the French army on the left flank of the Americans would not be ready at that time, Pershing had ordered a four-day delay. Here was the "phase-line syndrome" writ large. Having gone to extremes in defending Pershing against Clemenceau's challenge, Foch resigned himself merely to issuing a broadly aimed edict reiterating his desire to press the attack and reinforce success, and for each unit involved to keep moving regardless of the shape of the general front. Pershing interpreted the message from the Allied commander as an endorsement for his own tactical philosophy—concentrated rifle fire and victory through an infantry charge against machine guns. The Americans would attack. They would go forward against fixed defenses shoulder to shoulder, each division in a narrow sector, aligned with companion flanking units.

Pershing's plan envisioned an attack aimed at Sedan, twenty-five miles to the north. General Bullard's Second U.S. Army was not yet ready to stage a full-fledged offensive and was holding a line east of the Meuse River, a waterway running generally north-south and parallel to the projected line of the American attack. The first part of the offensive was to be delivered by the veteran divisions of the First U.S. Army under General Hunter Liggett. Bullard's forces were to conduct patrols, be prepared to move forward if the Germans began a general withdrawal, and make preparations for joining in the offensive after the first week of November. Since the Germans were heavily engaged against Haig's attack, it was believed that a serious American effort aimed directly northward would menace the German supply system for the lowlands and possibly provoke Ludendorff into acting to rescue his army by pulling it back to the Rhine River.

There was a bit of deception in the American scheme, but the opposing German army group commander, General Max von Gallwitz, was not entirely taken in. Two days prior to the assault Gallwitz informed supreme headquarters that air reconnaissance and prisoner interrogations clearly indicated an American buildup for a major offensive; however, he was uncertain as to which side of the Meuse Pershing would choose for his attack. When the Germans located the Seventy-ninth Division east of the Meuse in Bullard's Second Army sector, and when the American artillery shelled German forces east of the Meuse, Gallwitz canceled the movement of one of his divisions to the west bank of the river. He was ready for the Americans, but unaware that the effort was designed to take place almost wholly west of the Meuse.

With two hours of artillery preparation, the long-awaited American offensive was launched on a front of about eighteen miles at 5:30 A.M. on November 1. On the left, the Seventy-eighth Division attacked into a small wooded area, the Bois de Loges. To its right the Seventy-seventh Division assaulted north in open country, and on its right flank the Eightieth Division moved into the open as well. Farther east, the Second Division attacked north with the entire American inventory of available tanks—eighteen. To the right of the Second Division, the Eighty-ninth Division advanced through the northern tip of the Bois de Romagne toward the Bois de Barricourt. The right flank of Liggett's attack was led by the Ninetieth and Fifth divisions. The German artillery response to the American shelling was weak. The prime resistance to the U.S. assault was from machine guns.

Colonel Marshall's front-line pigeon reporting service was working. Between 7:30 and 8:00 A.M. the first birds arrived at Liggett's headquarters. The notes written on the battlefield were taken from the returning pigeons at the loft and read to Marshall over the telephone. Marshall then telegraphed the reported lead unit locations to each corps headquarters. In most cases division commanders learned of their own units' progress from the pigeon service earlier than from their brigade commanders. News from the tank-supported Second Division was encouraging; its progress was particularly rapid. However, toward the left flank the Seventy-seventh Division was stalled. By late afternoon, the deepest advance had reached about seven miles northward.

On the next day, November 2, the American drive continued. The flagging U.S. right flank got moving, pushing in seven miles from the starting point. The rush north caused the now-familiar problem of clogged roads. Artillery, headquarters contingents, follow-up reserves, and ammunition convoys became hopelessly snarled along the primitive road network. Communication with the front was lost. Elevated telephone lines could not be erected in time to keep up with the advance, and wires laid on the ground were soon cut by traffic and shell fire. Marshall's pigeons, now enjoying a well-deserved rest back at headquarters, offered no further solution. Motorcycle couriers took as long as four hours to thread their way through traffic jams between corps and army command posts. Once again the enterprising Colonel Marshall took to the air, this time using aircraft to drop orders to the advancing corps commanders of the First Army.

On November 3 a curious event occurred, one that signaled a distinct change in the nature of the war. The Second Division had been leading the pack since the beginning of the offensive and was determined to keep up the pressure. After an exhausting day of fighting, orders were received by the Third Brigade of the division to push out a reconnaissance toward the town of Beaumont, four miles ahead and only about ten miles short of Sedan, the American objective. Since there was a rather ominous-looking patch of woods to the front, the brigade commander decided to concentrate as much artillery fire there as he could call up. A devastating fire was placed on the woods and on each side of a pair of roads that seemed to run north, deep into the German rear. The idea of a reconnaissance gave way to the notion of a general advance, and as darkness gathered the entire brigade found itself in columns of twos, marching forward into the gloom. The roads joined deep in the woods and the Americans were now in a single column, two men abreast, being led by the capable foot soldiers of the Ninth Infantry Regiment. Moving quickly, the U.S. column brushed aside light resistance and began to intercept German soldiers shuffling to the rear. The surprised captives were merely passed to the rear as the Americans continued their march. Soon enemy artillery batteries were being bypassed, with some of the German gunners added to the catch. At one point the advance guard came on a lighted farmhouse and bagged a number of unsuspecting German officers. The commander adjusted his narrow formation, placing his German-speaking soldiers well to the front to better control and instruct the overtaken enemy. As dawn broke, the brigade was well out in front of the American army and overlooking its "reconnaissance objective." To the veterans of the Second Division, the night's events seemed more like a police raid than a battle. This was not the German army that they had known.

LIKE ALL ARMIES, THE GERMAN ARMY reflected the strengths and weaknesses of the people that formed its ranks, and from the late summer of 1918 on, the German people were losing their confidence in their government and losing their will to prosecute the war. The government had done much to foster discontent, particularly by its heavy-handed, overly optimistic propaganda program encouraging maximum public support for the spring offensive. Victory had been promised, but when the Allied summer counteroffensive began to succeed, reality dawned on German citizens. Stringent economic controls, continuous army manpower levies, and ill-advised "short-war" planning had resulted in German workers bearing a 30 percent decrease in real earnings for the past four years, a 90 percent reduction in meat consumption, a 95 percent cut in green vegetable consumption, and a 50 percent drop in the availability of cereals. The never-ending deluge of casualty lists left few German families without tragic reminders of the war's cost in killed and maimed. By fall the influenza epidemic was once again taking its toll, and Berlin absorbed 3,000 deaths in October alone.

Many Germans did not accept their fate stoically. A growing number of strikes began to cripple the kaiser's industrial complex. While some of the labor revolts centered on wage disputes, others had a more political basis. Workers began to demand decision-sharing and political agendas. Left-wing parties sparked a few of these conflicts, but in most cases the politicians simply attempted to ride the gathering wave of public discontent. At the heart of the unrest lay a fundamental belief: the controlling autocracy was incompetent, unfit to govern.

During the summer prominent politicians and some members of the aristocracy began efforts to reform the government by making the army more responsive to the national assembly, thus breaking the chain linking the soldier to the kaiser. The reform initiatives spread to diplomacy, industry, and civil government. All told, it was a widespread if somewhat disjointed assault on autocracy, and it both used and fostered discontent.

The unrest could not be isolated and kept away from the ranks of the German armed forces. In September several infantry unit commanders reported that their troops refused to conduct counterattacks. The men would defend, they said, but would no longer go forward. A number of rear-area military concentration points such as Brussels became crowded with deserters from front-line divisions.

In the long-idle German High Seas Fleet, word of a planned "suicide sortie" drifted below decks. To the sailors it seemed that their officers were planning a desperate last fling at the Royal Navy (indeed, this was the case). The sailors began to take matters in their own hands. The October Naval Mutiny reflected all the symptoms of an unstable, outdated society. Social class was more evident in the navy than in the ground arm, with officers treated to fresh bread daily and cakes on Sunday, while the lowly enlisted ranks had been reduced to potato bread for months. When the officers lied to their men, saying the forthcoming movement to sea was just an exercise, the knowledgeable sailors staged a sit-down strike. The fleet could not get up steam, and by October 29 the German navy was immobile and in revolt.

Demonstrations spread from the naval base at Kiel to eleven northern cities. Soldiers' and sailors' councils were formed in these urban areas, with deserters attempting to gain control of the German nation. The demands of these councils included the abdication of the kaiser and voting rights for all German citizens. The military and naval machine that faced the Allies in November had changed dramatically.

The German General Staff had long been aware of the growing discontent, and had been actively attempting both to stem the tide and to adjust to new conditions. As early as May, Ludendorff predicted the need for 200,000 replacements, knowing they would not be available. The first shock came in early August, with Haig's counteroffensive on the Somme. The Germans lost 50,000 men there. Losses for that month alone totaled 228,000 men, and there were only 130,000 replacements available.

The controversial crown prince, Wilhelm III, sensing the desperate situation, proposed renunciation of Western Front territorial gains—*status quo ante bellum*. The argument had its merits. Surrendering Belgian and French soil would undercut the French, British, and Belgian rationale for the war, and their forces were almost as fatigued and depleted as Germany's own. It would put the German soldier on his own land, behind formidable water barriers. Even if the Allies could muster the resolve to continue the war, the motivation of citizens and soldiers alike would be poor at best for the Allies, and relatively easy for Germany.

Ludendorff saw advantages in the proposal of the crown prince but he also saw the pitfalls. He knew that the propaganda campaign had raised public expectations to such heights for the spring campaign that a withdrawal to the homeland might have disastrous results. Second, without occupied French and Belgian soil there was little for Germany to bargain with. The enormous war losses had placed the stakes so high that any concession would be considered unworthy of the human sacrifice.

In mid-August Ludendorff decided. He argued against Wilhelm III. The army could hold ground long enough to extract concessions in any negotiation for an end to the war, he said. Germany had paid a great price and must get something for it. The general advocated a new propaganda campaign, one that would bolster the flagging morale of the dispirited German citizenry.

Throughout September German losses mounted, however, and Ludendorff's staunch position was undermined. Adding to an increasingly dark picture, the Austro-Hungarian chief of staff flatly told his ally that his army was collapsing. With Turkey and Bulgaria tottering, Berlin was subjected to the indignity of an uncoordinated Austrian peace bid that falsely claimed German backing. The Austrian diplomatic move was rejected by the Allies, but the damage was done—it signaled weakness. Ludendorff put out a dictum to hold on at all costs, but the German

General Staff was now paying more attention to the unsettled German public.

Two officers from the General Staff approached Paul von Heintz, the secretary of state for foreign affairs. Heintz had been a naval officer and had considerable experience in the diplomatic service. The staff officers suggested that public discontent could be diminished by political reforms that promoted a more representative government with greater control of the armed forces, at the expense of the kaiser's prerogatives. Heintz drafted a document and secured the approval of the kaiser, Hindenburg, and Ludendorff. These measures were considered necessary, since they might blunt the growing internal political dissent and respond to the American president's peace proposal, which specified negotiations only with a reformed German government. Having thus authorized preliminary negotiations with President Wilson, the kaiser launched his government on the uncertain path to peace. During September the German army suffered another 230,000 casualties.

All during October Ludendorff worked frantically to secure some measure of gain for Germany. Wanting now to begin talks so that the army could withdraw behind the Rhine and rebuild during the winter, Ludendorff pleaded with politicians, officials, and his fellow soldiers to keep up the fight while peace overtures were being made. His problem was that by mid-October many soldiers and officials considered the war to be lost, the German Empire at an end, and the German army incapable of further resistance. In a stormy meeting with the kaiser on October 26, Ludendorff insisted on maintaining some relationship between the army and the kaiser, while the German emperor now demanded the army's total subordination to the new political leadership. Ludendorff resigned, but Hindenburg was persuaded to stay, and the next day it was decided to accept the as-yet-vague American terms for peace negotiations.

SO IT WAS NOT SURPRISING THAT THE Americans found some dispirited German units in their attack during the first week of November. Germany was in revolution, her diplomats were making clumsy attempts to find a document to sign, and there was serious doubt as to just who was in charge in Berlin.

Not all of the German units were lackluster in their defense, however; some were fighting well. After the Second Division's easily achieved "reconnaissance attack," the Americans found tougher going. On the next day the Second Division faced the familiar stalwart enemy and took heavy casualties as the Germans began to be pressed to the rear, their backs to the Meuse River. However, the Americans were not to be denied, and drove forward. In two days they reached the Meuse south of Villemontry.

The progress of the Second Division was matched by that of the Eighty-ninth Division to its right. That division's attack had been bitterly contested at Beaufort, but the town fell on November 4. On the following day, the Eighty-ninth had cleared the forest overlooking the Meuse. Thus, by November 6 the American Fifth Corps was in firm possession of the river line, ten miles south of Sedan. A crossing of the river as far north as this would jeopardize all the German forces that were still south of the Meuse.

To the left and west of the Fifth Corps, in the American First Corps sector, progress was just as rapid. The U.S. First Army was able to keep its attacking divisions roughly abreast of one another during the offensive. The Eightieth Division had taken Vaux-en-Dieulet and Sommauthe against stout resistance on November 4, and then continued pushing the Germans during the night. By November 5 the American division was a bit north and west of Beaumont and again attacked during the night. It was relieved the next day. To the left of the attacking Eightieth lay the sector of the Seventy-seventh Division. Initially delayed on November 4, the unit got going on the fifth, and by the night of the sixth it too reached the Meuse, sending patrols to the river towns of Remilly and Villers. Still farther to the west the Forty-second Division relieved the Seventy-eighth Division after the latter unit had taken Les Petites Armoises on November 4. Here the Meuse was much farther to the north than in the sector of the Second Division, which was well to the east. The Forty-second began fighting its way northward and reached Bulson on November 6, about five miles short of the Meuse and the city of Sedan.

The day before, November 5, Pershing had directed his First Army to take Sedan. Previously the city had been clearly designated as being in the sector assigned to the French Fourth Army. The brief order that was transmitted to the First and Fifth American corps commanders contained few details necessary for coordination. It cited the opportunities now available, suggested that the attack should be carried on throughout the night, and stated that previously coordinated boundaries between units should not be considered binding. It was a formula for confusion, but the commander of the American Expeditionary Force was determined now to press the advantage and not give his enemy any chance to reorganize.

As the German forces backed up to the Meuse, their withdrawal became so rapid that Pershing's intelligence officers lost track of enemy unit dispositions. On November 5 the Americans counted seventeen depleted enemy divisions facing the American First Army, with twelve of them on line. Resistance was no longer in the form of trench lines filled with infantry; the attackers were subjected primarily to artillery fire and resistance from scattered machine-gun positions. The Americans now considered themselves to be in a pursuit phase. On the next day, November 6, intelligence officers claimed it was impossible to determine the status of the German forces. Citing the fact that their enemy was abandoning artillery pieces, the Americans concluded that their opposition was now thoroughly confused. Reports from the battlefield collected that night described enemy resistance as light.

During the night of November 6–7 the First Infantry Division began a trek designed to capture the city of Sedan. The "Big Red One" was about nine to thirteen miles south and east of Sedan, and had the American First Corps between itself and the famed French city. Wandering over, through, and in front of two U.S. First Corps' divisions during the night, the uncoordinated advance was in direct reponse to Pershing's orders, but it created sheer havoc throughout the night and the morning of November 7. The determined soldiers of the First Division even managed to "capture" the Forty-second Division's commander, Douglas MacArthur, and his staff. MacArthur took the whole episode in good humor, but the personalities in higher headquarters saw the incident in an entirely different light.

On the night of November 8, the Forty-second Division seized the heights overlooking the Meuse at Sedan. The newly won American position south of the river was all that was necessary to effect control of the rail lines through the city, and American artillery made short work of an important German lateral line of communications. The German withdrawal had been so disorganized that the four rail lines in Sedan were still crowded with loaded cars. Despite the shelling, vast quantities of supplies thus fell into the hands of the French, who were given the honor of retaking the city, a scene of humiliation for France in the Franco-Prussian war of 1870.

Far to the south and east, General Bullard's Second U.S. Army was nearing combat readiness. Visiting his units on November 9, Bullard realized that his younger officers were champing at the bit for large-scale action. Heretofore his army had been limited to making local attacks; now, on November 10, the entire Second Army went over to the offensive.

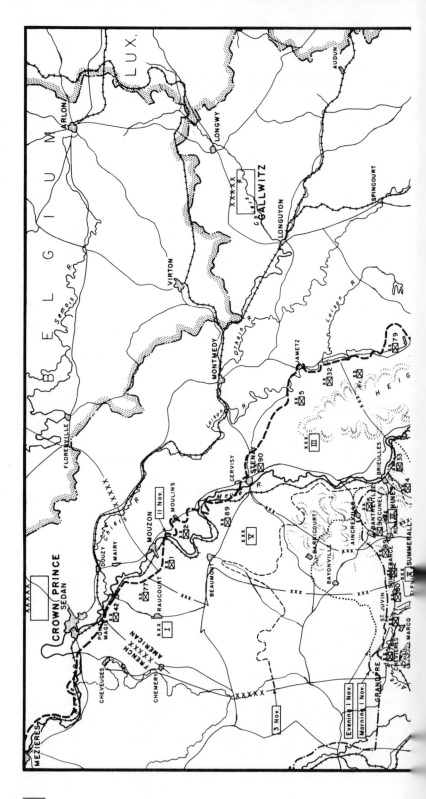

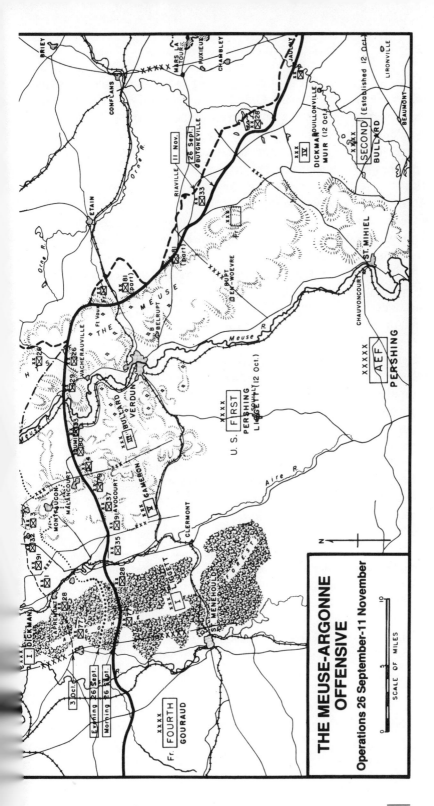

THE MEUSE-ARGONNE OFFENSIVE

Operations 26 September-11 November

SCALE OF MILES

Thus, as the first ten days of November faded away, two American armies were pressing forward. Only a few months before, the first corps-sized element of U.S. forces had been committed to battle. Now America was fielding a large, organized ground force, complete with its own artillery and air arm. The enemy the Americans faced, however, was not the enemy they had encountered during the early summer.

But the German general facing the Americans acted as if it was no concern of his who was in charge of the German nation, or whether the German army was capable of fighting. Max von Gallwitz had argued strenuously against any change in the government, and had strained every resource to keep Pershing at bay. Gallwitz was in the midst of a withdrawal—but it was a fighting withdrawal. The German general had been falling back on Sedan, and hastily organized a defense that incorporated as much of the Meuse River as possible. As it approached Sedan, the Meuse flowed in a more east-west direction, providing a well-oriented, sizable barrier to the American advance. Gallwitz had hoped to defend about thirty miles of the Meuse, along a line that ran generally southeast from Sedan. On November 4 a fierce battle had opened up at Brieulles, along the Meuse, thirty-five miles southeast of Sedan. The Americans crossed the river, were driven back, then the whole bloody process was repeated. At the end of the day, Pershing's troops were maintaining a precarious toehold on the German side of the waterway.

On the next day, November 5, the momentum of the American offensive had accelerated. General Gallwitz was now aware that the Americans were racing to the Meuse. At night their supply convoys were driving with their headlights on. His adversary had thrown caution to the winds. Gallwitz was dealing with an enemy that had changed tactics. Pershing had finally told his commanders to disregard fixed objectives and flanks.

The German general received orders to withdraw slowly north of the Meuse, and had to watch his exhausted soldiers yield one position after another. However, a number of his units made Pershing's men pay dearly. Gallwitz, often personally observing the fight through field glasses, described his enemy as attacking "in close, deeply arranged formations," "recklessly sacrificing their massed infantry," and charging "unconcernedly right into our machine-gun fire." That evening the old soldier learned that his government had dispatched a commission to Foch, seeking the Allied leader's terms.

On November 8 the long-awaited meeting was held. Later, when he heard the results of the first session, Gallwitz believed the Allied terms to be nothing short of a brazen and unjustified demand for Germany's unconditional surrender.

American units were informed that although negotiations were in progress, a cease-fire had not yet been agreed upon, and maximum pressure was to be exerted against the withdrawing German forces. Gallwitz had no troops left to throw into the fight. His forces were down to scattered groups—some still fighting, some trudging northward, and others simply awaiting capture and a bit of rest. All along the front the German army was a mere shadow of its once-proud legions. There was little use in continuing the battle. More Americans were en route to France, and Germany had no more to give. The Allies had gained a victory—a victory by attrition.

When Foch received a radio message from the German Supreme Headquarters requesting a time and place for talks, he responded, identifying a rail site in the Compiègne Forest, a spot near the front. Gathering his delegation together, he departed by train on November 7. The German plenipotentiaries—two government officials, one navy officer, and three army officers—arrived at the forest at 7:00 A.M. on November 8.

The head of the German delegation, Secretary of State Erzberger, had instructions to end the conflict under almost any conditions, but he insisted on wrangling with the Allied representatives, attempting to get the best possible terms for his country. Foch conducted himself like a cold, inflexible robot. Demanding that the Germans formally ask for an armistice before he would even reveal the required terms, he gave every indication that he and his delegation were quite prepared to walk away from the talks and continue the war if the proceedings did not go as he wished.

When Erzberger voiced the obvious, asking for an armistice, Foch stated the conditions. They were designed to render the German armed forces incapable of further offensive operations. The terms included evacuation of occupied territory; surrender of vast quantities of war stocks, weapons, and submarines; return of prisoners of war; internment of seventy-four warships in neutral or Allied ports; and the establishment of three Allied bridgeheads across the Rhine River.

It was 2:05 A.M. on November 11 when the German delegates finally received the authorization to agree to the terms and were ready to sign. Foch assembled his delegation at 5:05 A.M. as the lengthy, definitive text became available. Signatures were affixed by 5:10 A.M. Foch then dispatched orders—a cease-fire would begin at 11:00 A.M. The Allied representatives, consisting of three British naval officers, two French generals, and two interpreters, had finished their work. No British or American army officers were present.

THE WAR WAS OVER. THE COST IN HUMAN life had been enormous, and the totals were highly controversial. Governments generally minimized their own losses and exaggerated the estimated dead of their foes. Almost forty years after the event, one researcher, Arthur Banks, consulted over 1,300 works and concluded that the widely varying claims could be only roughly adjusted to some murky picture of actuality. Of the major Allied participants, Banks estimated Russian losses at 1.7 million, those of the British Empire at 997,000, and French losses at 1.39 million. Allied killed also included 460,000 Italians, 340,000 Romanians, and 116,000 Americans. For the Central Powers, Banks arrived at totals of 1.85 million Germans, 350,000 Turks, and 1.2 million Austro-Hungarian soldiers killed.

Allied combat deaths for five other nations, including Serbia, Portugal, and Japan, amounted to about 14,650. Bulgaria suffered 95,000 deaths in the cause of the Central Powers. It was little wonder that the figures were so imprecise, so clouded, and so masked by authorities. In the initial decades of the twentieth century, such unheard-of numbers were the object of shame.

It had been a world war—a great war, the first of the twentieth century's global conflicts. It set the pattern and sowed most of the seeds for the Second World War. Although its geographic sweep was immense, the critical battleground was the blood-soaked Western Front. There the strategic importance of the geography and modern mobilization procedures ensured that the belligerents would field huge armies that stretched literally across the better part of a continent, creating the conditions for stalemate and, in turn, the enormous casualty figures.

From the beginning of the Western Front stalemate, the generals labored long and hard to break the impasse, hoping to reintroduce maneuver on the ground. It was not until the first few months of 1917, over two years after the beginning of the conflict, that practical plans and new doctrine began to emerge. The Western Front leadership of 1917 and 1918 initiated the techniques and methods of warfare by maneuver. They would largely fail to achieve maneuver in this war, but what they created would be copied and would succeed in another war in 1939–45. The last phases of World War I provided the military beginnings of World War II.

The primary French contribution to breaking the stalemate in early

1917 was Nivelle's planned infantry penetration method. Based in part on Captain Laffargue's 1915 tract, the use of small groups of thoroughly trained foot soldiers to infiltrate through no-man's-land and seize specific objectives had worked well for Nivelle during 1916, although the upscaled version failed for the French in 1917. The flaw was not in the concept but in the army that attempted to execute it. Nivelle's army was shot through with dissension, and it was an army without a staff system that could implement far-reaching change on the battlefield in the midst of war. When the Canadians used the same technique at about the same time that Nivelle launched his offensive, they made it work. Their attack was small-scale and limited, but nonetheless a success. In early 1917 neither Nivelle nor probably any other French general could make the new doctrine work. But the concept was sound; it would be seen again.

After his failure Nivelle faced a military court of inquiry. While the French army was undergoing revolt and a subsequent revival under the hand of Pétain, Nivelle defended himself. The articulate artilleryman artfully dodged the blame, was cleared of any serious charge, and quietly left the country, assigned to the obscurity of North Africa. Six years later, in 1924, Robert Nivelle died in Paris.

Nivelle's successor, Henri-Philippe Pétain, was destined to live a tumultuous later life. He was already sixty-one when he took command of the dispirited army. He not only held the French army together, he nursed it back into an attacking force by 1918. The old man's methods included whirlwind battlefront tours and personal appearances in front of the troops, where he used his informal cartop talks to inspire confidence, patriotism, and anything that would motivate the French soldier. It worked. He ended the war a genuine hero. His leadership techniques would not go unnoticed. Another generation of military leaders would study Pétain and emulate him in the next world war.

In the latter part of 1917, through personal intervention and supervision, the elderly general changed the doctrine of the French army. He discarded the philosophy of bold attack and insisted on the massive use of firepower and carefully orchestrated assault. After World War I, Pétain took a direct hand in shaping the French army, becoming minister of war in 1934. France had a special experience in the Great War. She mobilized a higher percentage of her population and suffered a greater wartime death rate (3.5 percent) than the other participants. Naturally enough, postwar French views would favor policies designed to ensure minimum casualties by using fixed defenses and a reliance on firepower. Perhaps unjustly, Pétain was blamed by many for the rapid collapse of

France in 1940. At the age of eighty-four, he cooperated with Nazi Germany, heading the Vichy regime. After World War II the old soldier paid the price. Tried for treason, he was sentenced to death, but received a commutation to life in prison. Henri-Philippe Pétain died on the Isle d'Yeu in 1951.

Although Pétain created the style of leadership that some World War II leaders pursued, his sometime rival Ferdinand Foch provided the example for combined international command that was seen again in the next conflict. Unlike Pétain, Foch died before the accolades ceased. His cross-Channel allies granted him a highly unusual recognition in 1920, naming him a British field marshal. The position that he shaped for himself in 1918, half politician–half soldier, was readily re-created in 1943 for an American general, Dwight D. Eisenhower. On the surface, the role of a Supreme Allied Commander appears to entail merely the translation of political imperatives into military tasks. But as Foch knew, and his American successor would discover, the position actually requires seeing the whole of the problem and influencing the course of policy, as well as directing military events. Unlike Eisenhower, Foch spurned the opportunity for political office after his war. He died in 1929.

Not only was Douglas Haig's example not followed in the next war, it was studiously avoided. For the British, he set the pattern for what not to do, what not to be. Because Haig was usually immaculately dressed, succeeding British commanders prided themselves on casual or unconventional field attire. Because Haig had a reputation for rarely visiting the front, his successors eagerly sought opportunities to visit their troops and to be photographed while doing it. To this day the memory of Haig kindles to bright flame some smoldering coals of British irrationality. His many detractors reach shrill heights of vehement derision. His few defenders have always been his worst enemies, suppressing evidence, ignoring facts, and praising beyond reason.

The root of Haig's strange effect on British history can easily be laid to one word: Passchendaele. The major postwar argument centered on the question of who was to blame for that terrible bloodletting. Haig's defenders push the Fifth Army commander, Gough, as the target, while Haig's critics offer Sir Douglas as the chief villain of the piece. The controversy is so burdened by emotion that both sides usually focus on the battle and not the campaign, overlooking Haig's and Bacon's imaginative plan for an amphibious operation, a skillful but unused endeavor that provided the essential foundations for a later operation, the 1944 Normandy invasion.

Another sphere of controversy centers on Haig and the tank. His detractors point to his failure to foresee the machine's use as the ideal device to bring about maneuver, conveniently overlooking the fact that the World War I tank was designed from the outset as a slow-moving infantry support aid, that from 1916 on Haig pressed hard for large-scale production, and that he literally turned over the preoperational training of his army for the Cambrai offensive to the armor advocates. Also obscured in the continuing argument is the brilliant performance of both the British army and its commander during the 1918 Allied counteroffensive. In some respects, Haig was fortunate to have died in 1928, before most of the arguments became heated.

Ludendorff himself left little personal imprint on succeeding soldiers, but the system he headed, the German General Staff, was a meritocracy that featured ideas and teamwork, not personalities. The German team of 1917–18 had much to do with shaping the warfare of the future. Ludendorff's young officers designed the elastic defense to save the lives of German soldiers and quickly recoup the temporary loss of ground during major offensives. They skillfully used reverse slope defense systems, nullifying Allied observation and crippling accurate artillery fire by their enemies. Taking the opposition's ideas, they used Captain Laffargue's infantry penetration concept as the governing philosophy for the counterattack phase of their new defense doctrine. Then, in 1918, the German General Staff designed a coordinated offensive system that used the 1917 counterattack doctrine as a new method of attack.

As the war ended and major figures of the Great War passed on, the German staff team remained intact. During the interwar years they coupled British tank innovations and techniques with their own World War I infantry penetration doctrine. They substituted the tank for the 1917–18 German infantry light machine-gun organization. Realizing that the essential ingredient in their new method of warfare was rapid communications among and with the fast-moving cutting edge of their penetration forces, the staff selected an infantryman who had served in World War I as a radio communications officer to nurture and organize the new ground elements. Heinz Guderian proved to be an excellent choice. Erwin Rommel, another infantryman, was destined to be one of the most celebrated practitioners of the new doctrine, which would become known as "blitzkrieg."

The Allies had great difficulty grasping the new German tactic. When they first faced it in March 1918, they dubbed it "Hutier Tactics," attributing Ludendorff's successful staff work to a single Western Front field commander rather than to the work of a staff system. It would have amazed those German staff officers to know that sixty years after the event General von Hutier was still getting credit for the innovation in U.S. Army educational circles.

John J. Pershing brought enthusiasm and large numbers of sparsely trained soldiers to the war. Both were gone shortly after the conflict ended. Postwar America heard a plea from its soldiers, one that grew fainter with each passing year: the unanswered plea for war preparedness. The military leaders did not press a case for a large army. After all, they had become accustomed to answering the requirements of America's major ground wars through hastily contrived expansions. But even they were appalled to find themselves, on the eve of World War II, heading the world's thirteenth-ranked army. The American political leadership apparently recognized the need to have an army larger than Portugal's, but evidently quailed before the prospect of its exceeding the ground forces of Bulgaria.

In 1933 Douglas MacArthur, the U.S. Army chief of staff and veteran of the World War I Forty-second Division, vomited on the steps of the White House after a stormy and unsuccessful budget battle with President Roosevelt. The general had told FDR that American soldiers would die at the end of their enemies' bayonets for lack of war readiness. Nine years later MacArthur was tragically proven right during the Bataan Death March. American soldiers wanted planes, tanks, trucks, and machine guns—everything they did not have ready in World War I. What war matériel Congress and the president did provide was chiefly in the form of battleships, some of which failed to last out the first hour of the next war. With little combat experience during the Great War, American admirals offered the pleasing specter of insular defense during the 1930s and created one of the world's most powerful—and vulnerable—battle fleets.

Their soldier counterparts did, however, learn from their war experience. The U.S. Army officers of 1917–18 returned home to produce practical plans for total war industrial mobilization, to discard the failed doctrine of concentrated rifle fire, and to create a combined arms doctrine for mechanized warfare. The latter innovation was largely worked out under the supervision of Colonel George Marshall at Fort Benning, Georgia, during the 1930s. The change from Pershing's philosophy was accomplished without the bitter acrimony that accompanied similar doctrinal revisions in Britain. Industrial mobilization plans were accomplished by hardworking young officers who studied the miserable record of World War I and produced a workable system in time for its implementation in 1940.

The American solutions to the problems of World War I were nothing short of breathtaking when they were put into action during 1941–45. Not only did the Americans equip themselves with prodigious numbers of war machines, but the U.S. stores were vast enough to equip other armies as well. The speed with which the Americans launched their mechanized forces into a winning battle of maneuver produced a sense of wonder. The American veterans of World War I, many of whom served in World War II, saw their performance as the logical outgrowth of the Great War's lessons. They had simply coupled American fighting spirit with U.S. industrial power. Others, more critical of the United States, saw the Americans as able to win only with an ultimately dangerous overdependence upon machines, weapons, and supplies.

Pershing, blessed with a short, albeit bloody, American involvement in the Great War, emerged from the conflict as an unabashed hero. He was promoted to General of the Armies, a title that placed him only slightly below George Washington in rank. He won a Pulitzer Prize for his memoirs and became a figure of veneration. He survived all of his contemporaries in high command except Pétain, and lived to see the creation of the mechanized U.S. Army and its triumph over Germany in 1945.

World War I also gave birth to new air and naval concepts. The Atlantic convoy system of 1917 was so successful that it was quickly reinstituted during the next war with an improvement, the use of radar. Each of the Great War belligerents continued the development of interceptor, fighter, and close-support aircraft, but some differences arose over the utility of strategic bombing. The Germans, early advocates of city bombing in World War I, refused to put much stock in the practice after 1918. Postwar British and American airmen became the great champions of strategic bombing, and like the American battleship admirals of the interwar period, received substantial support.

The Great War produced many military innovations. Foch's method of combined command, the techniques of amphibious assault, Pétain's style of leadership, strategic bombing, and the convoy system were all developed in World War I and would be seen again in World War II. Blitzkrieg, American industrial mobilization, U.S. combined arms techniques, and British mechanized warfare all stemmed from the lessons of the first of the twentieth century's global conflicts. While some of the latter innovations were derived from the perceived errors of the Great

War, others were created and initially implemented during the last two years of World War I.

The military leaders of World War I are often depicted as unthinking, inflexible dolts, while World War II leaders are usually pictured as creative, dashing figures. In reality, most World War II leaders simply repeated what they had seen implemented under the direction of Foch, Pétain, Haig, Sims, Trenchard, and Ludendorff. There would not be much new in World War II; the changes were already in motion during 1917.

The last two years of the Great War also brought about the end of an era—a political one. The entire concept of empire, the age-old belief in a king's inherited right to control the destinies of his subjects, no matter how far-flung and diverse, died in the trenches during 1917–18. The czar's Great Russian Empire was first to fall, followed by the Turkish Empire, the Austro-Hungarian Empire, and finally the German Empire. In the space of about twenty months of fighting, a centuries-old political system all but disappeared. The only remaining empire of substance, the British Empire, also started on its path of decline. Unlike most of the others, the British Empire was not a thoroughgoing autocratic regime. It was a democracy—at least for its white citizens. Good soldiers, skillful generals, and astute politicians were on hand to ensure that the fall of the British Empire would be a gentle one. Nonetheless, after Passchendaele the British Empire was fatally weakened. In the years to come, the notion of empire was to become a subject for historical study alone.

There was also an ominous political birth. The prosecution of the Great War required the total mobilization of a nation's industry, its people, and their energies. Once centralized control methods were developed, it was natural to imagine what the result would be if they were left in place after the war, or reincarnated during peacetime. Unprecedented power would be available; the talent and energy of an entire population could be directed toward the achievement of rational goals. The state could have readily available military power at its command, cowing or conquering its external adversaries and subduing its internal opposition. People could be trained and educated into continuous service for the state.

The last two years of World War I brought forth the first modern totalitarian dictatorship: the Soviet Union. Three more would quickly emerge. Italy, Germany, and Japan, all belligerents in the Great War, followed the Soviet example by creating totalitarian governments, and banded together as the Axis partners of World War II.

In the midst of these changes, the last two years of World War I put another political system through a difficult test. Democracy not only survived, but seemed to prosper. When Foch entered the railroad car on November 8, he gave every indication that if the German emissaries offered the least resistance to his conditions, he could simply walk out. He knew that he could do so and the democracies—Britain, France, and the United States—would continue the war. The German negotiators had no such assurance.

Yet the French general also knew the German army had not been defeated, and that true maneuver had not been attained. There had been no bold stroke, no deft severing of the enemy's lines of communication. There was still only attrition—the grim business of providing more targets than the enemy could destroy. It was the soldier's dark horror of no room to move, a war that, until the very last, required bowed necks and movement straight ahead into the fire. No matter what had been tried, it all came out the same: maneuver had failed, and attrition was the only option. Yet the democracies were still fighting when the autocracies— Russia, Bulgaria, Turkey, Austro-Hungary, and Germany—had either failed or were in the throes of collapse.

Why would the democracies continue the killing, suffer the losses, and go on prosecuting the war? Though there are probably many reasons why the democracies triumphed while the autocracies failed in the Great War, one in particular stands out. The conditions of World War I, a total war, required each of the participants to focus maximum energy and resources externally. The autocracies, internally dependent on the use, or the threat of the use, of force, were largely stripped naked within their own borders in order to carry on an external war of attrition. The democracies also needed to use force internally, but to a far lesser degree, because they were blessed with a mechanism of change. Important, unresolved problems could be, and occasionally were, settled at the ballot box. The autocracies had no such self-correcting procedures, and were faced with growing weakness due to internal discontent. The autocracies experienced radical change, while the democracies enjoyed continuity. In this war, a war of total attrition, democracy proved to be more resilient than autocracy.

It was a world war, a tragic event of unprecedented magnitude. It was neither the first nor the last of the world wars, but for twenty-one years it stood as the all-time cataclysmic conflict. No one yet knows its human cost, but one estimate holds to 8.5 million combat deaths. It was a war that was not only destined to be renamed, but would come to be regarded as a military aberration. Its memory was swept away by another world war, the new war appearing to herald a return to maneuver warfare. Even as World War II opened, the conflict of 1914–18 was largely dropped as an object of study. Yet the First World War contained many of the new military beginnings, and was the cause of vast political changes. It also provided a brutal test for democracy, a test that yielded a reassurance in the strength and continuity of representative government.

ESSAY ON SOURCES

BACKGROUND AND GENERAL SOURCES

ALTHOUGH THE GREAT WAR IS PERHAPS one of the best-recorded global events of all time, analysis is uneven, documentation is suspect, and personal accounts are often focused on postwar arguments. Dr. Edward M. Coffman, a longtime student of the conflict, concluded that the intervention of the Second World War precluded the normal phase of research and analysis that usually follows a major war approximately thirty years after the event. By 1948 tempers had cooled and sources had been defined, but by that time there was no market for good books on World War I because the more recent conflict had displaced it in the public's memory.

Great War official histories and contemporary documents are often criticized for their lack of accuracy, and justly so. The researcher must keep in mind that the bureaucracies of the time had never experienced such an awesome event, and no participant was prepared to record such enormous figures and far-reaching facts. Numbers were shaded and disagreeable documents were destroyed, ignored, or altered. Readers of these sources must proceed with considerable skepticism. Memoirs should also be approached with caution. On the good side, there are many of them. But then, the authors had so much to "explain." There are paths through this mixture of fact and fiction. The following route is offered as one of them.

ANALYSIS REQUIRES RELIABLE BACKGROUND sources, and the best single-volume overview of the war is still Charles Cruttwell, *A History of the Great War, 1914–1918* (London: Oxford University Press, 1934). It is the starting point for diplomatic, political, and military matters. There are also several specialized reference works that are essential to serious scholars. Holger H. Herwig and Neil M. Heyman, *Biographical Dictionary of World War I* (Westport, Conn.: Greenwood Press, 1982), describes the major figures of the war and gives helpful clues about postwar disputes. Since a war of attrition is dependent on population figures, a recommended source is Brian R. Mitchell, *European Historical Statistics, 1750–1970* (New York: Columbia University Press, 1975). Thumbnail sketches of campaigns, weapons, and comparative casualty figures are available in an exhaustively researched atlas: Arthur Banks, *A Military Atlas of the First World War* (New York: Taplinger, 1975).

Analysis of a military campaign requires a careful reading of official histories, documents, memoirs, and book-length secondary sources. To do so is necessary, but the history of the Great War was blessed in 1971 with a fine series of article-length accounts by noted experts in a variety of fields. *The History of the First World War*, 8 vols. (London: BPC Publishing, 1971), edited by Brigadier Peter Young, contains hundreds of well-coordinated pieces. Its greatest value is that an authority on a given aspect of the war offers a detailed account of a campaign or activity, using the best sources and giving a well-illustrated text complete with superb maps. Most of the authors involved offer their own nation's evidence. The series was evidently not sold widely in the United States, but the entire set was reprinted in 1987 and is available at the U.S. Army Military History Institute in Carlisle Barracks, Pennsylvania.

There are more critics of the various official histories than there are supporters, but accounts by government-sponsored historians can be balanced with opposing views. For example, the fourteen-volume British version—Brigadier General James E. Edmonds, ed., *History of the Great War* (London: His Majesty's Stationery Office, printed over a period of 27 years, 1922 to 1949)—can be checked against the Australian and Canadian companion official histories that often take London to task. General Edmonds could not find it in his heart to criticize his superiors or look very carefully into numbers, but the "colonials" seemed to revel in such tasks. Perhaps the best approach to the troubled field of official history was inadvertently taken by the American secretary of war when he scotched the idea of a U.S. Army narrative history of the war, saying "no one would believe it." The result was a seventeen-volume documentary history with a minimum of editing, containing good maps, intercepted enemy messages, and postwar letters and notes. See U.S. Department of the Army, *United States Army in the World War, 1917–1919* (Washington, D.C.: U.S. Government Printing Office, 1948).

Institutional histories are essential to an understanding of the armies involved. Corelli Barnett, *Britain and Her Army, 1509–1970* (New York: William Morrow, 1970); Gordon A. Craig, *The Politics of the Prussian Army, 1640–1945* (London: Oxford University Press, 1955); and Charles De Gaulle, *France and Her Army* (London: Hutchinson, 1945) are all sound works. For the Americans, Russell F. Weigley, *History of the United States Army*, enl. ed. (Bloomington: Indiana University Press, 1984), is good, but Edward M. Coffman, *The War to End All Wars: The American Military Experience in World War I* (New York: Oxford University Press, 1968), offers more depth for the U.S. Army from 1911 to 1918.

Citizens of the Roman Empire no doubt scoffed at Caesar's *Commentaries* as being self-serving and slanted. All war memoirs are subject to well-founded skepticism. However, since most of the surviving notables of World War I rushed into print soon afterward, cross-checking is possible. The advantages of Great War memoirs are that just about all of the major figures had not only writing adversaries on the other side of the line, but internal rivals who were also proud authors. Thus General John J. Pershing's two-volume description, *My Experiences in the World War* (New York: Frederick A. Stokes, 1931), can be compared not only with Marshal Paul von Hindenburg, *Out of My Life* (London: Cassell, 1920), and General Erich Ludendorff, *My War Memories, 1914–1918* (London: Hutchinson, 1920), but also balanced against the often-contradictory views of General Peyton C. March, *The Nation at War* (New York: Doubleday, Doran, 1932). An entire volume of contemporary foreign views on the Americans at war is available in G. S. Viereck, ed., *As They Saw Us* (New York: Doubleday, Doran, 1929). Hindenburg's and Ludendorff's accounts can likewise be compared with the published diaries of Admiral Georg Alexander von Muller in Walter Gorlitz, ed., *The Kaiser and His Court* (New York: Harcourt, Brace and World, 1964). Douglas Haig had the good sense not to write memoirs, but one can find wide-ranging British accounts in Basil H. Liddell Hart, *Reputations: Ten Years After* (Boston: Little, Brown, 1928), and *The Real War, 1914–1918* (Boston: Little Brown, 1930). The opposite view is presented in John Terraine, *Ordeal of Victory* (J. B. Lippincott: New York, 1963). The truth about Haig probably lies somewhere between these two points of view. The hands-down best of the lot is Ferdinand Foch, *The Memoirs of Marshal Foch*, trans. Colonel T. Bentley Mott (New York: Doubleday, Doran, 1931). Relevant memoirs on the various campaigns of 1917 and 1918 are cited below.

THE 1917 ALLIED SPRING OFFENSIVE

The wartime evolution of German tactical doctrine is detailed in G. C. Wynne, *If Germany Attacks: The Battle in Depth in the West* (Westport, Conn.: Greenwood Press, 1976). The French Nivelle offensive and the mutinies are described in Richard M. Watt, *Dare Call It Treason* (New York: Simon and Schuster, 1963). The British and Canadian offensives are recorded in the respective official histories: Cyril Falls, *The History of the Great War: Military Operations in France and Belgium, 1917*, Edmonds, ed. (London: His Majesty's Stationery Office, 1940), and Colonel G. W. L. Nicholson, *Official History of the Canadian Expeditionary Force, 1914–1919* (Ottawa: Queen's Printer, 1962). Allenby's role is described in Raymond Savage, *Allenby of Armageddon* (Indiana: Bobbs Merrill, 1926). A German view is detailed in Ernst Junger, *Storm of Steel* (London: Chatto and Windus, 1929). Byng's contribution to the action at Vimy Ridge is explained in Jeffery Williams, *Byng of Vimy: General and Governor General* (London: Secker and Warburg, 1938). British air operations and techniques are described in H. A. Jones, *The War in the Air: Being the Story of the Part Played in the Great War by the Royal Air Force*, 6 vols. (Oxford: Clarendon Press, 1937).

THE 1917 LOWLANDS CAMPAIGN

Haig's contemporaneous arguments and actions are traced in his writings. See J. H. Boraston, ed., *Sir Douglas Haig's Dispatches* (London: J. M. Dent and Sons, 1931). The plan and preparations for the British amphibious operation are best detailed in Admiral Reginald Bacon, *The Dover Patrol* (London: Hutchinson, 1919). Gough's side of the story is found in his own *The Fifth Army* (London: Hodder and Stoughton, 1931). A good official account is in Charles J. H. Bean, *The Australian Imperial Force in France, 1917* (Sydney: Angus and Robertson, 1943). Plumer's view is presented by General Charles Harrington, *Plumer of Messines* (London: John Murray, 1935). John Keegan wrote a sound analysis of the campaign; see "Passchendaele: The Second Phase," in *History of the First World War* (London: BPC Publishing, 1971), hereinafter referred to as *BPC History*. Ludendorff's and Hindenburg's memoirs should also be consulted.

CAPORETTO

Italian accounts and testimony were translated by the U.S. Army War College after the war. They can be found at the U.S. Army Military History Institute, Carlisle Barracks, Pennsylvania. These papers include General Luigi Capello's war notes, General Ettore Vigano's description, and the testimony of General Cadorna before the 1919 Italian governmental investigation committee. Two Italian monographs also detail the battle: Luigi Villari, *The War on the Italian Front* (London: Cobden-Sanderson, 1932), and Mario Caracciolo, *Italy in the World War* (Rome: Edizioni, 1936). The U.S. Army War College translated General Krafft von Dellmensingen's description of German logistical preparations, *Durchbruch Am Isonzo* (Berlin, 1932). Captain Erwin Rommel's account is in his *Infanterie Greift Am*. The best translation was published by Athena Press of Vienna, Virginia, in 1979. A good secondary analysis is found in Ronald Seth, *Caporetto: The Scapegoat Battle* (London: MacDonald, 1965). Another sound but brief analysis is in Kurt Peball, "Caporetto," in *BPC History*.

CAMBRAI

The tank commander's view is provided in Ernest D. Swinton, *Eyewitness* (London: Hodder and Stoughton, 1932). Development and personnel aspects of the early British tank story are presented in Basil H. Liddell Hart, *The Tanks: The History of the Royal Tank Regiment and Its Predecessors*, vol. 1 (New York: Praeger, 1959). Training and doctrinal matters are best described in J. F. C. Fuller's recollections, *Tanks in the Great War, 1914–1918* (London: John Murray, 1920). Two German views are found in Ernst Zindler, "The 54th Division at Cambrai," *Wissen und Wehr* (Berlin) (May 1937), and Georg Strutz, *The Tank Battle of Cambrai* (Berlin: German Government Record Office, 1929). The official British version is contained in Wilfrid Miles, *History of the Great War: Military Operations in France and Belgium: The Battle of Cambrai*, James Edmonds, ed. (London: His Majesty's Stationery Office, 1948). Two short, thoughtful secondary accounts are found in David Chandler's "The German Counterattack" and Kenneth Macksey's "Tank Developments," both in *BPC History*.

THE GERMAN OFFENSIVE OF 1918

The German doctrinal evolution is detailed in Wynne's book, *If Germany Attacks*, and can be supplemented by Major Timothy T. Lupfer, *The Dynamics of Doctrine: The Changes in German Tactical Doctrine during the First World War* (Ft. Leavenworth: U.S. Army Command and General Staff College, 1981). Ludendorff's memoirs can be further extended with Barrie Pitt, "Germany, 1918, New Strategy, New Tactics," in *BPC History*. A detailed account of the influenza epidemic is in Alfred W.

Crosby, *Epidemic and Peace, 1918* (Westport, Conn.: Greenwood Press, 1976). German testimony on the domestic effects of the campaign and eyewitness descriptions are contained in Ralf H. Lutz, ed., *The Causes of the German Collapse in 1918: Report of the German Constituent Assembly, 1919–1928*, trans. W. L. Cappell (Stanford: Stanford University Press, 1934). French views are summarized in Major General H. Essame, "The Matz," in *BPC History*. The use of air support by the Germans and Allied countermeasures are described in Thomas G. Miller's analysis, "The Air Battle," in *BPC History*. The new Allied command and control arrangements are related in John Keegan's "The Doullens Conference," in *BPC History*. Foch's own view is described in his memoirs. The official British version of events is detailed in General Edmonds's edited series. See the volume entitled *Military Operations: France and Belgium, 1918* (London: Macmillan, 1937). The U.S. Marine role is described in Captain John W. Thomason's book, *Fix Bayonets* (New York: Charles Scribner's Sons, 1926).

THE AMERICAN CAMPAIGN

Pershing's memoirs should be supplemented by George C. Marshall's recollections, *Memoirs of My Service in the World War, 1917–1918*, ed. Brigadier General James Collins (Boston: Houghton Mifflin, 1976). Other memoirs include Major General Robert Lee Bullard, *Personalities and Reminiscences of the War* (New York: Doubleday, 1925); Major General Hunter Liggett, *AEF: Ten Years Ago in France* (New York: Dodd, Mead, 1928); and Major General Johnson Hagood, *The Services of Supply* (Boston: Houghton Mifflin, 1927). Dr. Edward M. Coffman's book, *The War to End All Wars*, mentioned above, can be supplemented with a number of battle descriptions in Major Edwin F. Harding, ed., *Infantry Attacks* (Washington D.C.: Infantry Journal, 1939). George S. Patton's notes and letters are found in Martin Blumenson's edited volume, *The Patton Papers, 1885–1940* (Boston: Houghton Mifflin, 1972). Blumenson also wrote an excellent description of Sam Woodfill's adventure, "The Outstanding Soldier of the AEF," *American History Illustrated* (February 1967). The St. Mihiel story is told by Major Robert C. Cotton, "A Study of the St. Mihiel Offensive," *Infantry Journal* (July 1920); Donald Smythe, "St. Mihiel: The Birth of an American Army," *Parameters* (June 1983); and J. W. Stock, "Americans at St. Mihiel," in *BPC History*. An excellent analysis of American tactical doctrine is provided by Major James W. Rainey in his "Ambivalent Warfare: The Tactical Doctrine of the AEF in

World War I," *Parameters* (September 1983). The Meuse-Argonne offensive is described by Philip Warner, "American Offensive: The Argonne," *BPC History*, and Captain Arthur E. Hartzell, "The Meuse-Argonne Battle" (Chaumont, France: HQ AEF, 1920). The U.S. Army official history volume for the St. Mihiel battle, volume 8 in the series mentioned above, is quite good, and contains many contemporary enemy communications. The opposing view, however, is best presented by General Otto von Ledebur, the chief of staff for Army Group C, which faced the American attack. See his account, "Rushing the St. Mihiel Salient," in *As They Saw Us*, ed. George S. Viereck (New York: Doubleday, Doran, 1929).

ATTRITION

A good firsthand source describing the desperate straits of the Allies during the Battle of the Atlantic, 1917–18, is Admiral William S. Sims, *The Victory at Sea* (New York: Doubleday, Page, 1921). That account should be balanced with a British view: Arthur J. Marder, *Portrait of an Admiral: The Life and Papers of Sir Herbert Richmond* (Cambridge, Mass.: Harvard University Press, 1952). The best analysis of the subject, however, is provided by David F. Trask, *Captains & Cabinets: Anglo-American Naval Relations, 1917–1918* (Columbia, Mo.: University of Missouri Press, 1972). The difficulties with the American air effort were largely centered in the United States, and are described in Irving B. Holley, *Ideas and Weapons* (New Haven, Conn.: Yale University Press, 1953). American operations are recorded in the official history: see Department of the Army, *United States Army in the World War, 1917–1919: Meuse-Argonne Operations of the American Expeditionary Forces*, vol. 9 (Washington, D.C.: U.S. Government Printing Office, 1948). The opposing view is provided by the commander of the German forces facing the Americans, General Max von Gallwitz, who was in command of Army Group C during the Meuse-Argonne Campaign; see "The Retreat to the Rhine," in *As They Saw Us*, cited above.

CONTINUITY AND CHANGE

Foch's memoirs are particularly good in describing the military aspects of events leading to the armistice, and of course detail the actual last-minute negotiations. The British and American official histories are useful and revealing about the last phases of fighting. The German side is provided by Hindenburg, but a better source for the thinking in Berlin is found in the Muller diaries, previously cited, and in the Constituent Assembly hearings cited above. These should be supplemented by several good articles, including Dieter Groh, "The Kiel Mutiny"; H. W. Koch, "Germany Accepts the Fourteen Points"; Jacques Meyer, "The Armistice"; and D. R. Shermer, "The Influenza Pandemic," all in *BPC History*. An excellent analysis of the U.S. contribution on the ground and an appraisal of the American army is provided by Colonel Paul F. Braim, *Test of Battle: The AEF in the Meuse-Argonne Campaign* (Newark: University of Delaware Press, 1987). Pershing's after-action report should also be consulted; see Commander-in-Chief, AEF, *Final Report of General John J. Pershing* (Washington, D.C.: U.S. Government Printing Office, 1920). The birth of "blitzkrieg" is to be found in G. C. Wynne's book cited above, and in Hans Guderian, *Panzer Leader* (New York: E. P. Dutton, 1952). The lack of Allied understanding of the change in German offensive doctrine is described by Laszlo M. Alfoldi in "The Hutier Legend," *Parameters* 5, no. 2 (1976). Postwar British development is provided by Dr. Jay Luvaas in *The Education of an Army: British Military Thought, 1815–1940* (Chicago: University of Chicago Press, 1964). The story of the U.S. Army's solution to the problem of linking America's industrial potential to wartime requirements is found in the first two chapters of R. Elberton Smith, *U.S. Army in World War II: The Army and Economic Mobilization* (Washington, D.C.: Office of the Chief of Military History, 1959).

INDEX